Homeless
in *Paradise*

ROB ROSENTHAL

Homeless

in

Paradise

A map of the terrain

TEMPLE UNIVERSITY PRESS   *Philadelphia*

Temple University Press, Philadelphia 19122
Copyright © 1994 by Temple University. All rights reserved
Published 1994
Printed in the United States of America

The paper used in this publication meets the minimum requirements of American National
Standard for Information Sciences—Permanence of Paper for Printed Library Materials,
ANSI Z39.48-1984   ∞

Library of Congress Cataloging-in-Publication Data

Rosenthal, Rob, 1951–
      Homeless in Paradise : a map of the terrain / Rob Rosenthal.
            p.   cm.
      Includes bibliographical references and index.
      ISBN 1-56639-129-6. — ISBN 1-56639-130-X (pbk.)
            1. Homelessness—California—Santa Barbara.   2. Homeless persons—California—
Santa Barbara.   3. Santa Barbara (Calif.)—Social conditions.   I. Title.
HV4506.S36R67   1994
362.5′09794′91—dc20   93-17275

This book is

dedicated to

M A R G A R E T   H A L M Y

and

H E R B   R O S E N T H A L ,

for the values

they taught;

K I T   T R E M A I N E ,

for starting me

down this road;

and

S U N N Y   B A N W E R ,

for holding me up

along the way.

Contents

Acknowledgments   ix

Introduction: Why Are They Homeless?   1

1 Paradise   7

2 Becoming homeless   19

3 Being homeless   45

4 Hanging on and hanging out   77

5 The homeless movement   95

6 Getting ahead and the barriers to escape   111

7 Homelessness and the American Paradise   143

Appendix Researching homelessness: A case history   173

Notes   197

Index   257

Acknowledgments

My thanks go first to Kit Tremaine. Not only did she provide financial support and constant encouragement for the Homeless People's Project, but the original idea for such a study was born of her well-known compassion.

Dick Flacks guided me through the original research with a light hand but a sure touch; Nancy McCradie, Suzanne Riordan, and Guadalupe Kennedy provided invaluable assistance during that period. Roger Friedland and Harvey Molotch were extremely helpful in reviewing an early version of the manuscript.

Doug Welch began as a research assistant but quickly became a colleague I learned from. Patty St. Clair, Philip Wichline, and David Linder provided help with computer analyses under trying conditions. Faculty and staff in the Department of Sociology at Wesleyan University were supportive throughout and cut me slack when I needed it; Sue Fisher, Charles Lemert, Alex Dupuy, and Mary Ann Clawson went beyond the call of duty by reading parts or all of the manuscript and providing detailed and helpful suggestions.

Mike Rawson, Matt Salo, Peter Dreier, and Douglas Harper also made many helpful suggestions in reviewing earlier drafts. A final draft might never have seen the light of day if not for extensive editing suggestions by Craig Reinarman, Herb Rosenthal, Rhoda Rosenthal, and Norman Storer. A coherent final draft would likely not have seen the light of day without Jim Baumohl's generous investment of time and energy in reviewing the manuscript. Janet Francendese provided me with encouragement in the crunch and highly flexible deadlines throughout the years. Debby Stuart and Jane Barry provided invaluable assistance in producing the final product.

Sunny Banwer not only put up with years of strange behavior but served as sounding board and critic for many of the ideas developed in this work. Sam and Annie Rosenthal were gracious enough to delay their respective arrivals so that this birth, too, could happen.

My greatest debt, of course, is to those homeless people in Santa Barbara who allowed me into, and guided me through, their lives. Special thanks to the members of the Santa Barbara Homeless Coalition. Keep on keeping on.

Some of the material contained in the Appendix first appeared as "Straighter from the Source," *Urban Anthropology* 20 (1991): 109–126.

Some of the material on the "Skidders" group first appeared as "Skidding/Coping/Escaping," in Sue Fisher and Kathy Davis, eds., *Negotiating at the Margins* (New Brunswick, N.J., 1993).

Homeless *in* *Paradise*

Introduction:

Why are they

homeless?

It is August 19, 1986. The City Council of Santa Barbara, California, is debating a proposal to rescind the city's "illegal sleeping" law, which prohibits sleeping outside of a residence from ten at night until six in the morning. The law, homeless people say, makes them criminals by their very status. The meeting has drawn the largest crowd in City Council history. Several hundred people jam the Council chambers, while an overflow crowd listens to the debate on loudspeakers outside.

Almost one hundred people rise to voice their opinions about the issue. Each stresses how long he or she has lived in Santa Barbara. Each expresses a deep concern for those truly in need. Each demands that something be done about "the problem." But what exactly is the problem?

The owner of a car wash located next to Fig Tree Park, a major gathering place for homeless people, says he is "incensed by your proposal to let people sleep at the Fig Tree":

> These people are foul-mouthed, they do not respect private property. They come on my property, drive away my customers.

A member of the local Mental Health Advisory Board says:

> Many of our homeless—and I'm speaking of the homeless in particular who are mentally ill, who have alcohol and drug abuse problems, that's probably 65 to 70 percent of the homeless in this area—need a stable environment to get back on their feet.

A man whose face plainly shows the signs of living outdoors says:

> I've lived in this city for seventeen years. I've owned a business in this city and I pay taxes in this city. I've also owned a home in this city. But I am homeless. . . . Our Constitution says, "We, the People." We are part of the people. We are part of the city.

The mayor attempts to sum up public opinion:

> People want to help the mentally ill, they want to help the women and children, they want to help those with jobs or seriously looking for jobs. A lot of people out there have had one misfortune after another happen to them. And this is a caring community. Everybody wants to help them. But there are some out there that none of us want to help.

While most of us who are housed encounter homeless people as we move through our daily lives, we are far from united in our perceptions of "the problem."[1] We cannot agree about who homeless people are, or why they are homeless, and therefore about what might be done about homelessness.

Researchers in the past thought they knew the answers to "who" and "why." Homeless men of the late nineteenth and early twentieth centuries were said to be hobos (who "work and wander"), tramps (who "dream and wander"), or bums (who "drink and wander").[2] Their condition was largely attributed to their own characteristics: "industrial inadequacy," "defects of personality," "wanderlust," and so forth.[3]

Researchers of the post–World War II era, although dealing with a very different population largely found on Skid Rows, maintained this focus on personal characteristics and similarly emphasized a more or less consciously chosen isolation from mainstream society. According to the leading theory of the time, the mostly elderly white men found on Skid Row were "disaffiliated."[4] Some researchers saw them as lifelong isolates whose situations were due to their "inept sociability";[5] others argued that homelessness involved not simply disaffiliation from mainstream society but also a reaffiliation with Skid Row or homeless society, a theory particularly applied to alcoholics, homosexuals, and other "deviants."[6] Although a few researchers suggested that homelessness and disaffiliation could be simultaneously produced by calamitous social events such as revolutions, economic crises, or natural disasters,[7] the prevailing image was of rootless, isolated people, detached—even willfully disengaged—from kin, community, and mainstream institutions. In the most severe versions of this image, homeless people were said to be isolated even from each other, incapable of the reciprocal relations necessary for social networks.[8]

An emphasis on prior and supposedly causative personal characteristics was again dominant when homelessness reappeared as a public concern in the early 1980s.[9] Those seen on the streets appeared to be mentally ill, substance abusers, or shirkers. We might sum up the image of homeless people as "slackers and lackers": those unwilling or unable to do the work of life. But the huge increases in numbers in a very short time and the increasingly obvious heterogeneity of those on the streets made it difficult to believe homelessness was simply an individual problem.[10] Either hundreds of thousands, possibly millions, of Americans had suddenly caught irresponsibility or incompetence like the flu, or more social, less individual causes must be involved. Thus arose what might be called the "displacement school," researchers who blamed the explosion in homelessness on specific governmental policies or, in a few cases, on the very structures of our society.[11] Whatever the personal problems of the individuals who become homeless, these researchers argued, large-scale economic and social trends—including unemployment (often tied to deindustrialization), holes and cutbacks in the welfare system, the mental health policy of deinstitutionalization, changes in traditional family structures, and, beyond everything else, the demise of affordable housing— have created a game of musical chairs: There are just not enough residences to go around.[12] In the current academic language, the emphasis changed from the "agency" of homeless people themselves—that is, their individual actions and behaviors—to the "constraints" imposed on them by social processes beyond their individual control.

But while most recent researchers have dropped the disaffiliation school's emphasis on personal characteristics as the primary cause of homelessness,[13] they have largely retained the image of homeless people as isolated and disaffiliated.[14] While some argue that disaffiliation plays at least a contributing role in causing homelessness (i.e., that displacement leads to homelessness for those with the weakest ties to affiliative networks),[15] almost all argue that people become isolated and disaffiliated in reaction to homelessness. Disaffiliation is thus recast as a *result* of homelessness that makes homeless life and ultimate escape from it more difficult.[16] At the same time, by implicitly or explicitly minimizing personal blame, displacement theorists have correspondingly emphasized a picture of victimization, rendering an image of homeless people as hopeless and helpless against the great social forces that grind them down. In a mirror image of older theories, there is now only constraint and no personal agency.

For almost five years in the middle 1980s, I was involved in a research and organizing effort called the Homeless People's Project (HoPP) in Santa Barbara, California, and thus spent much of my time working and passing time with homeless people there. Neither a picture of slackers and lackers nor one of hopeless victims resonated with what I was seeing. This work is an attempt to recreate that landscape of homelessness, to draw a rudimentary map of the terrain, rather than to create a census. It draws on my field experiences with homeless people, 44 in-depth oral histories I collected from some of those I came to know through my work,[17] and two data sets collected by groups serving homeless people: 518 intake interview forms filled out by screeners at shelters run by a coalition of churches in 1985, and more than 200 calls logged recorded by a homeless self-help group, the Single Parent Alliance (SPA), in the mid-1980s.

By conveying a picture of homelessness as it was presented by the people I met,[18] I examine how the great social processes described by displacement theorists actually play out in the lives of individuals. In particular, I explore the different kinds and degrees of affiliation homeless people have to each other, to housed people, and to mainstream institutions, and thus question the image most housed people have of homeless people as both different and separate from the rest of us (and therefore to be ignored whenever possible). Doing this requires exploring the various kinds of lives homeless people lead, the heterogeneous people, paths, and survival strategies that make use of an inclusive term like "the homeless" meaningless. But while tracing the many faces of homelessness, I continue to emphasize the contribution of displacement theorists, the understanding that individual homelessness cannot be understood without an understanding of the social roots of homelessness as a mass phenomenon. That is, I want to describe the lives of particular homeless people without forgetting to ask why there are any homeless people at all.

Chapter 1 introduces Santa Barbara and the development of homelessness as a public issue there. In Chapter 2 I detail the many paths into the "career" of homelessness. In some few cases these involve a prior disengagement from social networks. In almost all cases there is involuntary displacement from a situation of residency through one or more economic setbacks; in most cases there is an intermediate period in which the individual's or household's "social margin"—resources available through social networks—is used up in an attempt to avoid homelessness. The great variation in paths begins to show us why finding a single unifying "theory of homelessness" is likely to be futile.

I then discuss what daily life is like for those who have become homeless: the many ways in which homeless people obtain the resources they need for survival (Chapter 3), and their reliance on old and new social networks for both material resources and emotional support (Chapter 4). While some homeless people are isolated, most, I argue here, are far from being nomads in a distant world. They make and preserve formidable ties with other homeless people and with housed people—ties of resources, values, and sometimes friendship.

The next two chapters discuss how people resist homelessness, either collectively in the homeless movement (Chapter 5) or individually (Chapter 6). Returning to the question of disaffiliation, I argue that the trait is much more likely to appear as a *result* of homelessness than as a *cause*, but

I continue to challenge the characterization of homeless people as generally disaffiliated. In my view despair and disengagement are periodic reactions to their shifting circumstances, as are spurts of efficacy and engagement.

In the final chapter I return to the macro level, exploring why society as a whole has failed to move forcefully to eradicate homelessness and suggesting how that might be done.

My descriptions and prescriptions are framed by my definition of who should be considered homeless, a problem faced by all works on this subject. The narrowest definitions include only those on the streets without a physical roof over their heads, while the broadest definitions also include people "at risk *in* their housing or at risk of losing their housing."[19] Complicating the matter is the question of whether homelessness can be determined purely in material terms, or whether there are social and psychological dimensions as well.

After years of working with and among homeless people, I came to see the critical factor as whether a person has a home base to depend on—a place to sleep, eat, wash, store belongings, and so on—and, further, whether one has some degree of security, a sense that one will be able to return to the same place tomorrow. I will thus define homeless people in this work as those without sleeping quarters where they (or their legal guardians in the case of minors) have *legal* rights of residency for a period of at least seven days.[20] I therefore include those in shelters or doubling up with friends, for instance, as homeless, since they may be evicted without legal recourse. I do not include those living in Single Room Occupancy (SRO) or welfare hotels, or those threatened with legal eviction after seven days, as has been suggested by some researchers.[21] This, of course, is merely an arbitrary cutoff point, since the smallest setback—a delayed paycheck, a missed welfare check, a night of "inappropriate behavior"— can result in eviction and joining the "truly" homeless. As a result, the "nearly homeless" are often part of this discussion as well.

Chapter 1
Paradise

Most residents of Santa Barbara were surprised when homelessness surfaced as a local issue in early 1983. Located ninety miles north of Los Angeles on the Pacific Ocean, Santa Barbara enjoys a benign climate, miles of beautiful beaches, and a reputation—foremost among its own residents—as "Paradise."[1] Aside from its natural beauty, the city itself is quite pretty, testimony both to its major industry of tourism and to the character bestowed by several extremely wealthy neighborhoods in and around it. The streets are clean, the parks are safe, and there is comparatively little crime. Large and luxurious houses dot the hillsides; pleasure yachts are common in the harbor. State Street, the main thoroughfare, boasts the kinds of establishments the well-off patronize: banks and brokerage houses, fashionable restaurants, trendy boutiques. The garbage cans are decorated with ceramic Mexican tiles.

In part, however, the ambience of wealth is deceiving. Although there is extreme wealth in and around the city, there is also genuine poverty, and comparatively little in between. No heavy industry exists in Santa Barbara, and thus no sizable lower-middle-class workforce.[2] One finds the very wealthy, a professional class of fair size, and those serving the wealthy and the comfortable in service jobs. Median household income for the city in 1980 was $15,445, 15 percent below the state average and 8 percent below the national average.

Political developments in Santa Barbara reflect both the physical and the social settings. On one hand, environmental politics are important, including attempts to limit population growth, development, and oil exploration in the Santa Barbara Channel. Class politics, on the other hand, usually takes the form of battles over housing and its cost. Rent control was placed on the ballot (but defeated) three times between 1978 and 1988, and the issue promises to return.

Despite these ongoing battles, Santa Barbarans of all classes are prone to declare their city the finest place to live imaginable. In the "mellow and laid-back" California style so ridiculed by inhabitants of other regions, the tenor of the town seems to say, "We are special here, we have found the Good Life." This attitude notwithstanding, Santa Barbara is typical of cities experiencing homelessness in a number of ways.

To begin with, the emergence of homelessness as a social issue in Santa Barbara parallels its emergence elsewhere. In the 1960s and 1970s, homelessness was rarely considered a significant problem by most of the city's institutions. Emergency shelter for adults was provided by three religious organizations in the downtown area, while homeless youths could stay at the Klein Bottle/Social Advocates for Youth (KBSAY) shelter. In all, about a hundred beds were available, with the Salvation Army shelter reporting an average 25 percent occupancy in those years. Additionally, a number of programs offered shelter for people with specific problems,

Greater Santa Barbara, mid-1980s

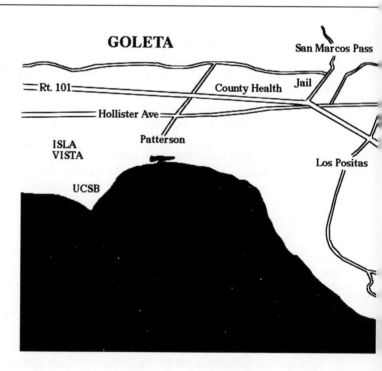

including alcoholics, those with mental illnesses, and battered women and their children, although few of these beds went to homeless people. Those working in the shelters and police on the streets described "the homeless" as largely older white men with drinking problems, often passing through town on their way to Los Angeles or San Francisco. In fact, the term "homeless" was rarely used: Such people were generically called "transients."

Beginning in the early 1980s, shelter operators and the police began noticing an increase in the number of these men, as well as the appearance of women and children. The police reacted to the growing numbers in the winter of 1982–83 by regularly dispersing those sleeping in an overgrown area near the beach called "the Jungle," forcing perhaps several hundred homeless people to move; merchants in the downtown area immediately began complaining about the "sudden" appearance of large numbers of "transients."

In reaction to the Jungle raids and the unusually wet winter, homeless people began organizing themselves into quasi-political organizations.[3] These groups' struggles gradually attracted housed advocates, first among

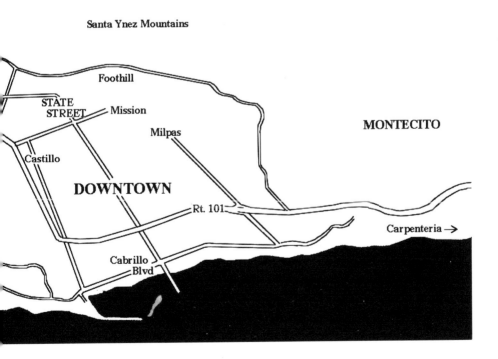

those politically active around issues of housing and social justice, and somewhat later among the religious community. As the activists and their advocates gained attention, a backlash developed. Letters to the local newspaper declared that homeless people should "move to Bakersfield,"[4] and some merchants threatened to pour bleach on their garbage to dissuade homeless people from "dumpster diving" (i.e., raiding garbage bins for food and other items). In December 1984 a homeless man named

This is A WARNING TO all "TRee people". You ARe NoT welcome here iN SanTA BARbARA. I will make life difficult FoR You AS I did mR. BuRR.

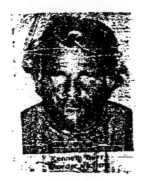

Victim #2

Although I Acted Alone, I have a faithful And Respected group of citizens behind me. You bastards ARe low life scum And will NoT enduRe. I promise you.

B. WARe

Kenny Burr was murdered by a single bullet fired at close range. The execution-like style of the killing (Burr was sleeping and none of his possessions was taken) convinced many homeless people and their advocates that Burr had been murdered purely because he was homeless. Most chilling of all was a flyer that appeared several days after Burr's murder threatening other homeless people with a similar fate. While its author eventually met with the police and was cleared of the actual murder, the leaflet generated profound fear on the streets. Burr's murder remains unsolved. Eight months later another homeless man, Michael Stephenson, was murdered by two students from a local military prep school, apparently in a case of mistaken identity.

During the development of the homeless movement and the backlash, local government moved toward action at a torturously slow pace. One City official was later to say that until the first interim report on my research appeared in June 1983, "We thought the homeless problem was thirty drunks on State Street." As the number of homeless people increased and homeless activists were joined by housing advocates and religious leaders, the City and County exchanged charges over whose responsibility homeless people were, while proclaiming that, in any case, they were only concerned with local homeless people and not transients. In an attempt at joint action, a city/county task force on homelessness met three times in 1985 and then disbanded. Eventually, however, the pure numbers involved, the insistence of merchants and the religious community that something had to be done (although their agendas for action were quite different), and media attention created a situation in which the City could no longer avoid acting.

The watershed event occurred in the summer of 1985. In March of that year, Mitch Snyder, a nationally known advocate for homeless people, had been invited to speak at a press conference called by the local Legal Defense Center. Snyder used the occasion to attack Santa Barbara's law prohibiting sleeping outside of a residence between ten at night and six in the morning. Perhaps attracted by Santa Barbara's manageable size and its prominence as President Reagan's hometown, Snyder vowed to use it as a test case to challenge "anti-sleeping" laws being considered across the nation. Calling Santa Barbara the "Selma of the 80s," he promised to return in September with large numbers of homeless people and celebrities who would court arrest under the anti-sleeping laws and repeatedly go to jail. The political risks of angering those voters who wanted to "preserve law and order" and "curb the homeless" were now balanced by the fiscal risks of dealing with a large demonstration, including the kind of negative national publicity abhorrent to a tourist town. In August the City amended the laws to allow sleeping on most municipal property, and the City/ County Task Force was resurrected to come to grips with a problem that political players finally recognized would not just go away.

Doonesbury

While a few aspects of this history are particular to Santa Barbara, the general outlines can be seen in most cities around the country: a surge in the size of the homeless population in the early 1980s; early recognition by shelter operators, police, and merchants of a growing problem; organization among homeless people and their advocates; counter organization among merchants and others opposed to the presence of homeless people in their town; and eventually political battles in which elected officials tried to avoid either angering the housed population or provoking large-scale confrontations with homeless people, while simultaneously acting to lessen the impact of homelessness on the daily running of the city.

Santa Barbara is typical in other ways as well. Most important, the social roots of homelessness identified by displacement theorists were all evident in the local explosion.

The Crisis in Affordable Housing

Throughout the United States, low-cost housing has for many years been substantially less lucrative to build and operate than luxury housing or commercial construction. The private market has responded by building the latter, often destroying affordable housing in the process (and often, as in the cases of urban renewal and gentrification, with the aid of the state).[5] At the same time, the federal government has largely abdicated its role in creating affordable housing. Funding budgets for public and Section 8 housing (i.e., privately owned units whose tenants' rents are subsidized) dropped as much as 80 percent in the 1980s, with the largest cuts coming in new construction.[6]

As a result, the country is experiencing a severe shortage of affordable housing, defined here simply as housing that costs (in rent or mortgage payments and related expenses) no more than 25 to 30 percent of a household's income.[7] The percentage of the population that could afford to buy a new house fell from nearly 70 percent in 1950 to less than 15 percent in 1982, while rents rose almost twice as fast as tenants' incomes in the 1970s.[8] The situation was even more drastic for low-income households: Rents for all tenants increased by 93 percent between 1978 and 1985, but rents for households with incomes under $3,000 increased 147 percent.[9] The median "poor renter" (i.e., below the poverty line) household was reported to be spending 65 percent of its income on housing in 1985.[10] In Santa Barbara, the percentage of tenant households spending over a quarter of their income on rent rose from 53 percent to 65 percent from 1975 to 1980; in the latter year almost a quarter of all tenant households were spending at least half of their income on rent. By 1985, the *median* tenant household in Santa Barbara was paying between a third and a half of its income on rent; for those households earning under $7,500, rents on average accounted for well over two-thirds of income.[11]

Coupled with rising rents were other pressures on tenants, particularly displacement due to conversions, demolitions, abandonment, and arson. Nationally, 2.5 million people are displaced involuntarily from their homes each year, while 500,000 low-income units are lost annually.[12] The least expensive housing has been particularly hard hit: Fully half of the nation's supply of Single Room Occupancy (SRO) units—a total of *one million* units—were lost during the 1970s.[13] Demolitions of residences doubled in Santa Barbara from the early 1970s to the early 1980s.[14] Between demolitions and commercial conversions, available SRO units declined 31 percent between 1975 and 1985.

Unemployment

Whereas joblessness idled an average 4.6 percent of the national workforce between 1946 and 1975, the late 1970s and 1980s saw an average official unemployment rate of about 7.5 percent, peaking at 10.8 percent in December 1982, the highest level since the Great Depression. And the jobs that unemployed people can find frequently pay less than their old ones as the country loses jobs in heavy industry and adds them in the service sector in the process known as "deindustrialization."[15] This shakedown in employment is most severe at the bottom of the occupational ladder. The weakening economy of the early 1980s appears to have wiped out many marginal jobs or replaced those holding them with other, more highly skilled workers, themselves victims of deindustrialization or recession.[16] (Ironically, economic upswings may *increase* homelessness by leading to new construction of commercial buildings or gentrified housing that displaces poor people.)[17] Unemployment in Santa Barbara County followed these national trends, rising from 5.8 percent in 1979 to about 8 percent for most of 1982 and 1983.

Holes in the "Safety Net"

In 1982 the U.S. Conference of Mayors reported that no human service program was serving even half of its eligible population; for some programs the percentage was as low as 10 percent.[18] As a result, "40 percent of the nearly 12 million households living below the poverty level in 1981 received no welfare, no food stamps, no public housing, no medicaid, no school lunches."[19]

The gap between the number of indigent people and the number receiving aid is a perennial problem, but one that the Reagan administration's attack on social service programs greatly exacerbated during the early 1980s by removing hundreds of thousands of people from aid programs, many of them members of the "working poor."[20] While the below-poverty-line population of Santa Barbara County increased over 9 percent during the recession of 1979–83, fewer people received public assistance. No program kept up with the increase in the poverty rate; the Supplemental Security Income (SSI) rolls fell almost 15 percent.

Deinstitutionalization

Deinstitutionalization of mental patients, broadly defined as their diversion from large state mental institutions to treatment in smaller, community-based clinics, has resulted in dramatic drops in state mental hospital populations (from 559,000 in 1955 to 125,000 in 1981).[21] But while the basic goal was to replace state hospital beds with community-based beds, less than 40 percent of the two thousand community mental health centers called for by the 1963 Community Mental Health Centers Act were ever created.[22]

Although deinstitutionalization has been heralded in the popular press as a major cause of homelessness, its effects have been generally misunderstood. Deinstitutionalization is predominantly implicated in the growth of homelessness not through the discharge of patients to the streets, but through tighter standards for patients seeking admittance to state mental institutions and the shortening of average hospital stays.[23] This policy coincided with the entrance of the baby boom generation into their late teens and early twenties, when schizophrenia and other major affective disorders are most likely to surface, "to produce a numerically significant population of chronically mentally ill individuals with specialized service needs"[24] at a time when gaining admittance to hospitals was

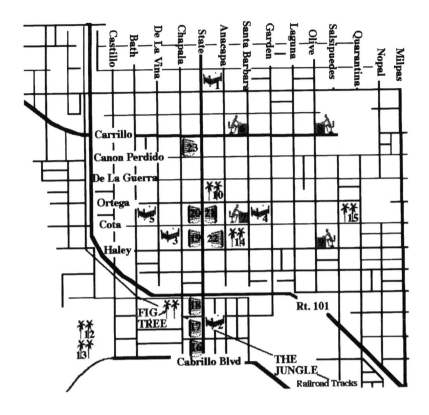

Downtown Santa Barbara, mid-1980s

Shelters	Agencies	Parks	SRO Hotels
1. KB/SAY Youth	6. Department of Social Services	10. De La Guerra (City Hall)	16. Californian
2. Rescue Mission	7. Employment Office	11. Fig Tree	17. Southern
3. Salvation Army	8. Social Security	12. Pershing	18. Neal
4. Transition House	9. Catholic Social Services	13. Plaza del Mar	19. Savoy
5. Wings of Love		14. Plaza Vera Cruz	20. Schooner Inn
		15. Ortega	21. Garvey
			22. Faulding
			23. Carrillo

becoming difficult at best, a trend furthered in the 1970s by the success of the patients' rights movement in curbing the powers of civil authorities to commit people to mental health institutions.

Further, the decentralization of what had been a fairly unified system of mental health care caused more patients to "fall through the cracks." Those patients least able to manage on their own—the chronic, "revolving door" mentally ill—were most likely to get lost in the transition from one form of care to another: not only in a one-time "deinstitutionalizing" from state mental hospital to community-based center, but repeatedly, every time they somehow found their way (often through the penal system) into a component of the mental health system.[25] The resulting community mental health system has been aptly characterized by Marjorie Hope and James Young as "a competitive, inefficient, inequitable, uncoordinated non-system. . . . A two-tiered approach has emerged: those who can pay privately, or have insurance, get one level of treatment. The poor get another."[26]

The effects of deinstitutionalization are difficult to quantify in Santa Barbara, although conditions there appear to be consistent with those in the nation as a whole. What is certain is that the number of local board-and-care facilities that served mentally ill people (and especially the affordable ones) decreased each year. In 1984 alone, ten board-and-cares closed their doors in the greater metropolitan area, perhaps a quarter of all such institutions.[27] Additionally, a number ceased to accept mentally disabled people and began to serve aged and developmentally disabled people, for whom state-regulated payments were significantly higher. Between changeovers and closures, the dearth of board-and-care beds passed the critical stage. In 1984 the County's Mental Health homeless project director observed that "literally days on end go by when there are no beds in the community" for people seen by County Mental Health workers.[28]

As with affordable housing and public assistance, federal cutbacks exacerbated the problem, both through decreased funding for direct services and through cuts for ancillary services such as Legal Aid and housing, weakening or removing many of the services that were necessary for a transition to a community-based system of mental health. Reflecting decreasing federal support, state funding to Santa Barbara County for mental health care dropped dramatically in the early 1980s, resulting in a shortfall of about $2.5 million from expected revenues in the three-year period 1981–83.[29] Most outpatient clinics and day care centers closed, and services were consolidated into one suburban location, making "service less accessible to clients who . . . will have to go to clinic by public bus, sometimes changing several times. This may prove impossible for less well organized patients."[30] Emergency, preventive, and educational services were also cut back. Whereas 3,700 people had been served by County Mental Services in 1978, only 2,080 were served in 1982.[31]

Changes in Traditional Family Structures

Finally, displacement theorists have spoken of changes in traditional family structures, such as the greater frequency of single-parent families.[32] The national divorce rate rose sharply in the 1960s and 1970s, from 0.22

percent of the population annually in 1960 to 0.52 percent in 1980.[33] Births to single women rose by 60 percent between 1970 and 1984.[34] By 1980 half of all children lived some "significant" part of their lives in one-parent families.[35]

Changes in social mores have made women more willing to leave unsatisfactory relationships. Yet patterns of employment and wages make women without mates, and particularly those with children, prime candidates for poverty. Women are significantly less likely than men to be working for wages, and today even those who work full-time earn 64 cents for every dollar earned by full-time male workers. It is not surprising, therefore, that over a third of female-headed households live in poverty, five times the rate for married-couple households.[36]

In addition, rising numbers of runaway and "throwaway" children (i.e., those whose parents are unwilling or unable to care for them) have joined the homeless population. The U.S. Department of Health and Human Services has estimated that "at least one-third of the million young people who leave home each year are 'technically homeless,' " unable to return to their homes.[37]

These changes were evident in Santa Barbara. The local divorce rate almost tripled between 1960 and 1980. Santa Barbara's only youth shelter, Klein Bottle/Social Advocates for Youth, estimated in 1984 that there were approximately 2,700 homeless children per year in Santa Barbara County.[38]

Although these trends collectively altered the social landscape, few Americans, and few Santa Barbarans, were acutely aware of them unless personally affected. Residents were perplexed by homelessness in Paradise. Many fell back on the comfort offered by the term "transient," the implication that these must be problems and people imported from elsewhere. The truth was that both problems and people were largely local, even as they reflected national trends and policies. This is not to say that Santa Barbara is typical in the sense that everything about it can be generalized to all other cities.[39] No single city presents a total picture of homelessness in the nation: hence the numerous endnote references to studies in other areas for purposes of comparison. But if we can understand how people can be homeless in Paradise, how the American nightmare of homelessness can exist within a city that seems to be the embodiment of the American Dream, we may have some idea as to what might be done about the problem, there and elsewhere.

Chapter 2
B e c o m i n g   h o m e l e s s

I wasn't born homeless," a speaker at the Santa Barbara City Council hearings told the crowd, "I just happen to be homeless now." The chain of events that leads a person from residency to homelessness typically involves three stages: a predisposing *vulnerability* to homelessness; *precipitating incidents* that directly lead to the loss of a residence; and an *inability to find substitute housing*.

Vulnerability

If homelessness were largely the result of individuals' irresponsibility or incompetence—if homeless people truly were simply slackers and lackers—the homeless population would be drawn from all economic classes.[1] Instead, homeless people are mainly drawn from a much larger group who are already in a financially precarious position, most frequently (but not always, as I will discuss shortly) those who have been poor for extended periods of time. Their vulnerability is in large part due to the gap between their limited incomes and their housing costs. Michael Stone has suggested that those whose housing costs leave them with less income than the Bureau of Labor Statistics calculates is the minimum for nonhousing necessities ($11,000 in 1980 for a family of four) are "shelter poor," forced to choose between shelter and other necessities. By his reckoning, 32 percent of all households in the United States—25 million households—were shelter poor in 1980.[2] For those living in shelter poverty, any loss of income may lead to displacement.

Sporadic employment is one cause of vulnerability. Twenty-five-year-old "Mayor" Max graduated from high school in Orange County, south of Los Angeles, and began studying at a community college. He dropped out to become an electrician apprentice, typically working on a construction project for weeks at a time and being laid off when the job was completed. Although he tried to get work on the larger projects that last for months or years, he found that each contractor "usually has a list of brothers and cousins and uncles who want to work already." Further, his apprenticeship is only recognized in Los Angeles County, forcing him to apply for less skilled positions when seeking work elsewhere. For years he bounced back and forth from relative security when working to extreme vulnerability when unemployed. A downward cycle developed: The longer he went without a job, the harder it was to find a new job as prospective employers noted his inability to give recent references. By the time of his interview, as was true of virtually all of the interviewees not currently employed, it had been over a year since he had held any formal job that lasted more than three days.[3]

Like Mayor Max, the majority of homeless people I interviewed in Santa Barbara (and those surveyed elsewhere) have graduated from high school; in Santa Barbara they were as likely to be high school graduates as members of the housed population.[4] Many had attended college; a few had bachelor's or higher degrees. Yet many, particularly those under thirty-five, had always worked in what Michael Piore calls the "secondary labor market" of low-paying sporadic manual jobs.[5]

Some reported a lack of opportunities in the small towns where they grew up, while others cited the desire to find work as quickly as possible, leading those from low-income families, in particular, to seize the first available job.[6] Many spoke of diminished opportunities for jobs that paid well as plants closed or moved away. Whatever the reason for their original entry into the secondary labor market, they then found few paths to the primary market: A job history limited to a series of secondary market jobs hindered them from launching a "career."

For those in the secondary market, and in the service sector generally, it is entirely possible to be both employed and poor (in part because the minimum wage was not increased between 1981 and 1989, despite a greater than one-third increase in the cost of living and an even steeper rise in the cost of housing). Liz is a thirty-seven-year-old college-educated mother of two (one of whom lives with her ex-husband). She has been employed as a social worker in a variety of settings and clearly sees herself as a Professional Woman (as her classified ad looking for housing proclaimed). She currently works, however, at a tennis club, and until her recent promotion to manager received $3.50 an hour. Although her promotion has extended her hours to a full forty-hour week, she fears her time may be cut back in the winter months. In local economies dominated by service industries (such as Santa Barbara's), both low wages and seasonal employment are the common condition for a substantial sector of the working class.[7] As I will explore further in Chapter 6, while willingness and ability to work are often seen as a matter of individual choice or character, larger processes—political decisions, the state of the local economy, deindustrialization, the level of union membership—are often of greater importance in determining whether employment at decent wages is even available.

Other people cannot work in any job because of age, disability, or responsibility for young children.[8] Theoretically, a number of government aid programs are available to those poor enough to be vulnerable to homelessness, but a substantial portion of the poor and unemployed population fall through the holes in the so-called safety net, receiving no benefits of any kind.[9] For instance, fewer than one in six guests of the Santa Barbara Church of the Month shelter were receiving public assistance when they came to their first Church shelter (the figure is 24 percent if one includes Food Stamp recipients).[10]

But even those who receive public assistance often remain economically vulnerable. Sonja is a thirty-seven-year-old mother of an infant daughter and a resident of Santa Barbara for the past twenty-seven years. Unable to work because of medical problems, she receives Supplemental Security Income (SSI) and Aid to Families of Dependent Children (AFDC) payments totaling nearly $700 a month. In order to pay the $525-a-month rent for her last apartment, she gave up many of the "luxuries" of her life: nursery school for her child, new clothes, babysitting, and "things that you don't think about, like repairs for your bicycle" (her sole means of transportation). Previously she had been paying only $160, her rent payments supplemented by Section 8 housing aid, but her landlord evicted her (illegally) when her child was born. A second Section 8 apartment fell through when her landlord left the program because he wanted to raise the rent above its allowable level.

In the early 1980s, the average one-bedroom apartment in Santa Barbara rented for between four and five hundred dollars. At that time the maximum allowable rent under the Section 8 program was $421, but the low vacancy rate meant that fewer and fewer landlords enrolled in the program. Social Security payments averaged $430 a month, SSI maximum payments were $460, AFDC payments averaged $405 for a family of two, and General Relief (GR) offered housing vouchers worth $195, along with approximately $100 for food and $11 for laundry and "personal needs." Between 1980 and 1983, AFDC and SSI recipients in Santa Barbara saw their payments rise half as fast as the cost of living; GR payments did not rise at all. (Nor is this merely a reflection of the inflated cost of living in Paradise. In the median AFDC payment state, benefits bring a family's income to half the poverty standard, and in three-quarters of the states, payments are less than 65 percent of the poverty line.[11] The real value of AFDC payments nationally is estimated to have declined between 30 and 36 percent from 1969 through 1984.)[12]

Sonja's medical problem is a physical disability; others are disabled by mental illness.[13] Mentally ill people are largely unable to work to support themselves, but they are often not organized enough to navigate the bureaucratic mazes leading to SSI or other forms of aid. Further, their episodically "bizarre" behavior strains their relationships with others, leading to increased isolation and diminished support, financial and otherwise, from friends and family.

One such person is Rachel, an alternately gregarious and withdrawn woman in her late forties whom I met while working as a shelter aide. Rachel has a long history of mental health problems dating back to her early childhood. By the time we met, she had been in and out of mental hospitals twelve times by her count. She has been arrested a number of times, occasionally for economic crimes such as shoplifting, but more often for outbreaks of inappropriate behavior, especially the destruction of property in SRO hotels when she has enough money to afford a room for a night. These arrests sometimes lead to jail time but more often send her back into the mental health system, which she distrusts and flees as soon as possible:*

> It's never helped before. I mean, they seem to just get a charge out of it. [They usually get you] hooked on drugs, prescribed drugs. . . . It never did cure anything anyway, it just makes you more tranquil and look more easy to manage for that group of people that was around you, but it didn't cure the symptoms.

Being physically disabled (she is missing an eye from a childhood accident and suffers from severe arthritis), as well as mentally disabled, Rachel is a prime candidate for public assistance, particularly SSI, but at the time I met her she was receiving no welfare payments of any kind. She had once received GR housing vouchers, but her episodically destructive behavior in SROs had earned her a reputation that made it impossible for her to rent a room in any SRO establishment. Most of her income for the

---

*In all transcriptions, comments within braces ({}) indicate a note written to myself at the time. Comments within brackets ([]) indicate an editorial clarification added for the sake of the reader. Parentheses are used conventionally, to indicate peripheral or clarifying comments written at the time. Ellipses (. . .) are used when meaningful but not immediately pertinent information has been deleted, or to join parts of an interview separated by follow-up questions. Italics (unless otherwise identified) indicate an original spoken emphasis. I have removed stopwords ("uh," "umm," etc.), except when they appeared to have some importance, as when expressing hesitation or uncertainty. Names of homeless people have been changed, as have some details of their stories, to preserve confidentiality or protect third parties.

last ten years had come from the men she stayed with, a series of tumultuous relationships, most of them short-lived. Although her parents and siblings are still alive, she is in touch, rarely, with only one brother.

While mental illness may increase vulnerability, what is crucial is its *interaction* with personal factors (relationships, family support) and structural factors (gentrification, demolition or conversion of SROs, availability of local board-and-cares, barriers to receiving public assistance). The same is true of substance abuse. Although the bulk of evidence indicates that the old wino image is no longer an accurate picture of homeless people generally (if it ever was),[14] substance abuse may interact with other factors to lead to the loss of job, family, and friends, as it often has for Jack, a twenty-seven-year-old native Californian from the Los Angeles area. Jack's father was "a real drinker," leading to his parents' divorce when Jack was in primary school. Jack himself had his first beer at thirteen: "I started getting drunk when I was fifteen . . . but I think it actually became a real problem . . . when I got out of high school." Since then, Jack has spent a considerable amount of time on the streets, often working as a prostitute or panhandling, "just for a little bit to eat, and something always to drink." He no longer is in touch with any members of his family: "They wouldn't help, you know, and I wouldn't quit drinking."

When sober, Jack is articulate and charming. Combined with his good looks, these qualities have helped him obtain formal employment in recent years, usually in casinos in the Lake Tahoe area, but he regularly loses these jobs by going on drinking sprees. As time passes, his reputation as a drinker has made it harder to find casinos that will hire him. As Jonathan, another long-term drinker, puts it, "You become a *suspect* rather than a *prospect*." Further, loss of financial and social support may combine with what earlier theorists called "drift" toward a milieu where drinking is not censured.[15] Those cut off from past networks of employers, friends, and family members who condemn their behavior naturally seek community among others who do not.

Substance abuse frequently interacts with other individual problems. Those with mental illnesses are more likely to have substance abuse problems as well,[16] often apparently as a form of self-medication. For others, problems at work or in relationships may increase, as well as result from, substance abuse. Structural problems, such as the loss of low-cost housing units,[17] cutbacks in social services, and higher unemployment leading to reduced marginal jobs, play a part. Whatever the configuration of factors, substance abuse is clearly a potent source of vulnerability for some people, although, most studies now agree, it is not the major cause of homelessness for most homeless people.

Economic precariousness may also result from incarceration or institutionalization. One generally leaves jail or prison without financial resources and thus without the means to reenter the housing market, which typically requires greater resources (to pay the first and last month's rent, plus a security or cleaning deposit) than simply continuing in a residence. Imprisonment also stigmatizes, creating a barrier to finding employment once released. Further, families and friends are often less willing to help out, reasoning that the individual is unworthy of worry and support.[18] Unfortunately, discharge plans for those leaving jail or prison appear to be virtually nonexistent.[19]

The same may be said of people institutionalized in mental hospitals: Upon leaving they are likely to lack resources and social support while facing labeling barriers to employment, and, in the wake of decentralization and deinstitutionalization, aftercare linkages are extremely weak.[20] In the early 1980s, it was apparently not uncommon to discharge patients without securing a stable residence and financial support for them: In "Greyhound therapy," patients were simply put on a bus to another community.[21] Although a majority of patients now appear to leave with comprehensive discharge plans, many still do not, and even those with nominal plans are often discharged without sufficient resources or support.[22]

The transfer to a new environment breaks ties with counselors and emotional supports from the old environment. Discharge typically means the total withdrawal of efforts by the old support network before connections have been made to a new one.[23] Rachel snorts derisively when I mention follow-up by hospital staff after discharge: "Most of the time there is nothing. It's up to you to go find somebody to help you."

Although long-term poverty obviously creates a vulnerability to homelessness, many people become vulnerable from a position of relative economic security. The costs and disruptions of moving to a new area may exhaust a person's resources.[24] Migrants from other parts of the United States typically move toward better climates, to be near friends or family, or in hope of obtaining employment or better employment.[25] For immigrants, civil unrest or repressive social conditions in their native countries may be additional factors. Dula and her husband fled middle-class lives in El Salvador on extremely short notice: "We were living in fear for our lives; we had nightmares day and night." Their hasty flight allowed them to bring few resources, and her husband, a skilled mechanic, finds it difficult to secure skilled work. As a result, they "have always had to live with other people, sharing living quarters."

Even when migrants and immigrants arrive with enough resources to secure housing, their financial resources may be stretched to the limit, rendering them vulnerable to homelessness if another financial shock is experienced. Poverty and homelessness can be avoided if employment and affordable housing are found quickly, but in a tight labor and housing market, contacts and networks are essential.[26]

Another group of people who fall from situations of relative economic security to extreme vulnerability are those who are dependent on someone else's income, a situation characteristic, in particular, of women in couples and of children. Women in couples are less likely to be employed than men in couples or single women.[27] "Unemployed" women in couples, of course, are working as homemakers. But in the household division of labor, the partner whose job results in financial remuneration can survive a split far more easily than his or her partner.[28] And even those women who do work for pay on average make 64 cents for every dollar a male worker makes.

When children are involved, vulnerability is increased. Tom Joe and Cheryl Rogers note that while female-headed families make up only 13 percent of the general population, they make up 34 percent of those in poverty.[29] Although children offer a strong incentive to work, they also make working problematic, especially when funds for day care are limited or lacking. Child support is supposed to prevent the financial costs of child-rearing from weighing more heavily on the parent retaining custody than on the ex-partner, but the grim reality is that comparatively few divorced fathers meet their financial responsibilities. A 1981 Census Bureau study found that less than half of the women awarded child support received it, about a third received partial payment, and a quarter received nothing at all.[30]

Lynn, a thirty-three-year-old mother of two, spoke for many such women when she told me: "I was raised middle class, I live like the lower class, and I aspire to the upper class." A long-time resident of Santa Barbara, Lynn's financial woes began with her second divorce:

> I was married until about 1980 and everything was fine and dandy, we were both working, we could afford the rent in Santa Barbara. The marriage didn't work out and we got divorced. I didn't want to go back to work in my field—because of [caring for] my kids—which is restaurant management. Too many hours. And I found that I couldn't afford the rent on what welfare gives you.

Lynn has never received "one single dime" of the $100-a-month child support her first husband was assessed, and now has no interest in collecting from him: "The state will take it because I've been on AFDC off and on and they'll take whatever they have to, to pay off the fund." After her second divorce, she became involved with the man who fathered her younger child. They moved in together, but two months later he became physically abusive and she moved out.[31] He too refuses to help with child support: "After I moved out, he said, 'Well, that's your problem.' He didn't want to have anything to do with that."

Women, as Diana Pearce and Harriette McAdoo, point out,

may be poor for some of the same reasons as men, but few men become poor because of "female" causes. Men generally do not become poor because of divorce, sex-roles, socialization, sexism, or, of course, pregnancy. Indeed, some may lift themselves out of poverty by the same means that plunge women into it: the same divorce that frees a man from the financial burdens of a family may result in poverty for his ex-wife and children.[32]

Children, of course, are completely dependent on their parents' income. Lisa is a fourteen-year-old native Santa Barbaran with an already tumultuous history. Since the age of ten, she has clashed repeatedly with her single-parent mother, resulting in her running away at ten, twelve, and fourteen to places as far away as Seattle and Houston. Although these clashes are mainly over Lisa's independence and "acting too old,"[33] her use of drugs (mainly marijuana, but also more dangerous drugs) is a serious, and related, point of contention:

> She wouldn't let me do what I wanted. . . . My mom didn't like the idea of her baby growing up. And being twelve and acting like a fifteen-year-old isn't really good, you know, and that's how I was.

For four years Lisa has bounced between the streets and various relatives, most often her mother, but also, for short stays, her father, stepmother, and aunt. Each time she leaves, her "income" ends: "I was really on my own, with no money, no nothing, yeah. No clothes, nothing, just the things I had on my back the day I left." In conversation she swings back and forth between a child's exuberance and the deep despair of someone who has seen too much pain:

> I tried killing myself 'cause I didn't want to carry on no more. . . . They called the Crisis Center, and here I am [at a youth shelter], you know. And still thinking about running.

Although vulnerability may stem from many causes and may take many forms, at the heart of virtually every story is financial vulnerability. This constitutes a first parameter circumscribing the pool of potential homeless people: those close to or below the poverty line who lack an adequate income gained through employment and whose financial precariousness persists despite theoretical protection by a system of supports, and those above the poverty line who have no legal or practical control over their family's income. As James Wright notes, "The nation would be facing a formidable homelessness problem even if there were no alcoholics, no drug addicts, no deinstitutionalized mentally ill—no personal pathologies of any kind."[34]

But some people are not only financially but also "psychologically" vulnerable to displacement. That is, they may have the financial resources to continue living in a home—although not necessarily to find a *new* home—but they consider leaving their housed situation because of dissatisfaction with their lives.

Sometimes the source of this dissatisfaction is a conflict within the household, particularly between children and parents, as in Lisa's case. Mental or physical abuse may predispose women to leave their homes, as Lynn described. The disproportionate number of veterans—and particularly Vietnam veterans—in most local homeless populations suggests some linkage between military service and a subsequent disengagement from mainstream society, a loosening of attachments to conventional life-styles.[35] But among the homeless people I met, the most common form of adult dissatisfaction was frustration with their housed lives because of financial difficulties. Typically mired in dead-end, low-paying jobs, they began to wonder if the work was worth the payoff. This was the story for Wendi and Bret, a couple in their thirties. They met and became involved in Chicago, and then moved to Denver, where they had heard life was less pressured and jobs more available. But although both found jobs in Denver, they were barely getting by:

> WENDI: . . . the jobs are three thirty-five an hour. . . . We were making enough to pay rent and that was it. Not eating too much. . . . We did leave Denver with enough to pay rent. But what's the use of living in a house if you can't eat or do nothing?

Many researchers have argued that vulnerability to homelessness is highest among those who lack social connections; some suggest that those who become homeless are characterized by a long-term lack of social connections, in some cases beginning with childhood abandonment or abuse. Whether stemming from long-term disengagement or more recent alienation, estrangement from "straight" life, it will be noted, sounds very much like what earlier theorists called "disaffiliation." But there is a crucial time element missing. Some people may be life-long isolates; others tire of their conventional lives and, gradually or suddenly, take to the road, breaking all affiliative bonds. Yet, as I will explore in Chapter 4, it appears that where disaffiliation exists, it is, for most, the last step rather than the first, a *result* rather than a principal *cause* of homelessness. While other factors contribute to vulnerability, they often have financial underpinnings and generally assume importance only because they have financial repercussions. Wendi's dissatisfaction with her housed life stemmed from her despair at spending all of her income on rent. Rachel's mental illness made employment highly unlikely, as well as contributing to the short-lived nature of her relationships with men (and thus access to their income). Jack's drinking led to his loss of job as well as family and reputation.

Neither financial vulnerability nor any of the other factors, however, is enough. The people who become homeless, in Santa Barbara and across the nation, are a fraction of those who are vulnerable. In 1983, thirty-two million people in the United States were living below the poverty level, while another twelve million were living close to that line; in Santa Barbara County in 1983, 33,231 people were living below the poverty line.[36] But most vulnerable people do not become displaced; Peter Rossi and his colleagues have estimated that only 3 percent of the "extremely poor" in Chicago become literally homeless.[37]

Homelessness from social causes may be compared to homelessness resulting from natural disasters. In both cases those who begin with greater resources and more control over their daily lives are more likely to avoid loss of home. Those who take greater precautions stand a better chance of weathering the storm. Yet even those without resources or foresight may escape with their homes intact, while those with both may not. Where the storm touches down and with what results are crucial, and yet due to chance. Similarly, the specific events that lead directly to the loss of a home are often largely beyond an individual's or a household's control. Vulnerability, personal circumstances, and social trends interact to produce "precipitating events," transforming a small segment of the vulnerable into the relatively few who are actually displaced.

Precipitating Incidents

Precipitating incidents break an individual's or household's established patterns of residence and social support. Whether a specific incident further increases vulnerability or leads to loss of home depends on the resources at each household's command. Precipitating events therefore should not be seen as in some way the "real" or "actual" causes of homelessness. Rather, they are the other shoe dropping for people whose vulnerabilities render them likely candidates for displacement. When money is scarce, housing is often the first essential need to be sacrificed. As Jonathan Kozol points out, "Housing is a nondivisible and not easily adjustable expenditure. . . . By contrast, one can rapidly and drastically adjust one's food consumption."[38]

For some, the precipitating event is merely an intensification of the same factors that produced vulnerability. Mayor Max's pattern of intermittent employment led to displacement when the wait between jobs was so long that his meager savings ran out. Similarly, Jack's drinking sprees sometimes left him both unemployed and without money to pay rent:

> I was working at Lake Tahoe, a seasonal job at a resort that I've been on and off at for five years. And I had a little girlfriend, so I

quit drinking for about three weeks . . . while I was with her. So one night, I went and got drunk. *She* wouldn't even talk to me any more. Shined me on. So I was totally devastated. . . . So then I started drinking *really* heavy, and I got fired from my job. . . . And I [had] saved up a thousand dollars, I was gonna move to Hawaii and all this stuff with these friends of mine. And I was totally devastated, so I didn't want to go to AA, 'cause I'd been there before, so I just kept on drinking, going out spending fifty or a hundred dollars a night, in the casinos and the bars. And that was the first week of August . . . and by the first week of September, all my money was gone.

Although the popular image of homeless people would suggest that the kind of personal "fault" involved in Jack's path is common, those I interviewed were far more likely to have lost their jobs through illness, seasonal layoffs, or company failure. While some layoffs involve individual characteristics, unemployment rates as a whole rise and fall not with variations in personal character but with large-scale economic trends.[39] Further, those employed seasonally, episodically, or in the secondary labor market in general are rarely protected from layoffs by union contract or other mechanisms, nor are they likely to get unemployment benefits. And once laid off, the worker has a diminished resume to offer the next prospective employer.[40]

Lisa's vulnerability also developed into displacement: Her conflicts with her mother came to a head when she failed to return home for several days after a big birthday bash some friends threw her: "After my fourteenth birthday, my mom said, 'You know, you're kicked out of this house for good. I don't ever want you back.' "[41]

In other cases of displacement, income remains steady, but expenses—notably rent—increase. In 1985, we have seen, the average tenant household in Santa Barbara was paying between a third and a half of its income for rent; those households earning under $7,500 were spending on average well over two-thirds of their income on rent.[42] Any rent increase in such situations may lead to displacement.[43]

In means-tested entitlement programs (unlike, for instance, Social Security), benefits are not indexed to inflation. Thus, Sonya was evicted for the second time when her landlord raised the rent above the maximum allowed under the Section 8 program, a common occurrence in a market characterized by a vacancy rate under one percent. Kathie, a physically and mentally disabled woman receiving SSI and eligible for Section 8, describes a common scenario in Santa Barbara in the 1980s in which displacement—rather than housing—appeared to be "trickling down":

Around the first of the year I received a notice from the County Housing Authority that I wasn't going to be renewed on my contract in the place where I was staying. And I had been there for four, four-and-a-half years. It just got to the point where the housing market is way above what's available [i.e., legally allowable on Section 8] for housing. I mean, you just can't find anything for the three-fifty, three-and-a-quarter any more. The place was a hundred sixty dollars when I moved in four years ago, and it's now going for, I think, four-and-a-quarter as of last raise.

[The place] that I'm in now—uh, that I *was* in—that are now four-and-a-quarter, they [landlords] can get that. They know they can still charge that amount to fill them. All those people that used to have houses are taking those places. And the people that used to be in the four-and-a-quarter apartments are now in rooms in a house, which are now two thirty-five, three hundred a month. And the poor people that used to be in the rooms are now tripling and quadrupling up with other people, or are sleeping under a bush somewhere or in a car someplace. I can't even sleep in a car, I don't even have a car [laughs], so that leaves the bushes.

Many with low-wage jobs find that although their incomes remain steady, their wages cannot keep up with rent increases. Danita immigrated to the United States from Mexico six years previously: "I work as a maid in a hotel. The pay is very low. . . . I used to have an apartment when the rent was cheaper [but] . . . I could not pay the [new] rent." (As we shall see, full-time unemployment is often coupled with displacement for immigrants.)

Other people become displaced despite a steady (albeit marginal) income because emergencies or other unplanned expenses arise. When one is living on a budget already stretched to the maximum, such unplanned expenditures can lead to eviction for nonpayment of rent. Rob spent part of his December rent on Christmas presents for his two small children. Although his landlord told him at first that he could make up the rest of the rent later, he was evicted in early January. Margie was living so close to the edge that a late paycheck was enough to send her into the streets:

I had a paycheck coming at the end of the week, but my rent was due on Wednesday. So I had no place to go. And I had asked them if they could hold out until the end of the week, when I could pay it. I'd been there for three months, paying rent every week straight. And—it didn't work out, and I didn't have any place to stay.

In contrast to these last-straw cases, other people are displaced through a more drastic reversal of fortune. The same factors that produce vulnerability for some produce actual displacement for others, either because the events themselves entail greater economic consequences or because the people involved have fewer resources.

For example, while migration often leads to vulnerability, in some cases it leads directly to displacement.[44] Some migrants leave their last housing situation without enough money to establish themselves in an expensive and competitive housing market; others use up their money in travel. Hank, a fifty-nine-year-old painter, divorced with three grown children, had been living in Florida with his sister, but left when her drinking led to friction. Having previously lived and worked in Santa Barbara, he thought finding work there would be relatively easy and set off with a car, "a full wardrobe," and $500. But car problems along the way used up most of his money, and he was eventually forced to abandon his car and clothes, making the rest of the journey by bus. Although he had never been homeless before, Hank was confident that his old contacts would produce jobs for him and allow him to rent a room in one of the better SROs, as he had done in the past. He was right: Within two weeks of coming to a homeless shelter, he had found two painting jobs and was waiting for his first paychecks to move into the hotel. But Hank's quick escape depended on his previously formed contacts in Santa Barbara, a resource most migrants do not have.

Immigrants from other countries face worse problems. Their savings, based on a lower standard of living, are likely to be insufficient to rent a place in Santa Barbara. They may face discrimination from landlords. They may not speak English, and so have little chance of getting any but the most menial and low-paying jobs. They may be undocumented, and thus restricted in their employment or access to public assistance.[45] Some people in Santa Barbara have fallen from middle-class to lower-class status simply by leaving another country to come to the United States.

Migrants and immigrants, it is important to note, move in order to better their lives, not out of a desire to become homeless wanderers. Typically, they make the move precisely because they believe their new location has greater resources to offer them, generally a job. Bruce, a forty-year-old writer with a master's degree, came down from Seattle with his girlfriend and her two children seeking work near Santa Barbara:

> That's [something] I want to stress. When we first came out, we figured, "Well, we're going to be in the camper for two or three weeks. Let's just do it and don't worry about it and then we'll get a place after that." I don't usually have too much trouble finding a job, money, and a car. . . . Vandenberg [Air Force Base] was starting to move a lot of the space shuttle things and I thought that I could get a job there as a check writer or an editor. It turned out to be real rough and we ran out of money. . . . I stopped going there to Santa Maria [looking for work] and cut off those employ-

ment agencies. It didn't seem feasible at all, it wasn't worth it. I didn't have the resources.

Similarly, divorce (or separation) may lead to displacement rather than mere vulnerability. Consuela and her husband immigrated from Mexico with their two children "with the intention of bettering ourselves." The move initially seemed successful when her husband found work, "but when my baby was born, my husband walked out on us. I wasn't working, so I couldn't pay the rent, so we had to move out."[46]

While the financial repercussions of separation are usually the cause of displacement, an emotionally stunned partner may "hit the road," leaving everything behind. Greg, a thirty-seven-year-old recently discharged veteran from Pennsylvania, explained:

> She said she's gonna file for a divorce. So I just turned around and said, "It's better I leave town then, and that way neither of us cause trouble for the other if we just start a new life over." So I just packed my bags and left.

Discharges from institutions also result directly in displacement for some, particularly when institutionalization (or incarceration)[47] has used up a person's financial and social resources. Eli, a fifty-eight-year-old chauffeur and cook, became homeless (in one instance) after nine months in an alcoholism program; he expresses a bitterness shared by many who become homeless upon institutional discharge:

> In my opinion, rehabilitation is to give a man something, spiritually, emotionally, and physically, which he can utilize when he leaves you. But they send you out with . . . no money in your pocket! . . . God said to feed My people, clothe My people, and lift My people up. But He doesn't mean to lift you up only in spirit.

Julia was employed when her husband had her committed to a mental institution. While there, she lost her husband, her job, and her apartment:

> [My husband] terminated my oral agreement with my landlord, packed up all of my personal belongings and left them in the apartment, brought me a suitcase with a few personal articles of clothing, and basically said, "It's all over, you have one week to get out of the apartment." He was on his way to San Francisco. I didn't have a job, I had nowhere to live.

But despite the grave problems with aftercare linkages discussed earlier, only a small number of former patients appear to become homeless immediately upon discharge from a mental facility. The apparent discrepancy between the small percentage of homeless people who cite release from a mental institution as a precipitating incident and the substantially larger percentage who report some previous hospitalization suggests that the path from discharge to homelessness is often delayed and indirect.[48] Deinstitutionalized patients commonly return to their families, but most families "are unlikely to have the resources, the patience, or the training to take care of them."[49] At some point the friction becomes so great that some choose or are asked to leave their family home. It is at this point that homelessness generally occurs. Leaving the structured environment of a home leads to a number of factors that worsen the mental condition of the ex-patient and greatly reduce his or her available resources. Many discontinue taking medications, or "self-medicate" with alcohol or drugs; some become highly mobile, thus separating themselves from whatever support systems they had.[50]

Those people with mental illnesses receiving SSI, and others receiving other forms of welfare, may suffer an abrupt change in their situation if their public assistance is terminated or they are shifted from one program to another.[51] Kathie became homeless (in one instance) when her SSI benefits were cut off in the early years of the Reagan administration's reviews of disability cases:

> The SSI was going well for two years and three years. . . . And then, for some unknown reason, they had a ruling that cut it off, cut me off. I had to go through a couple of court cases to get it back. While I was off of it, while I was having to contest it with two court cases, things were incredibly hairy as far as making it on a day-to-day basis. I mean, I was selling blood twice a week until my veins blew out, just to have money to eat. And welfare [General Relief] cut me off because they said they [already] gave me the maximum amount that they could allow.

Such stories are common among homeless people. New York's Human Resources Administration reports that families who become homeless are twice as likely to have had public assistance terminated temporarily as families on public assistance who retained their housing.[52] Perhaps the greatest irony of the Reagan cutbacks was that they fell hardest on the working poor population, making it more difficult, for example, to qualify for Food Stamps and Medicaid, and eliminating 400,000 CETA jobs.[53] Here again we see the interaction of factors: Those traditionally most vulnerable found public assistance more difficult to receive at the very time that deindustrialization and soaring unemployment were making jobs harder to find. Many people who had held on to housing in the past found this double onslaught too difficult to withstand, especially when combined with the disappearance of affordable housing.

Evictions can occur for reasons other than inability to pay rent, as when Sonja was evicted after her baby was born: "I was evicted because they didn't allow children, and I'd been living in that place for six years."

Although such evictions are illegal in many places (including Santa Barbara), they are extremely widespread. Since landlords are not required to state the reasons for eviction, legal action is difficult. Only 19 percent of Santa Barbara tenants have written yearly leases: Evictions for virtually any reason, or no reason at all, are always theoretically possible for the remaining 81 percent of tenants on thirty-day notice.[54]

Many evictions are rooted in the desire of landlords to protect their investments by avoiding "excessive" wear and tear on their property:

> DORA: I came from Guatemala, I came here because my brother and his family asked me to come and live with them. I've never had a home [separate from them.] I've always lived with my brother until two years ago when his landlord asked him to move out because he had a lot of people living in the house. Ever since, I have been rolling from one place to another with my six children.

Such evictions are exceedingly important because many people attempt to cope with their shelter poverty by "doubling up," moving two or three households into a unit originally intended for one. The Census Bureau reports that nationally the number of homes shared by unrelated households jumped from 1.2 million in 1981 to 1.9 million in 1982, the first major increase since 1950.[55] Sometimes the individual or family moving in has equal rights to residency, as when their name goes on a lease or when minor children live with their parents. In such cases, homelessness as I have defined it has been averted, although the arrangements may be far from ideal. Where an individual or family moves into a residence through the beneficence of another, we may speak of them as already homeless. Wherever the line is drawn, overcrowding leads to literal "rooflessness" when the strains of the arrangement lead to eviction by those with greater authority (whether it is based on legal right or not). It is important to appreciate how commonly the path to the streets or shelters includes a stop in a doubled-up situation. Most people do not willingly become homeless. Instead they fight it, calling on whatever resources they have available, including the homes of friends and family. But these resources, too, may be used up.[56]

In the mid-1980's, more than 6 percent of Santa Barbara tenants were living in officially overcrowded households;[57] many of those I interviewed reported coming from such situations:

> CHRISTINE: We got a group of friends together, seven adults [and two children in a one-family unit]. . . . We lived there until the end of the six-month lease, when they terminated us.

> JUANITA: My girlfriend and I rented a room in the Hotel Happiness. She had to take care of her two children [Juanita also

has two]. I saw there about twelve families with children [in shared situations].

Aside from the risk of eviction by the landlord, overcrowding creates other pressures toward displacement. The fear of eviction may in itself lead one party to ask another to leave; friction often develops over the use of scarce resources; sheer physical and psychological discomfort may eventually cause one or another of those sharing to move out.

Housing may be "precarious" even if not doubled up. Forced into physically inadequate housing, poor people can be evicted by housing officials when their units are condemned for substandard conditions (although such officials rarely help tenants find new housing). Tenants who find the conditions unbearable may choose to move out. Landlords may convert rental units to condominiums or nonresidential use, or upgrade a building to attract a more affluent clientele, and evict tenants while doing renovations, a threat that is greatest in rundown areas undergoing gentrification.[58] Those who become homeless often have long histories of frequent moves.

In many cases, of course, displacement results from a combination of factors. Rachel's last landlord, for instance, faced continuous complaints from her neighbors about her bizarre behavior, but she was not actually displaced until her boyfriend left her, leaving her not only in a financially precarious situation but without the person who had previously placated her landlord: "So I was evicted. So even if I had money—I had a little money left and I could have got some more from my brother—he [the landlord] wouldn't let me stay there."

Kathie's slide into homelessness, which began with her eviction from Section 8 housing, appeared to be averted when a friend offered to put her up, but her mental problems then created a situation that led to another eviction and ensuing homelessness:

> I thought as long as I can sort of keep to myself, and not have to have a whole lot of interchange with these people that I'm living with, things will be reasonably mellow. . . . But it was like I could just feel all this stuff churning in my stomach again. . . . And then, it just really—the shit just hit the fan, so to speak. Because I wasn't myself. . . . And so I basically got bounced out on my ear.

The stories I have related, and many more I heard, seem to support the view that homeless people do not choose homelessness as a preferred lifestyle. Are there then no people whose path to homelessness includes voluntary elements, who willfully disengage themselves from a housed situation? On the basis of my Santa Barbara experiences, I would say there are very few, and even in those cases the term "disengagement" oversimplifies a complex process.

Contact with life on the streets can whet some people's appetite for more street life. That is, they appear to be "pulled" rather than "pushed": "The rich can become globe-trotters," Box Car Bertha told Ben Reitman in 1937, "but those who have no money become hoboes."[59] Margie, an eighteen-year-old who has been on the streets since leaving her home at sixteen, told me:

> Once . . . I met this girl and she was seventeen years old, and she was telling me about living on the streets. And I was asking, "You live on the streets?! You mean you sleep in doorways, a girl like you?!" And I just couldn't get over it, that she managed to survive sleeping literally on the streets. And I felt as if, you know, she knew more than I did. She had something, you know, something more, something . . .

Similarly, some of those who tire of a work life that leaves them little after the rent is paid, such as Wendi and Bret, find that life on the streets looks no worse, and in some ways better, than the struggles of their housed lives. Despair over their finances deepens into frustration with "straight" life generally; their revolt against working simply to meet the rent deepens into a rejection of working for material possessions at all:

> B R E T : I was working, working, working, and never had time to do nothing. Only to pay bills, get enough groceries to last from week to week. Borrow money from one, by the time I got my check it was all spent out. . . . After a while I was working just to pay payments. Not to get nothing out of it. What little time I had to enjoy what I bought wasn't worth keeping. . . . So we just took off. . . . I don't need it, I avoid it by avoiding material things.

Many housed people apparently believe that a significant number of homeless people prefer homelessness. In part, this image is inherited from the popular and academic literature of previous periods in which homelessness surfaced as a public issue. In part it is perpetuated because the homeless people most visible on the streets today are the ones most likely to *claim* a voluntaristic path to homelessness:

> H E N R Y : I like the freedom and the enjoyment of just being able to kick back and enjoy the town, just like the tourists. We're more or less tourists. Just being able to kick back and, like, if you do want to go someplace like up north or down to San Diego, you just take off. . . . Living on the street, you don't have any worries. Do I have to make any money today? No. Where am I going to sleep? Anywhere I feel like, more or less.

But even these "volunteers" are far from disengaged. No one I spoke to took to the road merely out of a preference for homeless life. Even when individuals had felt a previous "pull" to the road, it required a breakdown of their housed lives, a "push" of some kind, before they actually became homeless. Henry, for instance, did not set out on the road until the campground he lived in was closed down and he lost his rent-free job as caretaker. Margie's admiration for the girl who lived on the streets was formed against the backdrop of unending conflicts with her own parents. I asked one of the apparent "volunteers" about homeless people choosing their lives:

> W E N D I : Some people, that's all they know. You can put them in a house and set them all up, but they'll be back on the street.
> Q : You got any idea what percentage that is?
> W E N D I : About four percent [laughs].
> Q : You don't think it's many?
> W E N D I : It ain't a whole lot.[60]

Instead of a desire for homeless life, financial setbacks—often tied to larger social trends—appear to be behind most precipitating events, pushing those already on the financial edge over the line into displacement. Rarely, mental illness, substance abuse, or emotional pain alone puts people on the streets and causes them to ignore potential or offered financial help. But for the vast majority of homeless people, no matter what other problems precipitate displacement, the bottom line is an event that takes a financial toll. Those who can pay the rent are eccentrics and drinkers; those who cannot are lunatics and drunks.

Thus while many people are vulnerable to displacement, only a few actually lose their homes through a precipitating incident. One further specification now needs to be made: Of those people who do lose their homes, only a relative few become "homeless." We now turn to the final stage in that process, the inability to find substitute housing.

Inability to Find Substitute Housing

Neither "slackers and lackers" nor alienated victims would be expected to struggle against their dispossession, and yet that is precisely what the vast majority of displaced people do. Most expect and attempt to find substitute housing before their eviction notices take effect.[61] Data from the Department of Housing and Urban Development (HUD) indicate that two and a half million people are involuntarily displaced each year,[62] yet most of them apparently find new homes. Those who cannot become truly homeless.

Displaced people, of course, typically reenter the housing market (or enter a new housing market) with relatively few resources, but often the extra cost of paying "first, last, and deposit." They are unlikely to be working full-time, and unlikely to be receiving welfare. As a result, they rarely have much in the way of savings. They are further unlikely to come from families or networks of friends with sufficient resources to share. Most homeless people I met came from lower-class or lower-middle-class families; those who did not were either immigrants who had descended in the class structure upon immigration or people who were estranged from their families, often (although not exclusively) those with problems of substance abuse (like Jack) or mental illness (like Rachel).

Theorists speak of people who have "no adequate support system to turn to . . . and [are] unable to negotiate successfully the various bureaucracies that might be able to assist them"[63] as lacking "social margin," defined as "all personal possessions, attributes, or relationships which can be traded on for help in time of need."[64] In Chapter 4 I will explore the degree to which this lack of social margin is due to estrangement (or disaffiliation) or, in contrast, to affiliation to others who also lack resources. But whatever the cause, those who are unable to find substitute housing are unable to secure the necessary resources either from their own efforts or from others.

A resource that may be shared, however, is housing itself: One temporary option for some of those who are displaced, as for many of the vulnerable, is to double up with others, often kin or friends. As a number of researchers have argued, "That so many of the extremely poor do manage to avoid homelessness is . . . almost certainly the result of the generosity of family and friends,"[65] and "a stunning achievement on the part of . . . low income families."[66] By 1985, half of Santa Barbara tenant households with three to six members were living in units with two bedrooms or fewer.[67] Those groups traditionally with the lowest incomes showed overcrowding rates two to four times higher than the city average, including 11.4 percent of African-American households and 23.4 percent of Hispanic households.[68]

These figures indicate that doubling up is a common strategy for low-income households, but also suggest that newly displaced households may find it difficult to receive help from friends and family members who are likely to be already overcrowded as well as poor themselves. A common result is that those seeking substitute housing through doubling up are only able to find it for brief periods,[69] and must leave when their hosts' good will or resources give out. Doubling up is in most cases a temporary solution. Preventing homelessness generally requires finding a place of one's own.

The greatest barrier to finding substitute housing is simply the lack of housing in relation to need. Both locally and nationally, the shortage is most acute for low-cost housing. Santa Barbara's overall vacancy rate in 1983 was reported to be 0.9 percent, with an even lower 0.4 percent for rental housing, the result of low rates of new rental housing construction coupled with demolitions and conversions of existing residential units.[70] The crunch was most severe at the bottom of the housing market, particularly given the decline in available SRO units.[71]

As the private market's ability and willingness to provide low-cost housing declined, subsidized housing in Santa Barbara proved to be insufficient to meet the growing need. While public units owned and operated by the Housing Authority continued to grow through the early 1980s, the loss in Section 8 units was even greater. As the Housing Authority reported in 1982,

> Our Section 8 leased housing program has not fared well in these inflationary times. Rising rents, a tight rental housing market, and a reluctance by Congress to increase the Fair Market Rents [i.e., the maximum amount of rent that may be paid to landlords] has reduced our ability to fill our 810 unit allocation. Presently, we have only about 600 units under contract and the future is less than encouraging.[72]

It was not until 1985 that total subsidized units again equaled the totals in 1979–81. By then, however, need had swollen through general population growth and the widening gap between income and rent for increasing numbers of households. The waiting list for public housing grew from 1,500 households in 1970 to 2,500 by 1983; at no time in that period was the average waiting time for public housing or Section 8 certificates less than two years (except for those few tenants already living in private housing who persuaded their landlords to enroll in the Section 8 program).[73] Although the 1980 census found 59 percent of tenant households to be low- or very-low-income, the 1985 Rental Housing Task Force found that just 7 percent of the tenants surveyed had ever received Section 8 assistance.[74]

Displaced people in Santa Barbara often expressed frustration about their inability to use Section 8 certificates, one of the major problems for single, low-income parents according to the leader of the Single Parent Alliance:

> I've known several people who've spent the night in the [Housing Authority] parking lot in order to be first on the list to get these certificates. And they've gotten the certificates, and they cannot find a place to live because the [rent] regulations are inappropriate to the market in Santa Barbara. . . . There are virtually no places in this area that you can rent for that amount of money. So it's a waste of time to get people's hopes up, they waste their valuable time and valuable energy looking for something that doesn't exist. People get more and more disappointed, and more discouraged, and they're getting desperate.

Again, this is a local reflection of a national problem.[75] In December 1986 the U.S. Conference of Mayors found that the average—but highly variable—wait for assisted housing, including Section 8 certificates, in surveyed cities was eighteen months.[76] In New York City, the wait for public housing was eighteen *years*.[77] The bottom line is this: Less than a third of low-income households, and 6 percent of all households in the United States, live in assisted housing. Both levels are the lowest for any industrial nation.[78]

The combination of a private market that has largely abandoned construction of affordable rental units and a federal housing policy that has abandoned low-income housing in almost all its forms makes finding substitute housing difficult even for those with some resources. Kathie, receiving SSI and eligible for a Section 8 subsidy, describes her search for a new home:

> I totally *exhausted* myself trying to find something. I mean I spent about eighty dollars on ads in the paper, looking for something with a maximum of three hundred fifty-three [dollars] including utilities, and it had to be either a studio or a one-bedroom. I even had ads offering to do work exchange for a place to stay. I didn't get *any* results. I mean, I got one guy that was sorta looking for someone to sleep with.
>
> I went up to Santa Maria; they didn't have anything up there either. They were sending all their people to Santa Barbara [laughs], so obviously, I gave up the idea of Santa Maria. . . . So I came back down here, and I saw this thing about the City Housing Authority. . . . But then I got down there and there were like two hundred people or even more in line. And when I got up there . . . they said that I had a priority of zero because I wasn't a veteran and I wasn't living in a car. . . . With a zero priority, it's probably a two-year waiting list. So in the meantime, what do you do?

The structural context of limited housing compared with need sets the stage for the individual struggles of displaced people to find housing. In particular, the limited supply of housing leads to two processes in which low-income people are bound to be losers: higher rents and greater competition for available units.

Although John Gilderbloom and Richard Appelbaum have convincingly argued that rents are not simply set by objective laws of supply and demand,[79] low vacancy rates are nevertheless one significant factor permitting higher rents. Low-income people are often forced to choose between avoiding homelessness and meeting nonhousing needs. Kevin, working twenty to forty hours a week, complained, "I would pay two fifty a month or something—that would be reasonable for me. I *couldn't* pay more than that. I wouldn't pay more than that."

Nor is rent the only financial barrier for displaced people seeking substitute housing. The Santa Barbara Rental Housing Task Force found that in 1984 almost a third of the tenants interviewed in a random survey had paid a cleaning deposit (median $185), more than half had paid a security deposit (median $275), and more than half had paid the last month's rent at the time of taking tenancy (median $450).[80] In many cases, of course, people were putting down two or three of these extra deposits. For a household or individual on limited income to come up with $900 to $2,000 is nearly inconceivable. Indeed, those receiving AFDC are prohibited by law from having more than $1,000 in savings.

Fierce competition for units also allows landlords to be "selective." Discrimination against children, for example, appears to be a major obstacle for parents looking for substitute housing:

> L Y N N : Let's just say that [children] are one step above or one step below having a pet. I don't have any pets, I don't need two strikes against me, but according to the Unruh Act [actually a court decision, *Marina Point, Ltd.*, v. *Wilson*, 1982], it is now illegal to discriminate against people with children, but they still do. You ask them what the rent is and they go, "How many *people?*" And if you say two, they assume it's two adults, and if you say three, they assume it's one child and the rent goes into the unaffordable range.[81]

Racial discrimination is also commonly cited by people of color in Santa Barbara:

> J O S E : When I used to say that my name was Jose when calling the places, I was immediately told there were no places available. When I resorted to saying that my name was Joe, I was immediately told that I should stop by and see the place. [But] as soon as I got there, I was told that the place was no longer for rent.

Data from the tenant survey by the Santa Barbara Rental Housing Task Force reinforce this picture: 23 percent of those with children believed they had been discriminated against in the past year, as well as 14 percent of those without children.[82] Unfortunately, the practice of discrimination is not restricted to landlords: Anti-child discrimination by prospective housemates is also commonly reported by single mothers.

Displaced people with behavioral problems associated with mental illness or substance abuse also suffer from the selectivity of landlords and potential housemates. Even when individuals have the financial resources and organizational ability to procure substitute housing, many people will not rent to them, or share housing with them, because of their label or behavior. Thus Rachel could not rent an SRO room even when she had a GR housing voucher because of her reputation as someone who periodically engaged in inappropriate and sometimes destructive behavior. Likewise, SROs and private landlords can afford to turn down those whose alcoholic behavior might cause problems. Those with physical disabilities have a severely limited selection of units that serve their needs, over and above generalized discrimination against disabled people.

Discrimination is not, however, the only problem faced by substance abusers and those with mental illnesses. Many have difficulty finding substitute housing because of the same kinds of individual problems that first led to their evictions. Doubling up may be difficult because they "have become isolated [from kin and friends] in response to their behavior," as the director of the Salvation Army's Hospitality House shelter observed of many of the mentally ill people who stayed there from time to time. Further, people with these problems are less likely to climb out of a situation that would be difficult for anyone to escape. Rachel's reaction to abandonment by her boyfriend and eviction by her landlord was probably not "rational" and certainly not productive: "I lived in my car for about a week or two. I kind of lost track of time because I was going looney tunes again. . . . I felt kind of a calling to come to Santa Barbara, that the Holy Spirit wanted me to come here to witness for him, so I did." The same might be said of Jack's drinking up the thousand dollars he had saved to go to Hawaii and make a new start.

But treating these individual factors in isolation from the context of macro-processes—disability reviews, deinstitutionalization, declining availability of board-and-cares, cutbacks in alcohol and drug programs, and particularly the diminished availability of low-cost housing—falsely elevates their significance. Twenty years ago most of these people, despite their personal problems, would at least have been housed. Although the incidence of mental illness rose in the 1970s and 1980s as the baby boomers came of age,[83] the loss of SRO units and other low-cost housing was an even more important factor in both precipitating incidents and the inability to find substitute housing.[84] Available evidence does not suggest an explosion in alcohol and drug abuse in the late 1970s and early 1980s,[85] but does strongly suggest that the loss of SRO and other low-cost housing made substance abusers less able to hold onto their residences or find substitutes.[86]

Kathie's history is a good example of this interaction between individual and structural factors. She attributes the loss of substitute housing in one case to her mental instability ("I wasn't myself. . . . And so I basically got bounced out on my ear"), but her loss of housing and inability to find another place also involved disability reviews, low vacancy rates, rent inflation and the failure of Section 8 rent limits to keep up with it, and limited Section 8 certificates.

Certainly both mental illness and substance abuse may contribute to vulnerability, precipitating events, and the inability to find substitute housing. But this contribution takes place within structural constraints beyond the control of individuals. Displaced people afflicted with mental illness or substance abuse problems face barriers of both rational and irrational prejudices against people "with problems," prejudices that can be operationalized in tight rental markets where "selectivity" is possible. Together, these factors render them the likely losers in the game of musical chairs—a game of structural constraints that someone must lose.

Once a person is homeless, a further dimension is involved: A major barrier to escaping homelessness appears to be formed by the very adaptations people make to their condition. A very small number of people actually come to prefer street living. Most face the downward cycles of homeless life. To understand these adaptations and cycles, we need to understand what homeless life is like from day to day.

Surviving homelessness requires the regular gathering of at least minimal resources. Escaping homelessness (episodically or permanently) requires the gathering of a substantial amount of resources. How those resources are gathered and used is the topic of the next two chapters, which detail the daily lives of homeless people in Santa Barbara.

Chapter 3
Being homeless

The fundamental truth about homeless life is that it is a *hard* life, filled with, in Orwell's phrase, " 'the terrible complexity' of dire poverty."[1] Work must be found or a long hejira through an entitlement bureaucracy must be navigated. A new home must be located. At the same time, a homeless person must fulfill daily needs for food, shelter, and clothing despite scant resources and an outlaw status: "The person who lacks shelter is constantly occupied with meeting daily and basic needs—eating, sleeping, washing, urinating, defecating—that are often illegal when performed in public. These are "status offenses" which inevitably result from the very existence of homelessness."[2]

A second fundamental truth about homeless life arises from the difficulty of meeting basic needs: Coping with homelessness is *hard work*, and often a full-time job in itself. Like any other job, it requires specialized knowledge, as I learned when I asked Mayor Max how he spent his time:

> On Monday, Wednesday or Saturday, [I'll] get ready to take a shower at the [Rescue] Mission, which is the only place available unless you spent the night at the Salvation Army. . . . [Then I] get something to eat. Depending on what day it is, there are certain places that are open, on certain days or times. You get breakfast at the Mission or Salvation Army if you stay there overnight [but there's a limit of] two nights at the Mission per thirty days, and one night per month at the Salvation Army. . . . When I was first living on the streets, I figured that when I was hungry, I'd go and find a grocery store [dumpster] and see if there's any food, and

there was. I learned myself. Nobody every told me. I was out here for about four days before I found any food, but I found it. And then I, you know, developed a route of the places that had food or the most food that's available.

And [then I] look for a job, occasionally on the weekdays. Then, go around, look for aluminum cans, or somebody to get some cash up [for the cans] so I don't run out of cigarettes. Be able to go to a restaurant for coffee once in a while, stuff like that. . . .

The Salvation Army will give you [clothes] if it's a real emergency, like if your pants are torn from the cuff to your butt, they'll give you a voucher to go to their thrift store to get one pair of pants. . . . If you talk to the right person, you know I shouldn't use his name, but if you talk to [deleted], if he can see that you're soaking wet, he'll allow you to get a change of clothes. . . . The Mission, when you take showers on Monday, Wednesday, or Saturday, you can get a complete change of clothes, including shoes once a week. . . .

During the rainy season, the Mission allows an extra fifteen or twenty people to sleep inside, even if you've used your two days for the month. It's just who gets there first, gets in, and gets a bed out of the rain. And then there's the boxcars, which I've slept in many a night when it was raining 'cause there was nowhere else to go. And, on occasion, I've just gone up to the Amtrak station, under the awnings, and stayed awake all night, until it stopped raining. I've stayed down in the Jungle, . . . under the bridge where we cook, up past the bridge, up the railroad tracks.

Although Mayor Max's specialized knowledge is of "street" resources, people in somewhat different circumstances have comparable knowledge. Single women with children, for instance, develop an extensive knowledge of the family situations of their housed friends, enabling them to predict when they might use friends' homes for a few nights. Kids on their own learn which houses are abandoned, when the cop on the beat comes by, and so forth.

Mayor Max's account suggests a third fundamental truth about homeless life: Meeting basic needs can be tremendously time-consuming. Here Jack, in his second week of sobriety, describes the previous day:

I had slept on the beach the night before. . . . I stopped off at the restaurant and used the rest room and I walked down to Sambos and bought a *San Francisco Chronicle*. . . . Bought that and had four or five cups of coffee. . . . So I got out of there at like about twelve-fifteen and ran over to the Mission and had lunch. And after lunch I walked up to State Street here, all the way up to the Social Services office up to Carillo. And applied for Food Stamps, and they gave me an appointment for Tuesday. Then I . . . went to the Employment Development office, to see about my unemployment. . . .

   I still had the front page of my *Chronicle*, so I came back down here, bought a Cherry Coke, and I went out here on the grass on the beach and finished reading my front page and rested my feet. My feet were getting really sore from walking around. And then this guy I'd met at the unemployment office came tripping up. . . . I showed him where the Wings of Love [shelter] was, and he got something to eat. And then we went to the Salvation Army and we checked out their program. And they loaned me a blanket, a really big fluffy blanket. So I got a blanket now. So then me and him, we went all the way down [to the beach] and got my bag [which he had hidden there], and we came all the way back here. And then we got his stuff out of the Mission. And then we went back up to the Salvation Army and we got some free bread. He had a can of salmon. . . . And then we went back to the Salvation Army and caught a shower. And then we sat down at the wall down here at the beach for a little bit. And then I took him out, showed him . . . the breakwater down at the marina. And then lights were just going out over at the softball game, so he went up the hill to bed, and I went over to the tennis courts and went to bed.

   In the course of this day, Jack has walked (possibly ten miles), made appointments, and rested. But he has probably also spent a great deal of idle time waiting at each step for official business: "When you're on the street, virtually every act involves a wait in line. . . . It is the inevitable outcome of too many people competing for too few resources and services."[3]

   Most of the services used by homeless people are within a mile-and-a-half radius of downtown Santa Barbara, but other needs take them far away from this central location. Sleeping in the immediate downtown area is difficult, and many instead find places on the beaches or in other secluded places (some are lucky enough to find a place on someone's floor). Job or housing opportunities entail journeys to all parts of the metropolitan area. The main health services are outside the city borders, six miles away, as is the jail. Even downtown facilities usually provide only a single service each. The contingencies of time and distance thus shape the survival and advancement strategies of homeless people.

   These stories together suggest one last important point about homeless life: Despite their lack of a home base or other supports for creating an orderly life, most homeless people continually attempt to create one, an effort that requires some level of competency. Resources are available but scarce; surviving—to say nothing of escaping homelessness—means developing reliable resource networks.

Homeless people, like housed people, spend time procuring the resources necessary for survival ("getting by"); time bettering themselves, in this case escaping homelessness ("getting ahead"); and leisure time that is not accomplishment-oriented ("hanging out").[4] For some people and subgroups, these activities overlap, as when Lisa hangs out in front of the State Arcade, where casual conversation might refer to Madonna's new record, a possible drug deal, or a tip on a place to stay. For Hank, on the other hand, hanging out is largely restricted to his time in the shelter, while he works at one job to get by and a second to get ahead.

To speak of "the homeless" is to conjure up an image of a homogeneous mass, yet truly "the only sure thing these people have in common is the one thing they all lack."[5] Homeless people are well aware of their diversity. Pushed by an interviewer, they may come up with complex and sophisticated categorizations that involve a myriad of factors, but in their daily lives the main division is between those who are "like me" and those who are not. Although age, sex, drinking habits, background, and so on play a role in these evaluations, the practical division is between those one might spend time with and those one does not. This, in turn, is largely determined by the resource networks each homeless person utilizes. Given individual attributes, social margin, and constraints, each homeless person creates individual resource-gathering strategies. Yet because all must cope with some common problems using a finite variety of possible resources, resource-use patterns emerge and coalesce into what I will call "lifestyles" (without suggesting that they are freely chosen).

Based on the criteria of how resources are generally gathered and whom a person spends time with, six major subgroups appeared in Santa Barbara: Street People, Wingnuts, Kids, Transitory Workers, Skidders, and Latino Families.[6] The first three subgroups are highly visible to most housed people, shaping the image of "the homeless" in the public mind.

Visible Subgroups

STREET PEOPLE

Mayor Max, Jack, Wendi, and Bret—these are the people many housed people think of as "the homeless." Such "Street People" are generally men (though women have become more common in recent years) between twenty and forty years old, rarely currently married or coupled, and rarely with children. They are more likely than other homeless people to be veterans, most likely to remain homeless for fairly long periods, most likely to be recent arrivals in town, and most likely to have arrived in Santa Barbara after already being homeless. As their label implies, Street People use the street resources of missions, food programs, and street barter, and often sleep outdoors or in homeless shelters; by day most are highly visible on the streets, often carrying their goods and bedding with them.

Although Street People use the resource networks of the streets, they have other options—Mayor Max's routine is "to look for a job" *before* looking for cans and metal to sell. A majority of homeless people, in Santa Barbara and elsewhere, are looking for work, and Street People, despite their image, are among the most likely of homeless people to be doing so.[7]

Desire for work, however, does not necessarily translate into employment.[8] Finding a job is more difficult for homeless people than for housed applicants, but for Street People—the most visible and identifiable of homeless jobseekers—finding a steady job is often a lesson in frustration. Getting oneself and one's clothes clean, and then keeping clean on the street, is imperative for both interviews and jobs:

> W E N D I : Places like Carrows [a restaurant], I went for five days in a row and I talked to the nighttime manager. She said, "We have plenty of openings, I'll put you down." I kept going back and they wouldn't give me an application for work. . . . The lady, she knew that we were street people and everything. She was asking us, "Are you going to be able to be clean?" To work in a job like this, you have to be clean every day, you can't crawl out of the bushes and then expect to go to work, especially in a place like this. You smell, you have leaves on you. If you can't take a shower before you go to work, you are going to smell.

If Wendi figures out a way to get clean—for instance, by sneaking into the marina washroom and using the facilities—the question of a home phone and address arises:

> W E N D I : They need residence, address. The last excuse that they gave me was they said I didn't have a phone number, so they couldn't call me. I needed a phone number before they would accept applications. They wouldn't even take my application.

The lack of a phone number is not merely a nuisance to an employer trying to make contact. It is a sign of transience, impermanence: "All employers are leery of me since I can't give an address or phone number," says Glen, another Street Person. "I'm a risk to hire."[9] In short, what bothers most prospective employers more than any logistical difficulties in getting clean or getting to work is *the fact of homelessness*.

> B R E T : Mostly people [say they] don't want to give us a job because we don't have an address, we don't have a telephone number, we

don't look pretty enough, we don't look clean enough, we don't smell good enough. Or we don't have local references or we aren't from Santa Barbara or we haven't lived here long enough. Every time it's a different excuse. You got long hair, and everybody's looking at that long hair. But the ones that are working have longer hair than mine.

As a result, the jobs Street People usually find involve unskilled manual labor, often part-time and almost inevitably of short duration, the kind of work most other people will not take. Most seek work on a regular—although not daily—basis by looking in the newspaper or going to The Wall, the traditional site outside the unemployment office where employers select daily laborers.[10]

Even Street People who find steady jobs may not keep them for long, as was the case with Kevin:

I started to work mornings [loading and unloading trucks] from five to nine, and I needed more hours. And I went around trying to get more hours, and I couldn't get them. So I asked if I could work nights too, the same shift. Five to nine at night, five to nine in the morning. And I did that for a while, and I just got burned out. It would just kill me. Because I would work in the morning from five to nine, and then take care of what I had to do during the day. And I'd come back and work from five to ten. . . . It just seemed like there was no break, even though there was that sleeping time. . . . I think that's when I blew up and put in my two weeks' notice, and said, "I need a vacation."

The decision simply to quit a job may demonstrate precisely the slacker's unwillingness to do the work of life that housed people suspect is the reason people are homeless in the first place. Yet Kevin worked at one job or another for almost the entire four years I knew him. In his case, and in many others, the decision reflected his analysis that, given his low wages and the high cost of escaping the streets, there was little point in continuing at this job:[11]

KEVIN: My back hurts me every damn day. And I look at that and I go, "Here I am busting my ass forty-five or fifty hours a week, and I just barely survive. . . ." All I am is getting a little bit extra for working. When I could *not* work and [still] survive.

Even the decision not to seek work can only be understood within a housing context that demands $1,500 in order to pay "first, last, and deposit" and thus escape homelessness. A number of Street People who professed interest in escape nevertheless maintained that it was rational for them to refuse jobs that did not pay enough to make a real difference in their lives:

> E L I : [The Welfare Department] tells me to go out here and do manual labor. Sure I can do it. But . . . what good will that check do me at the end of the week? When the rents are so exorbitant ,here? I still won't have a place to sleep. I'll still be going through what I'm going through. So I'd say, "What's the use?" and go out and buy myself a bottle of whiskey. See, to me that's being logical and sensible. Rather than take that job, I just refuse to do it, and that way I don't have to buy the bottle of whiskey, you see.

The ways in which this logic may serve Eli's reluctance to work should not divert attention from its kernel of truth: Many homeless people are not willing to take jobs that offer no imminent hope of escaping homelessness. Rather than work in order to be more comfortably homeless, many homeless people will choose not to work and to hustle more.

What percentage of Street People *can* work—that is, do not have disabling mental or physical conditions? Data from the Church shelters and HoPP interviews suggest that perhaps three-fourths of those in Santa Barbara can work.[12] How many of these are looking for work? The HoPP data suggest that nearly all Street People are, although only some are looking for full-time, ongoing jobs. How many Street People would take such jobs if they paid well or offered a real chance for advancement? We simply do not know, since this situation comes up so rarely.

Some Street People do find or hold on to work, including full-time jobs. While those working part-time may be either choosing to work just enough to get by or unable to find as much work as they would like, virtually all of those working full-time are actively attempting to escape homelessness. Mark was traveling with his girlfriend and her two small children, and clearly wanted to provide them with an escape from the streets. His description of his workday gives some idea of the effort involved:

> M A R K : This is getting up at seven o'clock [in the park where he sleeps], . . . shave, make sure my clothes are as clean as possible. . . . Jump on a bus, ride out to [the suburb of] Carpentaria. . . . Go through the shift there. . . . Get off of that job at four o'clock. . . . If I can get out at five 'til, I can *run*, greasy and slimy and everything, I can run to the bus stop and catch a four o'clock bus. . . . If I can get that four o'clock bus, I can transfer and it'll deliver me about a block and a half from Sambo's on the beach at four-forty-five. Which gives me fifteen minutes to walk a block and a half, get in, splash some water on myself, bring myself around, and go back to work. Get out of work about one o'clock in the morning. . . . Walk

back up here [to the park, two miles away], keeping an eye out for
any local authorities anywhere, 'cause I don't want the trouble.
And forcing myself to sit down and go right to sleep. Get up first
thing in the morning and do it again.

In part because of problems finding sufficiently remunerative or
tolerable "straight jobs," a sizable number of Street People work outside
the conventional labor market. Henry scavenges junk, repairs it, and sells
it on the streets. Mayor Max and his partner Sandman salvage metal and
cans from dumpsters, which they sell to the recycling center (a business
that "really took off," Mayor Max says, when they rebuilt some old
bicycles, greatly increasing the ground they could cover.) Max's friend
Charlie has learned to fashion jewelry from inexpensive components.
Barter among Street People often becomes an alternative to the money
economy:

> CHARLIE: I started buying beads after a while, trading for them.
> We're trading, trading, rocks, pretty rocks, just got a couple today
> for a piece of rabbit fur that was given to me a few days ago. I trade
> [beaded] necklaces [he makes] and stuff, mostly for luxuries.
> Sometimes I'll trade for steak or something, mostly it's for dope
> and cigarettes, food.

Many prefer "cottage industry" and barter to a "straighter" job
despite the uncertain economic payoff. Such jobs share with professional
jobs the advantage that your time is your own, without anyone looking over
your shoulder. Equally important seems to be pleasure in surviving on
your own terms: not letting the situation compel you to take a job that you
hate. Those Street People surviving by this kind of street entrepre-
neurship are proud of their ability to do so, while those who take on
mainstream jobs often dislike their work. But cottage industries are rarely
lucrative enough to provide the funds to get ahead, though they are
sometimes sufficient for getting by.

We have seen that some people become homeless because they
cannot or do not work but nonetheless do not receive welfare. This
situation continues—indeed intensifies—once they are homeless. Street
People rarely receive any kind of entitlements other than Food Stamps.[13]
Most notably, very few Street People receive General Relief, a program
their extreme poverty makes them prime candidates for. While GR is often
insufficient for preventing or escaping homelessness, it is certainly a
valuable resource for making ends meet while homeless. Why then, do so
few Street People receive it?

Some do not apply, occasionally because they lack accurate information about qualifications or procedures. Others feel that they would have to
sacrifice their freedom to get on an entitlement program:

H E N R Y : GR is one of those things that you constantly like have to
depend on, where like, I just take it one day at a time, moneywise.
If I don't make money, fine, I'll find some other way of passing
the time.

Some homeless people, as Ann Marie Rousseau has argued, refuse to apply
for welfare in order to protect their last shred of personal dignity.[14]

Street People who apply for benefits are often unsuccessful. Welfare
workers tend to see them as "transients" rather than residents and often
deny benefits on the basis of formal residency requirements.[15] Most Street
People have in fact been in Santa Barbara for the necessary two-week
period, but few can prove it. Until June 1985, residency could be shown
only through rent receipts or paycheck stubs. Advocacy efforts succeeded
in loosening these regulations somewhat, but lineworker procedures
remained largely unchanged.[16]

Discouragement, often experienced first-hand, has also become part
of the "street wisdom":

Z E K E : I *personally* haven't tried [to get GR], no. But through what
I've heard and through my friends, they just give you too much
run-around. I mean, why fight the system? When you know what
the system is gonna do?

Requirements other than residency may also act as barriers. Program
regulations are typically written with poor but housed people in mind, and
thus meeting them is often problematic for homeless people. Even
showing up for appointments is difficult without a stable address where
one can receive timely notification of such appointments.

The relatively few Street People who persevere and receive GR do
not thereby end their problems. Months typically pass between application and eventual enrollment; benefits usually run out after thirty days;
and even receiving GR may not ameliorate the worst aspects of homelessness. At a time when GR housing vouchers were worth $195, for example,
fewer than 90 SRO rooms were available at that rate in the city of Santa
Barbara, and even these were rarely rented to GR recipients.[17]

Besides work and entitlements, there are few ways for Street People to
obtain money. Studies elsewhere have reported blood donations and
panhandling, yet neither seems more than minimally used in Santa
Barbara.[18] The alternative is crime, a potent part of the image most housed
people carry of Street People, and one often endorsed by the police. Police
in Santa Barbara, for example, reported that "transients" were arrested
1,944 times in 1984, accounting for about 15 percent of the total arrests.
This is, however, largely a bookkeeping fiction, since anyone who gives no
address at the time of arrest—a common occurrence for many reasons—is
entered into the computer records as a transient.[19]

The HoPP interviews yield a substantially different picture of Street People's involvement in criminal activity. Undoubtedly some have been in serious trouble with the law at some time in their lives, but *current* trouble seems usually to involve misdemeanors and infractions rather than the major street crimes that housed people fear. Further, these are overwhelmingly victimless or petty crimes, and many are status offenses in which homelessness itself is the crime or creates a greater vulnerability to arrest than housed people would face for the same action. Some are as minor as Glen trespassing in the marina to take a shower. Many are alcohol-related, and these tend to be for "open container" violations (drinking in prohibited areas such as parks or city streets) rather than for public drunkenness.

Among the economically motivated crimes Street People commit most frequently are those related to drug sales, mainly small-time marijuana deals:

> HENRY: I had to sell a few nickels and dimes of weed to make ends meet sometimes when everything else failed.
>
> Q: Where do you get it?
>
> HENRY: Usually other people on the streets.
>
> Q: They sell it in quantity and you break it up?
>
> HENRY: Yeah, usually like ounces or half ounces.
>
> Q: And then what do you sell?
>
> HENRY: Joints or dimes. But around here, even the big people, they don't make more than about fifty dollars a day anyway.

Other resource-motivated crimes include breaking into cars to sleep and shoplifting from grocery stores—especially those with a reputation for being anti-homeless. But, at least as reported by the HoPP respondents, major crimes are scarce indeed—a finding mirrored in studies elsewhere.[20] (Similarly, of the 443 "criminal incidents" of 1984 reported by the police in the Fig Tree area—the base for many Street People—only 5 were for economic crimes as serious as burglary or grand theft from auto, and 4 were for violent crimes, limited to battery. In contrast, 104 were for being a "suspicious person.")

The observation that most criminal activity by homeless people, and especially Street People, is either alcohol-related or tied to resource-gathering challenges those analysts who stress a psychological basis for it:

> Nothing, perhaps, is so devastating to the human spirit as indif-
> ference. Under such circumstances, some seek what psychologists
> term negative strokes. In crime, hustling, prostitution, and a variety of
> other deviant activities they find some recognition, some affirmation
> of their aliveness.[21]

Such formulations miss the point: When people hustle, it is first and foremost in order to survive.

Although Street People are among the likeliest of homeless people to commit crimes, not all people on the streets commit even minor crimes. Less than half of the HoPP Street People reported committing crimes or had been arrested for any criminal activity other than illegal sleeping offenses:

> K E V I N : [Housed people] should know that homeless people are not
> everything the paper says they are. All this propaganda saying
> they're all scruffy thieves, or rapists or whatever. . . . Conscience is
> knowing what's right and what's wrong. And you know, I'd say 95
> percent of the people that I know that are homeless live by that.
> And that's probably why they're homeless. Criminals, now on
> the other hand, who are thieves, they don't got to be homeless,
> they're making plenty of money. . . . So that's one reason
> [people are] on the streets. 'Cause they're not going to go out
> and steal, they're not going to go out and burglarize, they're not
> going to go out and do anything, because they don't want to go to
> jail.[22]

In virtually all studies in which comparisons are made, homeless people are more likely to be victims of crimes than to have been convicted of criminal activity.[23]

When Street People cannot or do not obtain money from work, public assistance, or crime, they look to street resources for meeting their basic needs. The most pressing of these is shelter. Until the great explosion in homelessness beginning around 1980, finding a bed for the night in one of the religious shelters was fairly easy, but in the 1980s, in Santa Barbara and elsewhere, shelter beds quickly became a scarce resource.[24] As late as mid-1990 there were 557 beds (only 387 from spring through fall) in all of Santa Barbara County for an estimated three to four thousand homeless people;[25] several of the shelters limited stays to one to five days, while others excluded substance abusers, mentally ill people, or both.

Among the four emergency shelters, the Wings of Love (known to some of the homeless population as "The Wings of Death"), with the barest of resources and no screening procedures, is the last pick of most. Almost equally unpopular is the Rescue Mission, but for different reasons. The Mission is strictly screened, highly structured, and serves a relatively good meal, as well as having clothing and other resources available. But since its "Christ-centered" program is based on the belief that homelessness stems from "falling from God," mandatory religious services accompany almost every step from meals to beds, with the sort of sermons that homeless people call "earbanging":

> C H A R L I E : Mostly it's fire and brimstone. Once in a while they get
> somebody in that's a little mellower.
> Q : How do you feel about the service?
> C H A R L I E : [extremely dryly] I'd just as soon skip 'em [laughter].
> Breakfast I never minded too much 'cause I usually went to sleep.

Of the traditional shelters affiliated with religious organizations, the Salvation Army Hospitality House has by far the best street reputation, based on its comparatively good resources, an extremely well-respected manager, and the voluntary nature of all religious commitments. But in late 1983, reeling under the increased number of homeless people seeking shelter and armed with a new local commander's philosophy of providing more intense help to a smaller group of people, "the Sally" adopted new regulations that placed it virtually off-limits for many Street People, especially men. Free shelter was restricted to one night every half year (a charge of five dollars a night was then imposed if space was available), unless the person was sponsored by a social service agency.

Some of the slack was picked up when the first Church of the Month shelter opened in March 1985. Although the sponsoring coalition, the Interfaith Task Force on Homelessness (ITFH), took pains to stress that the shelters were intended for women and children and not "Fig Tree types" (a euphemism for Street People), it was clear to those familiar with that population that, especially in the beginning, a majority of the Church guests were in fact Fig Tree types. As time went on and the Church shelters operated more smoothly than virtually anyone had expected, more women and children began using them, in large part because of an increased willingness by local agencies to send local people there. But it was not until several months into 1986 that women and children gradually came to outnumber single men in the ITFH's permanent shelter, Transition House.

At the most obvious level, the Church shelters provided fifty or so people with a safe and warm place to sleep, a place to get clean, and a little breathing room to figure out what they needed and wanted in the coming days. But for some, the Church shelters (the least demeaning and regimented of the shelters) met a psychological need as well:

> Z E K E : Before I hit the shelter, I was worn down, pissed off at the
> world because of the things that I had gone through. . . . What the
> shelter is, you come into the shelter, and you see that you're not
> the only one there, okay? And then you get to know the people.
> And it lifts your spirit, to where [you think], "Hey, now I'm not
> the only one, I'm not the only one fighting this." You know, it just
> gives you a whole different outlook.

Opponents' fears that the shelters would become "open asylums" for the mentally ill, or permanent homes to a permanent underclass, or home to only the strongest and toughest while the most needy were driven off, did not materialize.[26] Unlike many shelters in larger cities, there were few problems with violence or drugs.[27]

Nevertheless, many Street People (and even greater numbers of other subgroups, as we will see) shun shelters out of pride, distrust of other homeless people, or an unwillingness to accept regimentation:

> MARK: On more than one occasion I've had problems with people up there, with their screening habits and everything. They already know what [my] situation is, they already know what's going down. I'm getting *tired* of telling them the same stupid things and getting, you know, terrible looks. . . . I got thrown out of the shelter once, told never to come back, because I told [a shelter worker] to fuck off when he turned the lights on at six in the morning and yelled, "GET UPPPP!" . . . I didn't feel that being yelled at was necessary. . . . Because of that kind of tension, I usually don't go.

Street People unable or unwilling to gain admittance to an emergency shelter have several other options. Earned or received money can be used for short stays in SRO hotels, which offer a safe, relatively comfortable place to sleep and a chance to shower and get clean. Such stays, obviously, are rare treats. Some Street People stay in one of the campgrounds a few miles north or south of the city or in secluded places not intended for camping. Their distance from the urban core area with its jobs and services, however, renders these sites less useful for most people, especially the great majority who are not "rubber tramps" (that is, those with access to a vehicle).

Most Street People do not sleep in campgrounds, hotels, or shelters, but in the nooks and crannies homeless people have traditionally found:

> CHARLIE: [I sleep] behind an office building. . . . It's got a roof overhead and the wall keeps out the prevailing winds. . . . I got caught there a couple of times, and then we stopped staying there for a while. And then I started going back and staying there again when it was under construction, even spent the night inside on the carpet one night before they got all the locks on the doors. And out back ever since. It's been two months.

> RAY: At nine p.m. we're out on the street or in the park. . . . I used to go to the beach, dig myself a little hole, crawl in, and bury myself in the sand.
> Q: What are you going to do in the winter when it starts raining?
> RAY: Get myself a poncho that's weatherproof.

The streets present three great dangers: weather, arrest, and attack. Even in a warm-weather state like California, sleeping outdoors at night in coastal communities can be health-threatening—as evidenced by the fact that more people each year die of hypothermia (subnormal body temperatures) in Los Angeles than in New York.[28]

While Street People choose their places carefully to maximize protection from cold and rain, they must also avoid notice that will bring about arrest:

> M A R K : I have to wait until ten o'clock [to bed down] to make sure
>   things are safe and cool. And if I want to sleep in, how can you still
>   be asleep when it's day, when it's broad daylight? You know,
>   you gotta be up by like five-thirty and stash yourself in the car
>   [belonging to a friend] for that last hour and a half. And even the
>   car, by seven o'clock there are too many people who are starting to
>   come by. You know, you can only be so obvious before you get in
>   trouble.

Although sleeping anywhere but in a residence between ten at night and six in the morning was illegal in Santa Barbara until August 1986, only a very small percentage of homeless people were ever cited or arrested for this offense.[29] But for those who generally sleep on the streets, the threat of arrest is a constant concern. Almost all of the Street People I interviewed had been warned, cited, or arrested for such offenses at least once.

Arrests, however, appear to do little to deter homeless people from continuing to live in Santa Barbara. Some acknowledge that arrest and fear of arrest caused them to change their sleeping place within the city; Bret and Wendi eventually took refuge in a friend's camper:

> W E N D I : We had a little tent, and we would change from places that
>   got tickets. We'd get a ticket, then move up, then move back
>   down. Back and forth. We were getting ticketed too much. Every
>   time we turned around, it was always the same cop. So we got
>   tired of that. Linda, she wanted some help and we got tired of
>   sleeping out in the bushes every night. We thought that [living in
>   a camper] might help us get a job.

More, however, agree with Henry that if you have a good place, the police will not find it. If they find it, you just find a new, better place. No one I interviewed or talked to in four and a half years said that the illegal sleeping arrests were going to drive him or her out of town; interviews with those who left town would be necessary to ascertain whether the anti-sleeping laws did induce some homeless people to move.

While Street People and some others on the streets fear the law, they are even more afraid of criminals who threaten their physical safety. The murders of Kenny Burr in December 1984 and Michael Stephenson in August 1985 brought home the fear of street crime to homeless people in Santa Barbara in a dramatic fashion, but most people on the streets have first-hand experience as well.[30] As Margie's story shows, even an "unsuccessful" assault is a harrowing experience:[31]

> One man tried to rape me in San Jose. . . . What happened was the bus terminal closed at twelve o'clock and there was noplace else to go. And I thought I'd just walk down the street someplace, because I'd seen a park someplace. I stayed at this place. . . . At about four-thirty I got up, and . . . I started walking back toward the bus terminal. Okay, there's this man. Standing by a telephone at five in the morning. I thought it was strange. And he just stood there, okay? And then what happened was, I was walking, and I knew, I just knew he was going to walk after me. There was only two people on the streets, me and that man.
>
> And so I thought I should just stay back and try to walk slow. Boy, was I scared, I was scared to death! I was walking, I was scared. The guy started walking with me. I don't know how long it was that we were walking. And I was talking and talking, I was so scared. And I was telling him that I wanted to be a nurse, and this and that. And then the next thing, there was this doorway. And he tried to push me up there, and he said, "Kiss me." And I said, "Oh, no! It's okay, we're just friends, I can't do that." I was so scared! I was scared stiff! . . .
>
> And so I just kept walking, and then I played as if I had no idea what we was talking about. And just before we got to the bus terminal, there was a street corner. And he said, "Okay, why don't we go around this way, and just walk over there." And it was dark down there. I said, "No." And he just kept pulling my arms. Then he pushed me down on the sidewalk, and I was scared. I didn't know what to do. And I was scared and I started screaming. I guess after I started screaming he just let me go or something. Because I broke off, running away. I was scared and I started running. And there was the bus terminal, getting ready to open. It was still closed, but there were two men standing together in the light.
>
> I was all, you know, together and normal, but all the while I was just breaking up inside. It was just terrible. And then I went upstairs in the bus terminal to the bathroom and I started crying.

Nor is this an isolated experience. The manager of the Salvation Army's Hospitality House estimates that half of the females who come there, generally Street People and Wingnuts, have been raped. He describes their general emotional state as "very vulnerable and very fearful." Rene Jahiel reports estimates that "the incidence of rape in the [total] homeless population is 20 times higher than that in the general population."[32]

Most of the violent attacks reported by members of the HoPP group were, like the Stephenson murder, perpetrated by housed people. Many on the streets fear that their appearance alone marks them as targets for street toughs looking for a good time "troll busting." While many Street People reported "tussles" with other Street People, typically when drinking, almost all the serious attacks they reported were by housed people.[33] Unfortunately, the most successful tactics homeless people can employ to prevent attacks are illegal, such as carrying weapons, or call attention to their illegal status, such as sleeping in large groups or in well-lit, public places.

Largely as a result of this fear, some Street People, usually elderly or disabled ones, seek alternatives to sleeping at night. In the older hobo terminology, they "carry the banner," staying awake all night and sleeping during the day, as described by fifty-eight-year-old Eli:

> I've walked the streets every night for these sixty days since I've been out there, with no place to lay my head except in bus depots or all night coffee shops. . . . I spend most of my time here at the Greyhound bus depot. And during the early mornings, when they first open up at six, I come in here from about six until eight, unless they wake me up earlier. And I catch a catnap right here.
> . . . Now when they close at night, I go to Carrows and I sit down there and I drink coffee, say from one a.m. to five a.m. At five I usually leave there and walk around until this is open here [at the bus depot]. And that's my routine every day.

Most Street People (as well as other homeless people in Santa Barbara) agree that food is the easiest of the survival necessities to find. Eli, for instance, spoke at great length about carrying the banner, problems obtaining employment, and his drinking problem, but when asked about food, he immediately replied: "I can do that on the street. I can definitely get food."[34]

Among the homeless subgroups in Santa Barbara, Street People are the most likely to receive Food Stamps, but the amount given is paltry— about forty-nine cents per meal in the mid-1980s.[35] Additionally, those who stay at shelters have their Food Stamp allocations reduced to reflect the meals the shelters provide. (Federal regulations adopted in late 1986 further reduced Food Stamp eligibility by counting rent paid to shelters and welfare hotels by the government as part of the income of the sheltered person.)

Street People must therefore supplement their Food Stamps or seek other ways of finding food. It is they who are the greatest consumers of the mission meals and, in many cases, practitioners of "dumpster diving." Most people on the streets report their diet has suffered through eating less, eating sporadically, and eating worse food. As Wendi said, "I used to eat what I liked; now I eat what I can get."

Despite their limited funds and their routine patronage of free food programs and missions for daily meals, one of the treats of street life is ordering coffee in a restaurant, sitting in a nice place (compared with the streets) for a while, stretching the refills, reading a paper. Occasionally, pay days may find employed Street People eating a real meal in a restaurant. While getting some good food is one objective, at least as important is the temporary feeling of well-being.

Clothing is less important for survival than food or shelter but certainly not inconsequential. If a person is looking for employment or otherwise attempting to fit into mainstream society, clean and decent-looking clothes are essential. Street People have two problems with clothing: how to get it and how to keep it without a home base. They rarely are able to own more clothes than they can carry with them, usually one or two changes. They tend to obtain clothing from the missions and social agencies if not working, and to buy at thrift stores if employed. A significant minority also go dumpster diving for clothes, usually behind thrift stores. Some trade for clothes in the barter economy.

Similarly, maintaining personal hygiene is important for dealing with members of the mainstream world such as employers, and for feeling good about oneself, as well as for avoiding illnesses associated with unclean conditions. Those most recently homeless are particularly concerned, but demoralization can easily set in, since keeping clean is so difficult:

> GLEN: For a while you're real careful and you try keeping your pants clean. Then after a week or so, your pants are filthy, you just drop that situation, you no longer care about your pants, and the next thing you know, you don't care about your face, and it's a little chain.

This situation is made much worse by the lack of public bathrooms in the downtown area. In some parks where Street People are known to congregate, existing public bathrooms were closed when park workers complained that the facilities were just too hard to keep clean. Similarly, those opposed to the presence of Street People complain that they "urinate and defecate" in public places. While this charge has clearly been exaggerated, there is more than a grain of truth in it, particularly concerning urination. But this is mainly due to a lack of facilities. In meeting after meeting, Street People asked local authorities to open bathroom facilities downtown.

In summary, the base for Street People is literally the street. Most sleep outdoors most of the time; many spend most of their waking hours on the streets; even the charitable organizations assume that the resources they provide (blankets, food that does not require cooking, etc.) should be usable by people who live on the streets. But it is important also to stress that Street People often look to other resources—most importantly the mainstream employment market, to a lesser extent the more formal "charity" of public assistance, and, as we will see in Chapter 4, friends and kin from their previous housed lives. Their primary ties are to "the street," but they have other ties as well.

WINGNUTS

A second highly visible group has increasingly become a prototype of "the homeless" in recent years: those with severe mental problems, occasionally due to long-term alcoholism, but more often due to mental illness. Such people are called "Wingnuts" on the street. Although their lives revolve around many of the same resources as Street People, including missions, soup kitchens, and dumpsters, Wingnuts are a separate subgroup, shunned by Street People (and often each other) and showing some important differences in the resources they can and do use.

A constant in the stories of Rachel, Kathie, and Julia (and, indeed, in almost all Wingnuts' stories) is how poor they have been since becoming homeless. Wingnuts are rarely hired for regular—or even irregular—jobs. While some occasionally engage in marginal street jobs, such as stuffing newspapers into plastic bags, few earn enough to support even a homeless lifestyle.

Yet a clear majority of Wingnuts (in Santa Barbara and elsewhere) do not receive public assistance,[36] although they are certainly among the people SSI and Social Security Disability Insurance (SSDI) are meant for. Like Street People, they may lack the necessary information to apply for assistance, but ignorance may be mixed with extreme confusion. Like Street People, those aware of how to apply may nonetheless shun welfare out of pride or fear. Those with past encounters with mental health or penal institutions are especially wary of being deprived of their autonomy again. Julia, for instance, never applied for any form of welfare despite her extreme poverty:

> Personally, I do not want to become a victim of the social welfare system. . . . I am struggling desperately to avoid that system. I'm having a hard enough time dealing with the issues of self-esteem that I'm dealing with, and abuse and torment and discrimination, without becoming a direct victim of that system. . . . I've made a decision to tell the truth. . . . Anyone who's dealt with these [social service] systems anywhere in the United States knows *you cannot tell the truth!* . . . If you tell the truth, they're going to work against you. To get you to lie, to squeeze you into their system.

Like Street People, Wingnuts may be discouraged by welfare workers, in some cases because their mobility makes residency requirements difficult to meet. Those transferred from mental hospitals to community health programs often face a Catch-22 situation: Benefits cannot be received from GR or SSI until residency has been established in the community, but residency is often impossible to achieve unless the patient has received income support.[37]

In general, however, welfare workers tend to be somewhat more accommodating to Wingnuts, who are seen as more "deserving" than Street People. (When the Reagan administration mandated reviews of disability recipients, however, hundreds of thousands of people, including Kathie, were denied benefits until the review process was halted by court order.) Nevertheless, many fail to receive—or lose—assistance because at some point they fall through the cracks of the system. Like Street People, and for some of the same reasons, Wingnuts may fail to carry out all the requirements to qualify, but obtaining documents and meeting timetables is made even more difficult by fragile mental health. Since the onus is on the applicant, those who falter at some stage are rarely rescued.[38]

The application process is long, and denial is frequent. The Department of Social Services worker who sees most of the homeless mentally ill applicants in Santa Barbara describes the typical application for SSI in this way:

> First you apply. The medical application goes to Fresno, and the Examiner there denies 95 percent of those. You then have sixty days to file for reconsideration. But street people usually don't know they've been denied in the first place, or how to get reconsideration. If reconsideration is filed, it's usually denied, and you then have sixty days again to appeal. It then goes to an administrative law judge, who's the first human the client sees in the whole process. You can have lawyers, DSS [Department of Social Service] people, advocates. Ninety-five percent of the appeals are successful at this level.
>
> Based on my eight years here, I'd say the whole thing takes nine to eighteen months. If you're ever found eligible, you get your money from the date you first applied. But if you drop out during the process and start all over, you're only paid—if you win—from that point. Billions of dollars are saved by this system for the government. And I might point out, I've never lost a case for a client when I've taken it to the last stage of appeal. But few people on the streets can hang in there that long.[39]

Many Wingnuts (and other homeless people) believe, as this worker implied, that discouragement is a deliberate policy of public assistance bureaucracies:

K A T H I E : There was one woman down there, ... she really made you
feel like a piece of shit. I don't know whether they still have that
same sort of policy of making you feel so disgusted with it that you
decide that you don't want to go through their trip, so you drop off
and that's one less person that they have to hassle with.

Between denials, appeals, and the waiting periods that are inevitable in
dealing with a large bureaucracy, many Wingnuts indeed abandon their
applications.

Some who are receiving benefits lose them when transferred from one
type of entitlement to another; others lose other necessary supports.
Rachel's initial application for GR was only granted through the intervention of a lineworker, who then acted for some time as her informal social
worker—a support Rachel badly needed, since she was constantly getting
caught up in the legal system because of her "acting out" episodes. After
nearly a year, and with his aid, Rachel was finally processed through the
Social Security Administration and began receiving SSI. Once shifted from
GR to SSI, Rachel lost her social worker, since he was attached to a
different program, and workers stay with their programs, rather than with
their clients. Although she now had enough money to have some chance of
finding a place, without guidance and support she could not carry out the
tasks necessary for getting off the streets. Her mental health, generally
reflective of the turmoil in her life, *declined* during her first months on
SSI.

Partly because they so rarely are employed or receive welfare, crime is
fairly common among Wingnuts, but typically these are minor infractions
or misdemeanors.[40] Some Wingnuts commit economically motivated
crimes; when her SSI checks were halted during the Reagan-mandated
eligibility reviews, Kathie was arrested for soliciting:

I tried prostitution until the cops picked me up. Luckily, they let
me off with a warning. But, you know, that's how low things got,
and I mean, I never in the world would have thought of doing
anything like that under normal circumstances. But, I mean, what
else could I do? Welfare's not there for me any more.

Kathie had used an ad in a local newspaper to solicit customers, which
requires some amount of planning. More common are spur-of-the-moment
crimes, particularly shoplifting, usually from grocery stores.

Many crimes committed by Wingnuts, however, are instances of
"acting out," as when Rachel threw a television out the window of her
SRO room because she believed it was being used to program her mind.
When first in Santa Barbara, she spent thirty days in jail for biting a
supermarket security guard who accused her of shoplifting. Such crimes

are not means to economic ends, although they may have economic antecedents.

In the face of their almost total lack of resources, Wingnuts face even greater difficulties than Street People in finding shelter. They are generally less aware of their options, and their options themselves are narrower. Most of the Santa Barbara shelters bar mentally disturbed people, although Wingnuts are sometimes able to find a sympathetic screener, especially when they are relatively balanced emotionally. Since most do not receive public assistance and cannot work, motels and hotels are usually not an option; as in Rachel's case, even when Wingnuts have some money (from SSI or GR, for instance), they are often unable to rent SRO or other temporary low-cost housing because the high demand and short supply allow landlords to turn away potential risks. As a result, most find the same kinds of nooks and crannies that Street People do, although they face the additional problem that Street People are usually unwilling to share hiding places with them. Without a secure home base, it is nearly impossible for Wingnuts to organize their lives. As numerous commentators have pointed out, the lack of housing has at least as much to do with worsening mental health as lack of treatment or any other single variable.[41]

Finding food, too, is a greater problem for Wingnuts than for other homeless people. Those not receiving Food Stamps through the SSI program are usually unable to navigate the Food Stamp bureaucracy. During periods of confusion, they may go days without eating, worsening their mental state. Their access to clothing, on the other hand, is similar to Street People's: Except in the minority of cases where they are receiving SSI or SSDI, they generally get their clothes from missions and service agencies. Like Street People, they are unlikely to have more than one or two changes of clothes, since they must carry their wardrobe with them.

Compared with most other homeless people, Wingnuts spend more time hanging out than getting by, and almost no time getting ahead. Occasionally there are appointments to be kept if one is lucky enough to be getting public assistance or linked to a mental health (or alcoholism) program. But for the most part, Wingnuts have large expanses of time to fill, and rarely anyone to fill them with:

> R A C H E L : I get on the bus and I come to town, and I either go to the library, go to the beach, or go to the park. I would go to one of the feeding holes [for lunch]. . . . Or I just sit in the park and eat. If it is raining or something, I'll get indoors, like the library. If I'm sleepy I'll come out here and take a nap. . . . Then sometimes, just to kill a day, I'll go to the courthouse and listen to the divorce court or criminal court, either one. Sometimes they are both dull and I don't stay but a few minutes. . . . The street people, I know

them, they know me, yet we are not really friends. . . . They seem to stay clear of me because they think I'm crazy.

KIDS

The third group of visible homeless people are minors living without parents or guardians.[42] Like Lisa, "Kids" are largely native Santa Barbarans, invariably junior high or high school dropouts, with long histories of episodic homelessness following clashes with their parents.[43] Kids have even less access to work that Street People or Wingnuts. They are legally barred from most jobs; even when old enough for legal employment, they are unlikely to be hired because of their appearance of instability. This is not universal: Margie obtained employment by lying about her age; Michael worked for his uncle under the table for months at a time; others engage in the same cottage industries as some Street People. But their employment opportunities are more severely limited than those of most other homeless people. As minors, they are ineligible for most entitlement programs (exceptions include teenaged mothers receiving AFDC). They are rarely in touch with any social service or entitlement agency, other than, perhaps, the Klein Bottle/Social Advocates for Youth shelter.

Largely because they have few legal ways of supporting themselves, crime among Kids is fairly common: often theft, and sometimes prostitution or drug dealing:[44]

> LISA: I'd steal people's jewelry. I'd bump into people and take something from their pockets. You know, make it so it looked like an accident. And, oh, go into stores and steal. I'd get drugs and sell them. . . . And at times, I'm ashamed to say that I did pull tricks. With men. Brought in a lot of money, but it also put my self-esteem real down, you know. Made me feel like shit. Made me feel like I was nothing.

Emergency shelters in Santa Barbara (with the exception of the KBSAY shelter) are barred by law from admitting children under eighteen without a parent or guardian. Kids rarely appear to have stable sleeping places, but tend to revolve through a set of alternatives, with their parents' homes during periodic reconciliations and the homes of friends' parents their two greatest resources. Spending the night on the streets or beaches is a last resort, since the streets are frightening to even the most hardened Kids. They are particularly vulnerable to sexual assault, and some are exposed to violence through their involvement with illegal activities:

> Q: Anyone ever rip you off?
> LISA: Yeah, *lots of times!* For my drugs. They snake 'em. They'll just say, "Shut up! Shut up! You don't want to get hurt!" . . . That's

why I'm so scared to go out there again. 'Cause I was always scared of getting killed out there. . . . [And when you pull tricks], it's scary because those guys are big, and if you don't give them what they want, they'll kill us, you know? And it's scary to think about when you do it, because after you stop and you go, "Okay, where's my money?" you know some of them will just look at you and go, "What money, bitch?" And that happened to me a couple of times, and I'm just like, "Oh shit, what do I do?" The first thing you do is get your purse and just get out.

Ironically, in order to avoid the violence of the streets, some Kids turn to crimes or trade sex for a place to stay.

Q: Where were you sleeping all this time?
LISA: Beach, bushes. Break into motels and stay there.
Q: How about when you were making money?
LISA: Just stayed in hotels. Or when I couldn't get money, I would just go stay with men.

Kids rarely stay on the streets of Santa Barbara for very long. If they do not return to their homes or get placed in foster care, they usually take off for the greater anonymity of a bigger city:

LISA: San Fr[anc]isco, it's big, police have a hard time getting around, you know, that kind of stuff. So many places to hide, all those vacant buildings, all that other stuff you can just hide in.

Food and clothing are easier to obtain than shelter, although some Kids report periods when they did not eat for days because they did not know where to find food. In general, Kids appear to have erratic eating habits due to their lack of steady resources, at different times using money from legal or illegal enterprises or from friends, or trading sex for food. Much of their shoplifting is from grocery stores. But since soup kitchens do not restrict by age, food is less of a problem than most other resources. Clothing is even less of a problem: Kids may obtain clothes through street trading or purchase them with money they have made, but most simply wear clothing inherited from the past and use periodic returns to their parents' home to replenish their wardrobe.

Kids, then, use a patchwork of resources, including some street resources, the homes of their friends or family, and (mainly) illegal enterprises. Much time is spent on the streets, hanging out with other children (both homeless and housed), waiting for something to happen. For Kids, getting by, getting ahead, and hanging out are very much intertwined. The streets are their "offices" where business is conducted or new alternatives are launched as easily as time is passed.

Hidden Subgroups

Street life, we have seen, is a hard life, and therefore almost always avoided by those with other options. Most people would rather sleep in the homes of friends or relatives, in campgrounds, or in a SRO room than stay under a bridge or in the bushes. The issue extends beyond comfort: Homelessness is widely considered an abnormal state, with legal, social, and economic ramifications. Besides limiting access to needed resources, obvious homelessness may lead to loss or denial of jobs, rejection by friends and kin, and legal penalties ranging from arrest for "illegal sleeping" to the loss of children. Many homeless people therefore go to great lengths to remain "invisible."[45] Strategies range from physically hiding (particularly when sleeping) to passing as housed.[46]

Their determination to remain hidden limits researchers' ability to estimate the size of this population. All three of the Santa Barbara data sets, however, indicate that a large proportion of homeless people have found places to sleep that do not call attention to their homeless status, including campgrounds, hotels and motels, friends' or families' homes, outbuildings (such as garages), or their own workplaces (see table).

Sleeping places, of course, are just one indicator of "hiddenness." Where people hang out and with whom, whether and how often they use public agencies, and the extent to which they attempt to conceal their homelessness in daily life all play a role as well. But the figures on sleeping places suggest that those seen on the streets are probably a minority of the total homeless population.[47]

Access to resources and access to mainstream networks are the main factors determining ability to remain hidden. For example, use of campgrounds and hotels or motels suggests greater material resources than are possessed by the visible homeless population. Staying in the homes of friends or kin suggests deeper roots in the community, even if one can

Degrees of visibility: Where do homeless people sleep?

	Street	*Vehicle*	*Shelter*	*Hidden*
Church	51.1%	11.4%	16.7%	20.8%
HoPP	29.7	8.1	24.3	37.9
SPA	0.0	14.0	24.5	61.5

Sources: Intake forms from church shelters, interviews for the Homeless People's Project (HoPP), telephone logs of the Single Parent Alliance (SPA). See Appendix for descriptions of the data sets.

Notes: Church figures are for the night preceding arrival at the first Church shelter. HoPP and SPA figures are for the current night.

make use of these options only for short periods. Church, SPA, and HoPP inter- and intragroup comparisons indicate that women, married people, people with jobs, Latinos, those with past histories of residence in Santa Barbara, and those without mental health or substance abuse problems predominate in this group.[48] Precisely because they are hidden, however, such people rarely come to mind when housed citizens think about "the homeless."

TRANSITORY WORKERS

As in the past, some among the homeless population are highly mobile "Transitory Workers," relatively cut off from family and community, traveling from town to town, staying months or years in a place, and then heading off to greener pastures.[49] Although they ordinarily live in SRO hotels and other low-cost housing, they occasionally fall on hard times or do not have enough money to negotiate their move to a new area when work runs out.

Typically, Transitory Workers have both job skills and a history of full-time work. As Hank's story suggests, their primary resource remains the world of mainstream employment. They are the most likely of all homeless people to be seeking work, and the most likely to find it, in large part because they typically combine job skills and past references with a go-getter attitude:

> HANK: I just went around and [when I] saw somebody working, [I] stopped and asked them if they needed any help. In two days I found a job. . . . I've got two jobs, in fact. I've got one steady job, [and then] somebody I used to work with had some apartments that needed some painting done on them, so I told him I'd do them on the weekends for him. So I'm going to be working seven days a week starting next weekend.

Transitory Workers are generally loath to apply for public assistance. Many, in fact, do not consider themselves welfare candidates (or even homeless). Once she reached the age of eighteen and began working fairly regularly, Margie felt that receiving assistance was both demeaning and inappropriate: "It's just disgraceful to be dependent on them. . . . And it's just for people who really need it. I feel that since I'm working, I can take care of some of my basic needs."

Most never become desperate enough to apply for Food Stamps or GR. Those who do apply feel that they too are discouraged by welfare workers:

> HANK: I went to get General Relief and they said, "Well, first of all you have to show us a two-week rent receipt and without that we

can't help you." . . . They're so opinionated about people who come in there. . . . If you told them you just got off the Greyhound bus, or just hitchhiked into town, boy, whooo! [laughs]. They wanta get you out of there fast![50]

Although Hank was refused welfare, his ability to find work quickly obviated any need to raise money through criminal activities (an option he never considered). For Transitory Workers in general, both their relatively good access to resources and their self-conceptions as independent and "decent workingmen" (or women in a few cases) make crime highly unappealing—as it is for all hidden subgroups.

This underlines a general point: Transitory Workers rarely use the options and resources that the visible groups use. They rarely eat at free food programs, instead using their meager savings or wages in fast food restaurants or getting Food Stamps in times of extreme need. Similarly, they rarely obtain clothes from social service agencies, partly because of their general disdain for street resources, but also because, as earnest jobseekers, they place great importance on having "presentable" clothes. As in Hank's case, often the first money from any job goes to "put my wardrobe together."

The one exception to this rule is shelter. Usually without previous experience of homelessness, and typically lacking a conception of themselves as homeless, Transitory Workers seek to avoid the alien environments of the streets and the traditional religious missions. In Santa Barbara work-seekers have been given high priority at the Church-sponsored (but secularly run) shelters and their successor, Transition House. These provide free temporary housing while Transitory Workers save up enough money to get into low-cost housing, typically a SRO, which requires no first, last, and deposit. Screeners recognize this pattern and reward such people with easier admittance and by bending the rules at times—for example, by allowing those working to enter the shelter after the 6:00 p.m. curfew. The Church shelters also provide a place for workers to get themselves and their clothing clean for job interviews, and often a place to store their "interview" clothes.

Because they are unaccustomed to shelter life, however, Transitory Workers often find it demeaning and hard to tolerate:

HANK: You can't leave here [after 6:00 p.m.], you know? It's kind of like being on the Work Release Program I would say here, almost as if you're in jail. . . . And after being on my own, being my own boss my whole life, it's a little tough to say, "Now you gotta be here at five o'clock, and you cannot leave the premises. . . ."
That's the worst thing about the whole thing, the fact that you're almost a prisoner here of these people.

Yet most agree that, as Hank said, "It beats being out there on the beach, going through the garbage cans by a hell of a long shot."

Transitory Workers are typically homeless for very short periods and then, finding work, move back into low-cost housing. While they are homeless, they are rarely identified as such by housed people. By day, they blend in with other workers, looking for jobs and generally finding them. By night they stay in shelters, their cars, or SROs when possible, invisible to most of the housed world.

SKIDDERS

While Transitory Workers, like the other adult subgroups,[51] are likely to be men, "Skidders" are overwhelmingly—but not exclusively—women. Like Lynn and Sonja, they are usually Anglo women in their thirties who grew up and spent at least part of their adult lives in middle-class or upper-working-class families,[52] but "skidded" into homelessness as divorced or separated parents. Loss of an income-producing partner leads eventually to inability to pay rent and eviction; finding substitute housing is further complicated by anti-child discrimination and the difficulty of accumulating first, last, and deposit.

Some Skidders have full- or part-time jobs, but many are unemployed. Skidders are among the least likely of homeless people to be actively looking for work: The high cost of child care hampers both the search for work and the ability to work (or work more). Former homemakers' lack of a recent work history is another problem. Although many Skidders have at least some college, few have extensive job skills, and most have not done professional or skilled work. Few have enough free time to enroll in the various job-training programs they qualify for, even if they believed (as few do) that such efforts would be productive.

Skidders are the most likely subgroup to be receiving welfare (exclusively AFDC), a circumstance that fits both their demographic composition (largely low-income women with children) and their largely middle-class upbringing, which prepares them to negotiate the bureaucracy.[53] Fear of losing their children, however, holds some back from applying. The Single Parent Alliance advised its members that if they revealed they were homeless, "social services may refer your case to the Child Protective Services. In practice, we were told, this decision is made at the discretion of the individual workers and tends to be made on the basis that according to his or her opinion, your children look 'dirty' or 'neglected.' "[54]

Others are ineligible because of their income, although it may not be enough to escape homelessness.

> R O G E R : I got my tax return and the welfare—I was on welfare for a
> while—they knocked me off of welfare because of my tax return,

> measly $1,048. . . . I basically spent all of it on clothes and having
> a good time with the kids, which they haven't had for so long. . . .
> I got the check in April and then at the end of April when it was
> pretty much all gone, they said that I wouldn't be getting any
> money from them.

For most, some question of pride and humiliation is involved. Bruce
(sometimes Transitory Worker, sometimes Street Person, now coupled
with a Skidder and her two children) explained:

> Oh, I'd known about welfare before. I never really planned to do
> that. [In the past] I would have been overwhelmed, scandalized to
> think of it. Then you get that desperate. You've got kids with their
> hungry bird mouths pointing up in the air without food, and you
> have to put something in there.

Like Transitory Workers, Skidders do not obtain resources through
crime. No Skidder I ever spoke to had been arrested for any crime
(including sleeping offenses), nor, at least by their testimony, had any
committed a crime. This seems plausible, given both their superior
resources—and thus alternatives to crime—and their links with mainstream society.[55]

Most Skidders were once housed residents of Santa Barbara (although
a few become homeless upon migration to Santa Barbara from a housed
situation elsewhere); once homeless, they seek many resources primarily
through their networks of family and local friends from their housed days.
For instance, Skidders generally do not use the emergency shelters.[56]
Instead they stay episodically and temporarily, with friends or family
members.[57] Such hidden arrangements, however, are not easy. Skidders
are well aware of their dependence on the good will of their benefactors
and must be careful not to intrude too much. In addition, most live in fear
of detection by a landlord who will object to the extra wear and tear caused
by more people, or demand additional rent.

The common denominator of these arrangements and the alternatives
Skidders use periodically—including motels, campgrounds, and their
vehicles—is impermanence. Since the Skidder has no long-term legal
control over her or his housing, frequent changes of residence are the rule.
Christine and her baby, for example, lived in her van at a house, moved her
van to another house, moved into a group living situation, moved into her
van in a friend's front yard, housesat for a friend for a month, housesat for
another friend for a month, housesat for a third friend for three weeks,
moved in with a couple for several months, and then began living
clandestinely at another friend's place—all in a sixteen month period.

Only when the situation is desperate will Skidders even consider the
shelters. Both their fear of the environment and their conception of

themselves as middle-class militate against using the shelters and make their unavoidable stays brief. For the most part, however, they are able to avoid them through the use of their still viable social networks.

Similarly, Skidders do not use street sources of food. Those on AFDC receive Food Stamps as part of their benefits. Other use money received from work, family, child support (in a few cases), student loans, or savings to buy food at conventional stores. Skidders do not use Food Stamps if they are not on the AFDC program, nor do they eat at any of the religious missions, even in the worst of times.

Their social networks also serve Skidders well in terms of clothing. Although some buy clothes (typically in thrift or other low-cost stores), using their wages or AFDC income, they are much more likely to have access to their stored clothes. Similarly, hygiene and laundry needs are more easily met when living with friends or family.

But Skidders have a problem the groups previously discussed do not have: They are parents.[58] For them (and for Latino Families, discussed below), a crucial imperative is making their children's lives as "normal" as possible. Lynn and her children, for example, have been circulating through a series of friends' homes, but she tries to maintain the same schedule wherever she finds herself: She rises around seven, gets her children dressed, fed, and off to school, and then attends classes at the local community college from nine to noon.[59] After noon she takes a bus to a suburb north of the city where she works in a medical clinic until five, takes a bus back to her children's school, picks them up, and then takes them to wherever they are staying for dinner and bedtime.

Most Skidders worry even more about the psychological damage being done by homelessness than about its physical effects. They do not need to consult the growing volume of literature on the impact of homelessness on children and family relationships:[60] They see it daily. The strain of homelessness often affects the parent–child relationship:

> R O G E R : I am yelling at my kids more often than I have done before. That's not good. That is another form of abuse on children. I'm raising my kids and you can see that I am a concerned parent. When it comes to not having a place for them and I have to struggle doing what I have to do to find a place and not getting anything accomplished, and when they start doing their little things, it just builds on the negative that is already in me. I just scream and holler. I see other [homeless] parents doing it too. . . . It used to be if I saw a mother or father yelling at their kids needlessly, I would say, "Calm down a little bit." Today, I just pat them on the shoulder and I say, "I feel for you."

Many Skidders feel guilt over their inability to provide a conventional home for their children:

LIZ: I am supposed to have a career and have a place to live for my kid. I'm supposed to have some kind of security for her, so she doesn't turn into a basket case. All these things I'm supposed to be doing for one reason or another, I'm not doing. The guilt is real heavy.

The ultimate worry for Skidders is that their children will be taken from them because of their homelessness, a practice reported to be increasing nationally in the late 1980s and early 1990s.[61] While such incidents are rare in Santa Barbara (and not official policy of the Child Protective Service) widespread fear is evidenced by the continuing stream of articles on the topic in the SPA newsletter.

In summary, Skidders' primary links are to people from their former economic class; they are rarely have any links to street life. Their larger social margin, including networks among middle-class people and past residency, as well as individual characteristics in some cases, allow them more options than the visible populations or Transitory Workers. But the additional problems associated with children weigh heavily.

LATINO FAMILIES

Parents are also found in the last hidden subgroup, "Latino Families," probably the most hidden of all homeless people in Santa Barbara. Unlike Skidders, however, Latino Families usually have two parents typically immigrants from Latin America who have lived in Santa Barbara for several years, often alternating between housed lives and bouts of homelessness. Latinos (defined ethnically) may be found in other subgroups as well, but "Latino Families" emerge as a lifestyle subgroup because of their crucial reliance on social networks within the Latino community, the Catholic Church, and Catholic Social Service for meeting their daily needs.

Latino Families generally have at least one employed breadwinner, often working full-time. While some were skilled workers, managers, or professionals before immigrating, their past and present jobs in the United States are almost always low-paying, nonunion, and in the service sector. As maids, janitors, and gardeners, they enjoy little job security and no unemployment benefits. In most cases the family breadwinner is looking for more work, a search sometimes hampered by a lack of relevant job skills or English fluency and the time-consuming tasks required merely to get by. When looking for work (or additional work), Latino Families tend to use family, community, and past employer contacts.

Despite their employment problems, Latino Families generally steer clear of most kinds of public assistance. With the exception of a few single mothers receiving AFDC, these homeless families are much more likely to use the private charity of the Church and Catholic Social Service, or the resources of friends and family, as one activist explained:

> [From] my own experience, I have seen it is hard for Latin people, it is hard to say, "Hey, help me, I need assistance." They will go to the Catholic Social Service and talk to the nuns. They are ashamed even to go there—it is bad enough that you are in that position. You have a person [in government programs] that treats you like a beggar and that hurts. They [the CSS staff] know how bad they are [hurting]. They live with the nuns.

This reluctance may be in part cultural and in part due to lack of information, but it also reflects the fear of attracting any official attention on the part of undocumented members of this community. In addition, like Skidders, they fear losing their children if their homeless state is discovered. As with Skidders, however, the longer they reside in Santa Barbara, the more likely they are to apply for and receive AFDC. (Those residing in town longer are, of course, more likely to have become legal citizens.)

The reliance of Latino Families on resource networks within the Latino community is perhaps best seen in their shelter arrangements. Throughout most of the 1980s, Latino Families were almost never seen in any of the emergency shelters,[62] and virtually none used the GR housing voucher program. Instead, they called on the resource of families, friends, or acquaintances, staying in facilities over which they had no legal control, most frequently garages and outbuildings. In one style of resource pooling seen only in the Latino community, many people contribute toward the rent for an apartment whose kitchen, bathroom, and laundry facilities can be used by all, though only a few can regularly sleep there (or hold legal rights of tenancy).[63] In other cases, a resident household will pick up extra peripheral members who may sleep in the garage or in their cars while occasionally having use of the facilities:

> E M I L I O : Now we're staying in a garage. It's not too sanitary because we don't have a kitchen and only a small bathroom. I fixed our meals only once in these people's kitchen. The kids eat things that don't have to be cooked: sandwiches, cereal, etc. . . . [We live] like alley cats.

Similarly, these networks, rather than welfare or street resources, provide food, clothing, and cleaning needs. Use of Food Stamps or GR vouchers is almost nonexistent. Those who have access to cooking facilities purchase basic staples from grocery stores or, when hard pressed, receive them from Catholic Social Service, but they rarely eat at the religious shelters. Clothing is purchased at thrift or low-cost stores when money is available; when not, Latino Families rely on family or friends' donations and, when most desperate, vouchers given by Catholic Social Service.

As with Skidders, Latino Families are anxious to protect their children, physically and emotionally, and often report that homelessness puts pressure on the parent–child relationship:

> JUANITA: I was snapping at the kids. The kids were talking back, it was affecting us. . . . They were getting into fights with other kids. . . . They were hyper and unhappy. One of my kids one time sat down and cried: "Why do we have to go through life like this? Why doesn't God love us any more?"

Getting by, "simple survival" for homeless people, is not simple, in any sense of that word. Survival is difficult, requiring hard work and endurance of hard conditions. Survival is also complex, with each subgroup (and each individual) creating, maintaining, and sometimes transforming resource networks in order to make ends meet. These resource networks, from the most rooted Skidders to the least rooted Wingnuts, all have in common an attempt to create stability. This is a far cry from the public picture of homeless people as inept or voluntary wanderers, blowing from town to town, or the newer picture of anomic losers crushed by large-scale societal processes. Such resource networks are grounded in contacts with other people, both housed and homeless.

Chapter 4

Hanging on
and hanging out

T hrough all their trails, most homeless people attempt to live as "normally" as possible for as long as they can. They strive to preserve or create roots, to find jobs and a home, and to "carve out a modicum of meaning and personal significance in what must, from the more privileged perches of the normative order, appear to be an anomic void."[1] Conventional wisdom—mirrored in many academic theories—instead portrays homeless people as adrift in a different world from the rest of us. Disaffiliation theorists have often stressed a prior disengagement from conventional life while displacement theorists stress an unwilling displacement, but there is general agreement that the *result* of homelessness is disaffiliation from mainstream society and other people in general: "To be without a home is to be cut off from the rest of the world."[2]

Perhaps we can best begin by defining "affiliation." We say someone is affiliated when he or she is embedded in social networks made up of multiple relationships characterized by reciprocal (though not necessarily symmetric) exchange of resources, including material aid, advice, and companionship.[3] Presumably, those with affiliations are able to secure social support from others in their networks.[4] Although the concept of reciprocity is typically used in analyses of the more or less equal exchange of similar or identical forms of support (companionship, material aid, etc.), it also lies at the heart of the exchange of roughly equivalent but dissimilar resources in more formal market relations: An employer expects a certain amount of labor for a paid wage; a merchant expects payment for his or her goods.

Disaffiliation (and many displacement) theorists have argued that homeless people lack such ties with mainstream institutions such as the employment market, with housed friends and kin, and, in many accounts, with each other.[5] This characterization suffers from what Stan Hall and Barry Wellman have called "a vaccination model of support (an individual either has it or not)."[6] Certainly some homeless people are isolated—in particular, those who are mentally ill. But this condition is far from a general or permanent state for most homeless people. In this chapter I argue that homeless people retain or create meaningful ties with mainstream institutions, housed friends and family members, and other homeless people far more often than is commonly thought.

Indeed, as we saw in the previous chapter, because mainstream society controls most of the resources that homeless people need to survive, many homeless people get by through maintaining connections with housed people, employers, social service workers, and merchants. Many, particularly Skidders and Latino Families, are closely linked to housed friends and kin. Those who lack such ties are likely to have created meaningful ties to other homeless people in which reciprocity is the norm.

Further, homeless people strive to preserve or create *emotional* resource networks as well as material ones, and often these overlap. For the more rooted subgroups—notably Latino Families and Skidders—these may be stable, long-term relationships that began before and continue beyond the time spent homeless. For less rooted homeless people, found particularly in the visible street populations, the relationships are less stable, but, for the weeks or months they last, they constitute routines and supports that homeless people come to depend on. Overall, these arrangements suggest that a monolithic image of homeless people as socially incompetent and isolated by will or circumstances is inaccurate. Maintaining ties requires social skills, the more so when one's material resources are slim; the desire to maintain these ties remains strong among homeless people.

Relations with Housed People

Since affiliations involve reciprocity, retaining ties with housed people is problematic. Homeless people have few material resources, but the problem lies even deeper; it involves housed people's suspicions that homeless people have little of value *on any level* that is worth exchanging.

The perceived danger of unequal exchange is greatest when the tie is of a formal or market character, for here the housed person (an employer or merchant, for example) is likely to be responding to the homeless person less as an individual and more as a representative of "the homeless." Since housed people tend to see homelessness as a characteristic rather than a condition,[7] they tend to distrust those who appear to be "one of them" rather than "one of us."

Interactions between homeless people and merchants are almost entirely governed by expectations built on these divisions. Merchants fear that those they recognize as homeless will violate the principle of reciprocity, stealing instead of paying for their goods, or generating little in sales compared with the problems they create. Most fundamentally, they worry that homeless people will scare away customers who *would* observe the principle of reciprocity, either by their very appearance or by failing to observe the expected rules of decorum in exchange for access to shopping areas:[8]

> Last week there was a fellow going up the street, cussing as loud as he could in a mule skinner's oath. And when you have ladies that you're trying to attract to downtown, this is the best way in the world to help [competing shopping centers].[9]

> Basically they sleep in the doorways. They urinate on the windows. They defecate in the doorways and stuff.[10]

Homeless people are well aware that many merchants view them as examples of a type rather than as individuals:[11]

> MAYOR MAX: There's certain places that have in recent times taken a look at me and said, "Well, we don't want you or your kind in here any more." And it's not because I've done anything wrong; it's just because I don't have the availability of a bathtub.

As a result, many on the streets "take great care not to look street," as Glen described his own strategy. Members of the hidden subgroups rarely report problems with merchants.[12]

In general, those who are obviously homeless report far different treatment from housed people (including police, prospective employers and landlords, and social service workers, as well as merchants) than those who pass as housed. It is precisely for this reason that many homeless people go to such great lengths to appear housed, sleeping sitting up on park benches to prevent their clothes from getting wrinkled, giving prospective landlords a housed friend's telephone number as their own, lying to authorities or prospective employers about their homeless status.

The ability to remain "invisible" in this sense varies by subgroup. Latino Families and Skidders have greater access to cleaning facilities, but they must still cover their tracks verbally to keep their homelessness a secret from prospective landlords and employers. Transitory Workers' greater ability to get into the emergency shelters aids their job quests, since they are able to use the bathing facilities and keep their clothes relatively unwrinkled. Lack of a phone and home address may blow their cover, however, once they have achieved a job interview.

Wingnuts are the least able to appear "normal," and, in many cases, the least likely even to have that as a concern. They are thus the most visible of homeless people, heavily influencing the public picture of what homeless people are like and often reinforcing housed people's fears about both mentally ill and homeless people. Kids, on the other hand, probably worry less about passing than any other subgroup, because children in general dress casually, and because they are rarely involved in finding a job or housing.

Street People vary considerably in their desire and ability to appear housed. Those least interested in escape are least concerned with invisibility, while those highly concerned with escape go to great lengths to avoid being stigmatized as homeless:

> J A C K : I don't like doing this, but I have to do it so people don't relate to me as homeless—I stashed my bag in the bushes . . . which I'm terrified of doing, 'cause I've been stuck with nothing, with just the clothes I'm wearing. You never know when a bum will see that bag and say, "Hey, I can use that bag, that's a nice bag." But see, I still won't walk around with my bag, just to avoid that [label].

As time goes on, cleanliness—and therefore invisibility—becomes more difficult:

> G L E N : When you are on the street, most [attention] is unwanted. People notice that you are dirty or unshaven or whatever, so you try to stay low-key. . . . I know a lot [of homeless people] are [trying to stay invisible]. It seems like a lot of them just get to the point where you stop thinking about things like that.

Despite these difficulties, many homeless people do enter into or remain in formal or market relations with at least some housed people. In some cases this is because they have been able to hide their homelessness; in others it is because they already had such a relationship before becoming homeless (e.g., an employed Latino Family member), and thus have already demonstrated an ability to reciprocate, to meet the terms of the implied contract, which takes precedence over the housed person's general beliefs about "the homeless." In other cases, homeless people still have something that housed people want. For those who seek daily labor at The Wall, their homelessness may actually be perceived as a positive attribute, since it ensures that they will work for the lowest wages. Because mainstream resource networks have such vast resources compared with most alternatives, many homeless people regularly—and most homeless people at some time—attempt to connect with them, even though this requires creativity.[13]

Homeless people also often continue to have relations with housed friends and family. Many researchers have argued that such ties are typically weak, and that contact is likely to be infrequent; some argue that the presence or absence of such connections most strongly accounts for who remains among the "domiciled poor" and who becomes homeless in the first place.[14] Housed people in Santa Barbara often ask: "Where are their families? Why didn't the communities they came from take care of them? Why aren't they getting the help they need from their relatives or friends?" One answer is that many people *are* getting such help (as the figures on overcrowding suggest), and that is how they can remain among the nearly or hidden homeless instead of descending into the fully visible homeless population. Yet it is also true that those who become "roofless" as well as homeless, almost by definition, have been unable to rely on their families or friends to save them from the streets. This suggests two possibilities: that they have lost contact with housed family members or friends, or that such people are themselves too impoverished to help. Most observers stress the former possibility,[15] with some validity. Homeless people *as a group* are unquestionably less connected to housed friends and families than housed people *as a group*, but this statement needs to be qualified in a number of ways.

Comparisons with housed populations are difficult. What constitutes "contact," and what time period is to be used? Using national population samples for comparison,[16] local studies elsewhere appear at first glance to demonstrate that homeless people are significantly more isolated from relatives than others. For example, while 92 percent of the national sample report contact at least monthly with relatives, only half of shelter guests in the Twin Cities do so.[17] There are, however, significant exceptions: For example, Irving Piliavin and his colleagues' study of both sheltered and unsheltered homeless people reports that 90 percent of those interviewed had contact with relatives in the previous month.[18]

The appearance of widespread isolation from family is in part an artifact of methodology:[19] Many of the data showing lack of contact are obtained from shelter populations, which are likely to contain the most isolated of homeless people, those without any network of friends or family to offer a place to stay the night. Even mixed shelter and street surveys miss those hidden in the homes of kin or friends, thus entirely omitting those I have classified as Skidders and Latino Families. The previously discussed national data on overcrowding, for instance, are apparently not reflected in many of these lower estimates, although they are powerful evidence of homeless people's bonds with their families.[20] Demographic and environmental differences also produce significantly varied results. For example, women, rural homeless people, and homeless people with family members living nearby are considerably more likely to be in contact with their families than men, urban homeless people, and those without local family members.[21]

The data in Santa Barbara vary widely by data set (reflecting the proportion of different subgroups surveyed; see the Appendix for details). Over a third of the less rooted Church guests could not (or would not) even provide an emergency contact number (family member, friend, or social service worker) to screeners, and the percentage rises with the length of time spent homeless.[22] In the more rooted HoPP and SPA groups, however, over 80 percent were in contact with their families.

Latino Families, Skidders, and Kids are likely to have family members living in Santa Barbara. Latino Families and Skidders are almost without exception in touch with their families, whether their families live in Santa Barbara or not; Kids tend to be out of touch when not living at home, since their departure inevitably follows some blowup with their parents. Some Wingnuts have no contact with their families—or none they would speak of; others retained some ties.[23] Transitory Workers typically cite "slight" connections to family—a letter now and then, knowledge of their address. Street People have a higher rate of contact with their families than much of the literature would suggest: The HoPP interviews and my conversations with them suggest that a majority are in fairly regular contact, and perhaps another quarter in occasional contact. Those with family members in the area are much more likely to report contact than others.

For a variety of reasons, then, a characterization of homeless people as largely lacking contact with housed relatives is questionable; even if the most severe figures reported elsewhere were to be taken at face value, they would still indicate that the great majority of homeless people retain some, often significant, contact with housed relatives.[24] Conversely, many housed people show substantial evidence of disaffiliation, as Erving Goffman has noted among fanatic hobbyists and as Felix Berardo documents among aged widowers.[25]

A similar picture emerges for relations with housed friends: While less pervasive than among housed people, most studies indicate that at least a majority of homeless people retain such contact.[26] Further, a number of studies have found that poor people generally "have fewer friends than people in other classes [but] they seem to depend upon their networks more than do people in affluent areas," a pattern noted in some homeless studies as well.[27] Again, the widespread practice of doubling up with friends goes unrecorded in most surveys, although it is evidence of the closest of ties.

Connection to housed friends also varies by subgroup. Mobile groups—Transitory Workers, Street People, and Wingnuts—are least likely to have maintained friendships, and their present homeless status makes it difficult to form new friendships with housed people. Kids tend to have active social lives, making friends with those they encounter on the streets, a mix of housed and homeless children and adults. Some have friends from their previous lives as school children, but sometimes report that these ties are weakened by lifestyle differences and their own episodic mobility. The most rooted Skidders and Latino Families invariably report fairly long-term and constant friendships with those they were friendly with before the onset of homelessness.

Contact with housed relatives or friends, however, does not necessarily translate into support. Estimates of the percentage of homeless people receiving cash or other material aid from housed kith and kin generally range between 10 and 30 percent in other studies.[28] Some evidence suggests that lack of aid from families often stems from the precarious financial situation of the housed family members rather than from a lack of significant bonds.[29] For instance, although the vast majority of HoPP members were in touch with their families, only three of forty-four interviewees reported receiving money from them, and this lack of aid was most frequently attributed to their families' poverty. Julia, for example, retained a link with her working-class parents, but was not willing to burden them any more:

> [In the past] I have received limited funds from them when I am extremely desperate. I try to avoid that. They are both physically handicapped. They have severe medical problems and they have financial problems. They're not in a position, and either am I, to derive funds from them.

The backgrounds of HoPP Latino Families and Transitory Workers promise little hope of support. The former are largely rural and poor, and the latter are working-class. Street People come from a wide span of backgrounds, from very poor to upper-middle-class, but those with middle-class and higher backgrounds are either estranged from their families, long out of the house, or, in a few cases, unwilling to ask for assistance. Only the Skidder subgroup had ongoing contacts with middle-class parents, and this subgroup presented the only cases of parental financial support.[30]

Far more likely than outright financial support, however, is the sharing or giving of other resources, which almost all HoPP members with families in Santa Barbara enjoyed. Some Latino Families, living close to relatives (in some cases on the same property), share meals, laundry facilities, child care, and other everyday needs, as well as having clothes passed on to them. Skidders, who live more often with friends than family, are nevertheless able to approach their families from time to time for shelter, child care, clothing, or a meal. Even those few Street People who have family living in Santa Barbara or nearby tend to leave the streets for brief visits that involve, among other things, using resources:

> KEVIN: If I don't have a dollar fifty [for the public shower], and I'm really dirty, and my clothes are dirty, then I'll try to scrape up 50

cents and I'll hop a bus down to [a small town south of Santa Barbara] and use his [his father's] washer and dryer, and shower, and kitchen. And then come on back to town.

Some families refuse to share resources for a variety of reasons, ranging from Jack's drinking, to Mark's banishment after a marijuana arrest as a high school student ten years earlier, to Lynn's mother's feeling that she had already paid her dues and was no longer obliged to house her grown children.

Homeless people in Santa Barbara may also call on the resources of housed friends. Skidders and Latino Families may appeal to friends for temporary shelter, child care, outgrown children's clothing, and an occasional shared meal, but outright financial support is virtually never asked for or given. Shelter itself is always precarious, since, as previously described, the most unobtrusive guests eventually wear out their welcome.[31] Kids may appeal to their housed friends, although they, in general, have few resources not under their parents' control. Transitory Workers' new friendships with housed fellow workers and jobseekers are rarely of use in gathering resources other than job leads.

Where contact with friends or family has ceased, it is not necessarily because of disengagement by the homeless person.[32] Again, reciprocity is key:

MARK: What has happened is on more than one occasion I've been hit up by [his girlfriend] Anna that, "Well, you know, Jackie's working, why don't . . . you go borrow a hundred bucks from Jackie?" Or, "We don't have anywhere to stay tonight, how about if we hit Barry's floor?" or something. I've just been unable to repay. And I've just burnt too many friends trying to take care of this situation, waiting things out. So that really, I'm basically sitting in town with basically, at this point in time, *no one.*

Housed people may fear that they will keep on giving material and emotional support to a homeless person who has "nothing but trouble" to offer.

The reverse is true as well: Homeless people may find their inability to reciprocate too heavy a burden to bear, and thus cut the ties to their friends or families. Others cut such ties, as Goffman has written of stigmatized people generally, to conceal their "discreditable secret."[33] For most of those I talked to, loss of contact—where it occurred—was far more likely to postdate than to predate the onset of homelessness:

MARGIE: See, you don't start losing out from your family and your friends. You lose contact with them. Because you can't really relate to them, [or] because they don't care about you any more. And you are fed up with your own life and depressed by it.

Relations with Homeless People

Those without significant ties to housed friends or family are most likely to create new ties with other homeless people.[34] While disaffiliation theorists largely argued that homeless people lacked significant reciprocal ties with each other, a number of recent works contend that there are often meaningful relationships between homeless people, although these are typically seen as bounded by individual survival needs.[35] Carl Cohen and Jay Sokolovsky propose that "Bowery men . . . have an *intermediate* level of intimacy. In other words, their levels of intimacy are not as intense as community [i.e., housed] men but their relationships are not devoid of feeling and empathy."[36] Anne Lovell reports support relationships among virtually all of the street people she worked with, characterizing their state as "marginality without isolation."[37]

Attachments between and among homeless people may be envisioned in two ways: connections between friends and a more general feeling of membership in "homeless society." Santa Barbara's homeless population, like all homeless populations, is too large and heterogeneous to allow a collective group feeling that encompasses all subgroups, and the sense of belonging even to a specific subgroup varies widely.

Latino Families and Skidders display little solidarity—though much empathy—with others in their subgroups. This is hardly surprising, given their frames of reference, which are determined by their prehomeless social ties. None of the HoPP Latino Families or Skidders said that many or all of their friends were also homeless, and about half said that they had no homeless friends at all. Their ties are first to their families, and secondarily to the housed friends they see routinely.[38]

Their empathy with others in their subgroup, moreover, rarely extends to other subgroups. When asked about types of homeless people, most Skidders see a simple dichotomy: down-on-their-luck, hardworking citizens like themselves versus street people in the most negative sense of that term:

> LIZ: I notice they had a lot of street people there [at a news
> conference called by homeless activists]. People that live on their
> bicycles. I mean, really, the scuz of the earth. And to lump all of us
> into this, that is what the media picked up on.
> ROGER: I'm not a street person. I won't live on the street. . . . The
> money they make, they buy drugs and drink. It seems like that is
> their whole life. . . . I think something should be done about them.

Transitory Workers, who do not see themselves as homeless, feel no bonds to a homeless community. They—like the hardest-working Skidders—tend to be especially critical of those who do not appear to be looking for work:

> H A N K : There's people sitting right there [at a Church shelter] that absolutely are not gonna do anything. They lay in the park every day, they're not looking for a job. They're not doing anything. . . . And they have no other ambitions in life other than just to get something for nothing from everybody they can get it from.[39]

Thus few Transitory Workers, Skidders, or Latino Families identify themselves with either "the homeless" in general or their own subgroups. Skidders and Latino Families identify themselves with the housed groups they came from and still live within. Transitory Workers see themselves as workers and regard their current position as an accident that will be rectified with their first paycheck.

Kids tend to identify themselves mainly by the social groups they run with ("punkers," for example), which typically include both homeless and housed children. They evince solidarity against the symbols of oppression—school, cops, parents, adults in general—but they have little means to help each other. The episodic nature of their homelessness, combined with their high mobility to other cities, further militates against lasting group arrangements. Wingnuts, too, given their general isolation, show little if any sense of community. Some identify themselves with the Street People, but this is rarely reciprocated.

Street People, at least those who stay in town for some time, evince by far the greatest degree of community:

> B R U C E : I have a lot of acquaintances that are homeless. When I stay in a park, you run into people—you can tell by the way they look. They have a certain look. One dog can recognize another. . . . Anywhere you go. It's a fast kind of comaraderie. Never a middle-class type. You are too damn close to one another. You have a common interest. There is not that kind of distrust.

This feeling of community was most evident among homeless activists and others using the Fig Tree as a base:

> M A Y O R M A X : Usually there's about four or five people, they usually go around looking for food, and they bring it back, and whoever's under the bridge at the time will go ahead and start the fire. . . . And whoever cooked it, cut it up, and got the vegetables eats first, and whatever's left over, we give it to whoever else is hungry. And a lot of people stop through, you know, that wasn't even around to offer help.
>
> Q : Is there any problem with the people who are doing the work being pissed about people who aren't working getting to eat?

MAYOR MAX: They don't mind people eating, and they by no means get pissed or mad about it. All they do is suggest that, you know, "Come help us next time. Help carry something back if you want to. If not, just try and do what you can." That's how they recruit a lot of people. You know, one or two people are always doing it, but every couple of days, one or two new people help them. So everybody eventually gets into donating time and help with the food.[40]

Yet street life is often characterized by distrust and animosity as well, and periodically by intragroup crime and violence. A few Fig Tree regulars claim that the norms of the community prevent crimes within the group:

FIELD NOTES, 4/4/83: [People I had just met] talked about, showed, and eventually sold [drugs] right there with me and three other people they didn't know watching. I asked Benny, a buyer, if he wasn't afraid to be flashing money (actually $30 worth of Food Stamps) around, and he said, "No, if you have friends they'll back you up, and if you rip someone off on the streets, you can't come back to this town since everyone knows."

But most Street People report that petty thefts are common:

DEMO DAN: I've been ripped off. Stuff stolen from me, money stolen out of my pocket when I was drunk a few times. . . . I know people who have stolen and the next day they're right there [at the Fig Tree] saying, "I didn't take anything."

CHARLIE: I've had stuff ripped off sometimes. Nothing I consider major. Sleeping bags, stuff I leave lying around. Stupid, you know. You got to carry it around with you and watch it like a hawk.

In fact, two codes are found among Street People: one valuing loyalty to the group, exemplified by Benny's belief in street justice and Kevin's declaration (quoted in Chapter 3) that Street People have consciences; the other valuing street smarts and cunning. More than a few Street People commented favorably on the former while conceding the need to live by the latter when times got hard.

Solidarity within the homeless community (or subgroups) is strongest when political groupings seem to promise group progress (as I will discuss in the next chapter) and when danger threatens the group as a whole.[41] When Kenny Burr was murdered in December 1984, many previously low-visibility homeless people surfaced to voice their fear and anger. The reaction of Greg, a housed-looking Street Person, was fairly typical:

The only times I got the [illegal sleeping] tickets was when I was in large groups and we were out there, knew we were going to get the tickets. But it was for a cause. Slept at the Fig Tree, out in the middle of the open, right after Kenny's murder. Got a ticket. I slept at the train station a couple of times [that week] and got tickets.

Similarly, the trial of a prep school student for the murder of Michael Stephenson the following year brought out many once hidden homeless people, as did the City Council hearings on amending the anti-sleeping law in 1986.

While the sense of community seems to vary considerably with political and social conditions, smaller bonding patterns appear to be more constant, and it is in such relationships that a collective feeling and reciprocal exchange are most common.

This is least true, however, for Latino Families and Skidders, partly because they are connected to housed friends and family, and partly because caring for their children takes so much of their available time:

> D U L A : I see my husband off to work, and when I have a chance to use the kitchen [in the house where they are temporarily staying], I fix him a lunch very early in the morning. Then I take my little girl to her preschool. I come back and I wash clothes, play with my baby boy. After I pick my daughter up from school, we walk and I take them to the garden located in front of the Goleta Community Center. After, I go to the house and see if it's possible for me to cook for my family. . . . Afterward, I bathe my children, put them to bed, and a little later we do the same in preparation for the next day.

Like most Latino Family members, Dula spends what little free time she has with housed friends and kin.

As single parents, Skidders have complete responsibility for their children's needs but also a reason to go outside the family unit in order to enjoy the company of other adults, invariably housed friends from their previous working- or middle-class lives. These, however, are almost exclusively friendship relations: Very few report dating or other romantic connections for which most say they are too tired, too nervous, or too busy. Their social lives are further limited by their lack of a place to entertain in and their lack of money:

> L I Z : [I'm] just not having any fun in my life. I just come home [to a place where she is temporarily housesitting]. I better not go to the movies or out to dinner because I have to save every dime.

Transitory Workers, whose lives are in a sense on hold during their periods of homelessness, seem to have almost no social life. They are totally focused on finding work and making enough money to move back into a place of their own. Without social connections in Santa Barbara in most cases, they rarely have friends to pass the time with. The regulations of the shelter, where I met most of the Transitory Workers I came across, further restrict their hanging out:

> H A N K : Six o'clock we get up. . . . I eat breakfast here and get on the bus. . . . I go to work, to lunch, go back to work. After work I get on the bus and come out here [to the Church shelter] and go through this [intake] procedure, and eat dinner, and take a shower and shave, and go to bed. Because you can't leave here [after intake at six], you know.

They may make friends with other Transitory Workers, but their mobility (geographically and out of homelessness) often renders such friendships brief.

Kids, on the other hand, are typically quite social, but their patterns of mobility and episodic homelessness also make lasting friendships difficult to sustain.[42] They instead seem to form a succession of temporary bonds with others in similar situations, often referred to as being "best friends." While these last, there is the expectation of mutual aid, but the resources each commands are generally minimal.

Wingnuts do little bonding with others in similar straits.[43] For some this is deliberate:

> J U L I A : Number one rule when you're on the streets: No friends. No friends. *Not one.*

But even Wingnuts who desire bonding find that others on the street are unlikely to reciprocate:

> R A C H E L : I get lonely for friends. . . . Nobody ever wants to be with me during the day.

Jonathan's account of "a typical day" poignantly displays his yearning for contact with other people and the underlying reality of profound isolation:

> J O N A T H A N : A typical day is daybreak, a little place down at the beach, away from the police and others. . . . Come out from underneath the bushes. Walk along Cabrillo Boulevard. We go walking, we're walking with Jesus Christ, he's our best friend. . . .
> Then a tour through the parking lots, see. Got this thing in mind that boozers are losers, yeah, boozers are losers, lose it all. So I walk through the parking lot because they lose things. Dollar bills, often they smoke these funny little [marijuana] cigarettes and [I] find a roach, and that immediately alters the thing, you know. Finding a roach, smoking it, heading for Fellowship Hall, finding anonymous alcoholics, Alcoholics Anonymous. That starts

the day. You know, a tour of the parking lot. . . . It helps to have a routine. So, make the early bird meeting, seven o'clock, Fellowship Hall. And then, stay until the spirit moves me to move. . . .

So up State Street to the Fox Arlington Theater. Back down around to the plaza, possibly over to Club One [a drop-in center for alcoholics] over on Canon Perdido, and back to De La Guerra Plaza. Often over to the museum over there, it's a really quiet, meditative spot. . . . Then, if I'm hungry, the Wings of Love is open from nine to four. Yeah, not bound by any kind of time limit, but available if necessary. Oftentimes the dumpsters. . . . From Wings of Love usually to Fellowship Hall for a meeting, Alcoholics Anonymous. Yeah, go there at noontime, then afternoon, depending on the way I feel, sometimes maybe a walk down to the beach. Oftentimes go to Club One. Quite often, yeah, because it's one of those kinds of things where you can need it quite often.

After Club One, around and about through the streets of Santa Barbara, you know, reading and writing a lot. And whatever happens, yeah, just whatever happens. You know, usually it's until I get tired, fatigued, and most times I will stay awake until after dark. Usually another meeting at Fellowship Hall or Club One at five-thirty, six in the evening.

Q: You never go down to the Fig Tree?

JONATHAN: Yeah, I do not go down to the Fig Tree. I go *by* it, I go by it quite a bit, and *watch*.

Of all homeless people, Street People are the most likely to form lasting friendships with other homeless people. When not employed, looking for work, or applying for benefits, they hang out at specific locations, usually parks. Acquaintances and friends come to know each other's routines and to congregate at these locations, expecting others in their informal groups to be there, but not surprised if someone does not show up, since so many things—arrest, a job, leaving town—may come up.

Subgroups within the subgroup of Street People tend to have their own areas, their own turfs:

DEMO DAN: I walk into a black group, it's like I feel tense. Like the car wash is a typical place [where homeless black people hang out]. . . . They kind of run that block. Like six months ago there was like a Mexican–black kind of thing happening on that corner. I don't know what they were fighting over. . . . What I think is worse is that Mexican thing. You see a bunch of them, [homeless Anglos say], "I don't want to go over to those dirty Mexicans."

Nor are the divisions merely, or even typically, racial. For instance, most long-time alcoholics spend their time among themselves and away from other Street People, although they may welcome those who join them from time to time if they bring in additional resources.

Fig Tree Park is the largest and best-known gathering place for Street People. Perhaps a hundred people, with maybe thirty regulars, appear there each day. Hanging out is intertwined with getting by and getting ahead, as it is for Kids. There may be trading, in which Food Stamps are the basic currency, but trades can involve "anything you can find somebody willing to trade with," as Charley said. Tips on jobs or other resources are passed back and forth, as are street rumors and old-timers' wisdom. Deals, both legal and illegal, are struck.[44] Other Street People have found the pressure downtown, either from police or street life, too intense, and have relocated to parks further uptown. A few groups congregate in parking lots, or outside sympathetic marginal business establishments, or in nooks and crannies, such as under bridges.

Faced with common problems, common threats, and a common constellation of available resources, Street People do constitute a community of sorts, but each Street Person lives his or her life principally within a framework of ties to mainstream society, a small group of friends, and an established routine. Within their hangouts and marketplaces, like the Fig Tree, such groups may operate on a semicollective basis. While everyone understands that each person is ultimately going to go his or her own way,[45] these groups may exist for many months, and feelings of reciprocal responsibility, collective well-being, and mutual support are important. Mark describes one of these:

> There's Sammy. . . . He owns this little red car [which Mark sometimes sleeps in]. His size and mine are about the same, so we pass clothing back and forth all the time. He hasn't brought any, hardly any, income in at all, but he has a lot of company and a lot of time to give. . . . Then there's Jerry. . . . He's always got pot to offer, and he's always got, you know, thirty or forty dollars in his pocket. There's Mike. Mike just broke up with his wife. . . . And when Earl's sober, there's Earl. . . . [We help each other out] as far as the fact of realizing somebody hasn't eaten and going out and bringing them food, making sure they eat it. . . . There's still a lot of that kind of thing going around with food. And then passing back and forth on joints, or liquor, or something like that.[46]

Those Street People who travel particularly stress the importance of having a buddy:

MAYOR MAX: It's better to have a partner 'cause you can never always watch your back. And you got somebody there, it gets you an opportunity, if you're carrying a lot of possessions with you, it's good to have somebody you can trust while you make the errands, go check your mail, you know, groceries or something else.

For those settled in one town, the sense of community may lessen the need for a specific partner:

> C H A R L I E : Oh, I have to have a partner when I travel. . . . Somebody to talk to when you're sitting on the [freeway] ramp for hours. . . . But when I'm just doing Santa Barbara, I'd rather just do it by myself. Around the Fig Tree there's plenty of people to talk to. When you're traveling and you're in a place where you don't know people, [you need a partner] so you can leave your pack. But I can leave my pack at the Fig Tree [without a partner] a lot of times because I can have somebody watch it.

Although Street People display solidarity with their immediate groups and, less intensely, with Street People in general, loyalty clearly takes a back seat to their individual needs. Most solutions appear to be individual ones:

> M A R K : There is a lot of empathy, there's a lot of sympathy. But what I'm finding in my own situation now is that my need to get out of here is greater than anybody else I'm associating with. And I've got to take care of this need for myself. It's *got* to be done.

Thus while collective loyalties are important and meaningful, they are also often fragile and transitory. Few homeless people want to think of themselves as part of a homeless group because few want to think of themselves as homeless, given the connotations of that word. For example, when asked to classify the homeless population by subgroups, homeless people invariably report that their personal history places them outside the classifications they make for others:[47]

> G L E N : I am pretty much different from the people out in the street. I guess I'm more knowledgeable about the social-economic ladder, in other words.
>
> T E D : Most of them don't have a grounding anywhere. They are really like most children. I feel a great deal of compassion for them. So basically I see a lot of compassion coming from my circumstances, and yet I see that as separating me from the people that I feel compassion for.

Fear, as well as pride, may be involved in such distancing: "It terrifies the young ones to see the old ones—to feel that they're just one step away."[48]

The picture I have drawn here is of homeless people facing and enduring greater isolation than most people, but at the same time retaining and creating more ties than most theorists and housed people would predict.[49] While homeless people are rarely involved in what social network analysts call "dense" networks (in which multiple ties involving exchange of resources exist among many members of the community),[50] many are involved in meaningful and reciprocal relations. These may be of relatively short duration, or they may last months and even years. They may be with other homeless people, as they generally are for Street People, or with housed people, as is generally the case with Skidders. Humans are social creatures, perhaps by nature and certainly because of the structures of our social world. Getting by, meeting material—and, for many, emotional—needs, requires connecting in some way to other people.

The conditions and structural constraints of homelessness, however, bound these relations. Homeless people's affiliations are fragile, complicated by differing needs, competition for resources, the lure of individual escape, the labeling process and fear of that process, social divisions (both between housed and homeless people and between subgroups of homeless people), and often spatial boundaries (thus "the double meaning of being a 'Fig Tree type' ").[51] The networks they create are not constructed randomly but within the context of societal processes and the local structures and institutions that mediate those processes.[52] For instance, the "triaging" of different homeless people into different shelters—for women, for those who are mentally ill, for children—influences whom a person comes into contact with, and thus makes friends with. The labeling process, dominated by the definitions provided by mainstream institutions (but interpreted by homeless people based on their own experiences), further frames the options available for hanging out. Those perceived as the "deserving poor"—such as Skidders—are loath to associate with Street People "scuz"; Street People avoid Wingnuts, whom they see as less "normal" than themselves.

Further, their networks are impoverished, both in terms of material resources and in terms of the number of people who are willing and able to share resources with them. Yet while the structural context of their lives makes affiliations difficult to maintain, the *desire* to retain or create affiliations is not, as is often suggested, thereby extinguished. As Mark expressed it, "There's the pressure, the tension, the lack of having. . . . You've *got* to belong *somewhere*." Certainly some homeless people—particularly Wingnuts—have so little social margin, so little social status in the eyes of others (including other homeless people), that they are rarely able to create such networks, but even in many of these cases, the *yearning* for contact is there.

Most homeless people act on that desire, creating networks—for longer or shorter periods of time, in varying intensities, and involving varying reciprocal obligations—that fulfill their needs for *both* emotional and material support. Latino Families socialize with the housed friends and families they sometimes receive temporary housing or material help from. Skidders socialize with friends from their former station in life, people they housesit for, store their belongings with, or trade child care with. Kids hang out on the streets with other children, both for social interaction and to get leads on ways of supporting themselves. Street People hang out with other Street People who share and accept their lives without condemnation, while concurrently a good deal of sharing of meager material resources goes on. Transitory Workers, to the extent that they socialize at all other than in their mandated evening stays at the shelters, hang out with other workers who may lead them to job opportunities. Wingnuts, with few ties to organize resource providers and no social margin—no resources on any level that anyone else is interested in—generally hang out alone.

Hall and Wellman have argued that the resources exchanged in relationships and networks

> can vary in *quality* ([for example] whether the tie provides emotional
> aid or companionship), *quantity* (whether it provides much emotional
> aid, frequent companionship), *multiplexity* (whether it provides only
> emotional aid or both emotional aid and companionship), and
> *symmetry* (whether both parties to a tie exchange roughly equivalent
> amounts of . . . aid).[53]

Most Street People's ties with other Street People are fairly intense along all of these dimensions, as are the ties of most Skidders and Latino Families (though symmetry may be weak) with housed friends. Kids and Transitory Workers show greater isolation from reciprocal arrangements, often because of their mobility, but certainly such relationships occur in the short term. Only Wingnuts show little reciprocity along any of these dimensions with anyone.

While solitary and affiliation are typically fragile and tentative, and largely limited to an immediate circle of (housed or homeless) friends, there is one setting in which they are the norm. That setting is the "homeless movement," to which we now turn.

Chapter 5

The homeless
movement

Most theorists, and particularly those who hypothesized weak links between homeless people, did not anticipate collective political activity among that population, since "power derives from affiliations."[1] Theodore Caplow declared, "There is no reliable report of a skid-row population engaging in collective action or even in mutual self-defense."[2]

Such views did not preclude the possibility that homeless people might have political opinions, and such opinions are clearly evident in Santa Barbara. Many homeless people display an automatic antipathy to the status quo:

> RACHEL: Well, of course they are going to say, "Let's throw off our chains and join the Communist Party," why not? I mean, they've got something to offer them. We are not giving it to these poor guys who come from Vietnam or Korea or whatever war we're in. They come home and find no apartment they could afford, even if they did get a meager three-fifty-an-hour job. What could they afford? Nothing.

> SONJA: I guess I've gotten to the point that I am so angry and tired and drained from my own experiences. I know that a lot of other [homeless] women are desperate and are getting worse. I know that there are going to be more people joining them. It looks like the economy and everything and Reagan and unemployment and housing—I think people have to start doing something about it. At least trying.

Viewed from the outside, the chance of translating such feelings into collective political activity would seem slight, and the chances of homeless people actually organizing themselves even smaller. They have few material resources and many have little surplus time. The conditions of homeless life may induce exhaustion, confusion, and resignation. Even the most basic organizing tasks are extremely difficult when movement members and potential members with no phone and no fixed address cannot be summoned on short notice to meetings or demonstrations.

Perhaps most crucially, homeless people lack any obvious form of leverage with which to compel concessions. Organized workers, for instance, can strike and affect the profits of owners. Tenants can sometimes withhold rents and affect the profits of landlords. Organized interest groups can threaten to withhold votes and affect the futures of politicians. Homeless people do not have these options. They are not organized together in a workforce. They do not pay rent. They are rarely voters—indeed, they have been barred from voting in some localities.[3] Their only source of leverage is the threat of chaos, as Piven and Cloward have remarked of other "poor people's movements," and this is ineffective if not carried out on a grand scale.[4]

Aside from their lack of resources and power, homeless movements must somehow maintain an active cadre of workers. This is difficult, not only because homeless people must spend so much time and effort on their individual survival needs, but also because activism requires identifying oneself publicly as homeless, something few people want to do.[5] While there is solace in banding with others in a similar situation, public disclosure of one's homelessness makes individual escape more difficult. Homeless people are thus trapped between a need for a social movement that may alter their collective fate and the labeling process that makes identification with other homeless people a liability. And unlike those movements that can win as a class, homeless people can only truly win by escaping their class, and most do so as soon as they are able.

Despite all these barriers, two political organizations arose among homeless people in Santa Barbara in 1983. The first, the Homeless People's Association (HPA), was created by Street People in the winter of 1982–83. (The origins of the second group, the SPA, are described below.) The HPA was largely the product of the complex relationship that developed between the police and homeless people.

Interactions with police, like those with merchants, are greatly affected by the appearance of the homeless person. Those whose appearance least conveys their homeless status report few problems with the police,[6] while many of the more visible Wingnuts and Street People report repeated run-ins, some stretching back over years. Interactions have taken different forms during the three periods defined by the growth of the homeless movement in Santa Barbara. Perhaps no other relationship says so much about the relations between homeless people and housed society, about how perceptions and self-perceptions regarding the homeless population have changed over time, and about the role of construction and labeling in the development of "the homeless problem."

In the late 1970s and early 1980s, the police, sensitive to the growing number of "transients," became increasingly likely to stop, question, and often arrest visible homeless people for a variety of offenses, while homeless people reacted as isolated individuals. Homeless people, especially those on the streets, expected to be arrested for offenses that other people would not be arrested for, often simply to get them off the streets:

> R A C H E L : They say that the police round up people in the parks because it is tourist season and they don't want it to look bad, especially with the Fiesta [the big tourist event of the summer] coming up.

In these early years, most Street People saw the police as their main enemies, engaged in what one Street Person called "a war on the poor":

> D E M O D A N : That's your job [as a cop]. You move tramps out of town, and the way you do it is scare tactics. . . . Like when they go down to State and Cota. They'll go up there and go, "Get off of my block. . . ." So people are trying to save themselves, trying to keep it together, but they know what the war is all about.

The police saw these encounters differently. They flatly denied discriminating against homeless people: "You cite Mr. Bank President for crossing the street against a red light, then you cite a transient for doing the same thing. You don't give special consideration to one group of people."[7] Instead, police believed they were merely acting in accordance with the modern police emphasis on being "proactive" rather than "reactive," defusing a situation before it becomes a problem:

> It makes our job difficult, even challenging, to be able to identify who are the problem people, who are the ones preying on the others in the same condition and on society. Its very easy to classify everyone [who is homeless] as a bum, but they aren't. . . .
>
> The most offensive group are the younger alcoholics. They are generally the homeless-out-of-choice category. . . . Panhandling, begging money, a lot of petty theft, shoplifting, that sort of thing. On a more serious scale . . . there are assaults, stabbings, and robberies that go on down there, more so than a lot of people realize that live here. It's an almost daily occurrence. . . . On a lesser scale there is burglary and breaking into stores, and breaking into cars, stealing. To sustain their lifestyle, they need to do that. A lot of them are involved in drugs that cost money.[8]

Yet it is difficult to see how proactive police work can fail to become, at least from time to time, active discrimination based on appearance and visible homeless people complained that they were singled out for police attention and sometimes arrest on that basis.

This proactive stance was apparently behind the decision, in the winter of 1982–83, to begin nightly sweeps through the Jungle:[9]

> Sleeping in the Jungle isn't the biggest problem in the world. But we've had rapes, murders, assaults, fights down there all the time. A lot of which goes under cover. A lot of those problems are from people sleeping down there. . . . Granted, [serious crimes] don't happen every night, but there is the potential for problems to happen if you just let the condition go without any policing or anything.[10]

The combination of an unusually rainy winter and the Jungle raids (generally regarded by Street People as an intrusion into an area that had been unofficially sanctioned as a sleeping place) led directly to the establishment of the HPA and its initial demand for a safe and legal sleeping area:[11]

> B R U C E : We were standing down by the railroad tracks at the bottom of Santa Barbara Street, talking about our situation. . . . I hand lettered a flyer on the foot of a truck, went down and had them copied, passed out about seventy-five copies all around that area, and had a meeting at which about twenty people showed up. At that meeting we put together plans for actions we could take to help gain for us a livable camping situation. Housing situation if possible. At that time we were just thinking about camping. The notion of housing was even just a bit too grand. But just a place to camp, safe from police harassment, safe from criminal harassment. That was where it began.

The HPA soon set up an information booth at the Fig Tree, which had become the daytime replacement for the Jungle. Run-ins between the police and the HPA over the legality of the booth and deeper questions of turf escalated. These clashes were probably more crucial to establishing the HPA's reputation than the actual information provided. The fact that the HPA stood up to the police to protect the booth provided many homeless people with a new conception of their rights, ushering in a second stage of homeless–police relations in which homeless people— principally Street People—collectively and militantly resisted police actions.[12] A number of previously apathetic Street People were drawn into the fight by this new, aggressive stance:

CHARLIE: When I came back from Oregon in June, they had the table set up, so I just stuck around for that. . . . I though it was a real positive thing, something worth sticking around for.

At the same time, HPA members arrested for illegal sleeping developed a strategy of demanding jury trials instead of accepting the normal routine of spending a night or two in jail awaiting trial, pleading guilty, and being released for time served:

MAYOR MAX: I was one of the first people that got my case dismissed because I asked for a jury trial and a public defender. And so, since then, I've been asking everybody else to ask for the same jury trial and a public defender. And so far, about 99 percent of the people who have gone to court and asked for it have gotten dismissed cases.

This tactical success led to a general leap in confidence, and HPA members became considerably bolder in their dealings with the police:

HENRY: With me, I know the law quite well, so I'm like the person who quotes the law back at them. . . . If you quote the law to them, they will think twice about harassing you.

For some people on both sides, the question rapidly became who was going to "control" the Fig Tree area. Each move by homeless people was met with a countermove by the police in a continuous chess game in which even the most mundane actions became loaded with political significance. In one (now legendary) incident, grocery store employees were detaining a homeless man for shoplifting when Kevin intervened by purchasing the items in question:

I walked outside the store, and the other guy that was working there was holding Billy by the arm. At the time I had a cast on my foot, I was walking around on crutches. . . . So I lifted up one of my crutches and I said, "Let go of him! He didn't do anything!" So the guy lets go of him and Billy took off down the street toward the Fig Tree. . . . I didn't even know [him] at the time, I never even seen the guy before. I knew he was homeless. . . . He was all scruffy and scrungy and I knew he was homeless like I was. . . .

I could see these lights and a police car pulled over on the side of the road, and I . . . said, "They're going to try and arrest him and take him to jail, and he didn't steal anything. He didn't come out of the store with anything. I bought the two beers." So I caught up to him while he was being questioned. And I said, "What are you doing to this guy, he didn't do anything. Why are you asking him?" I'm sitting there thinking that there was no way they could

arrest him because he didn't steal anything. The only thing he
was being accused of stealing I had right there, and [it] was paid
for. And after ten minutes the police officer talking to the guys in
the store, he came back and said something to Billy, and turned
around and started handcuffing him.

And at that point I started arguing with the police officer. I said,
"Why are you arresting him? He didn't do anything . . . " I don't
know exactly how the argument went, but it was just back and
forth and back and forth. He started yelling at me and I started
yelling at him, and we got *that close*, yelling at each other. And
finally I just got so mad, 'cause he was going to arrest him, there
were no ifs, ands, or buts, he was going to arrest him and take him
away. And I got so mad that I just dropped one of my crutches and
I picked up the other one by the bottom of it, and instead of
hitting the police officer, the police car was right to my left, and I
just swing the crutch right through the windshield.

Of course, not every incident between Street People and the police
involved those at the Fig Tree or HPA members, but a disproportionate
number did. Only nine of the forty-four HoPP respondents reported
having been ticketed or arrested for illegal sleeping in Santa Barbara. All
were Street People,[13] eight had a home base at the Fig Tree, and five were
active in the HPA. In a two-year period, these eight Fig Tree regulars were
arrested more than fifty times for such offenses. Arrest became so frequent
for some that Henry was able to report, without sarcasm:

With me, I only get like maybe twelve times thrown in jail out
of the last two years. I got maybe twenty other times in jail, but
that was like on tickets that I forgot to pay.

Because of the police–HPA hostility, however, any incident between
police and Street People became charged with political and turf overtones,
regardless of the political stance of the homeless person involved.

As time went on, the HPA activists became increasingly concerned
with creating and circulating their own alternative vision of who homeless
people were and what the homeless "problem" was, focusing blame on the
City and County for their failure to help "citizens" in distress. They were
engaged in a battle with representatives of the status quo over the cultural
interpretation of homelessness.[14] When the police spoke of "transients,"
the HPA cited the long-term residency of prominent members. When
merchants spoke of "freeloaders," the HPA displayed signs reading "work
wanted." When housed people spoke of "bums," HPA members carried
the American flag and stressed their status as wartime veterans. At every
opportunity, the HPA sought to pose the question: "Are we the problem or
are we the victims?"[15]

Crucial to this effort was a strategy of emphasizing the civil rights of homeless people, first fought out over their right to vote. With the help of the Santa Barbara Legal Defense Center, HPA members successfully sued the County registrar to allow them to register. Buoyed by this victory, the HPA increasingly mixed protest with legal and parliamentary tactics.

Changes in the political situation now altered police–Street People relations once again. Several months after the formation of the HPA, the Single Parent Alliance (SPA) was independently created by homeless Skidders:[16]

> SUZANNE RIORDAN: I was at the newspaper, putting in a classified ad one day, where you can put them in for free, and on a *whim*, I put in an additional ad saying, "Single parents unite! Free listings of housing," and my phone number [i.e., that of a friend with whom she was temporarily staying]. . . . And I got, within a month's time, I got about forty calls, between forty and fifty. . . .
>
> We had an initial meeting and it was pretty well attended, twenty-five came. . . . We took up *three hours* at the first meeting, simply going around the room and introducing ourselves. The introductions were long and painful because everyone wanted to tell about their own trauma. In fact, it was necessary to let that happen.

Several months later the SPA received the first of several grants from a local benefactor that financed an office, a telephone, and small salaries over a two-year period.

In contrast to the HPA, the SPA's focus was on self-help groups and on lobbying local government for programs aimed at homeless families. Especially popular was a series of "rap groups":

> LIZ: When you are in this situation, you need a lot of support. Whoever is going to help us, we need a shoulder to cry on while we are doing all this. If you have kids involved, when you break down, they do, then you feel guilty because you are affecting them that way. And yet, where do you let this out? Where do you go where someone says, "I know what you mean, I know what you are feeling. Let's see what we could do about that." Because I felt like I was doing this alone. . . . We need a support group. Emotional support, that's a big one.

The SPA moved steadily toward operating as a social service agency as the HPA moved steadily toward operating as a social movement.

In the fall of 1983, organizers from the HPA, the SPA, and I attended a meeting in Chicago, of the National Coalition for the Homeless. That meeting led to the organization of the Santa Barbara Homeless Coalition, uniting the SPA, the HPA, and random advocates, both homeless and housed. Although the local Coalition went through a series of strains and fissures, mainly around the differences between Street People and Skidders and the contrasting public images each projected, for a time the Coalition became a somewhat unified voice for homeless people.

With the formation of the SPA and the Homeless Coalition, homelessness became generally regarded as a political issue, bringing both homeless people and the police under greater public scrutiny. Through a number of public gestures, including the release of a report charging that arrests for illegal sleeping costs the City and County over $100,000 in 1983,[17] the Homeless Coalition and others helped make the widespread use of the law against homeless people less acceptable. At the same time, as they entered the public and political arena, the HPA and other homeless people became more interested in long-term, general solutions and less in individual standoffs between themselves and the police. Many Street People began adopting a more sophisticated analysis in which the police were seen to be, for the most part, merely carrying out what the housed community wanted done:[18]

> K E V I N : Now I don't think that it's just the police. It's the whole city. The people that are making the laws and the rules. And they're telling the police to enforce them. I realize that it's not just the police, though there are a lot of asshole cops.
> C H A R L I E : Some of them are all right. . . . We all know that when somebody has a warrant, they get caught, they gotta go to jail for it, you know. That's the way it goes.

As a result, the HPA began directing more attention to the laws that guided the police. Foremost among their new tactics was a suit challenging the City's anti-sleeping and anti-camping laws, brought by the Legal Defense Center in 1984. In 1985 the anti-camping law was held to be constitutional, but the anti-sleeping law was overturned. Each side appealed the decision it had lost, with an appeals court ruling in late 1985 that both laws were constitutional. A further appeal to the U.S. Supreme Court was denied (without prejudice) by that body, since the cases on which it was based had not yet been heard on the local level.

Uncertainty over how the courts would eventually rule, the emergence of homelessness as a bona fide political issue, and the HPA's change in emphasis all helped to cool the hostility between the Street People and the police. The police still used the anti-sleeping law, but less often. Ticketing became more common, and arrest less so. By August 1986, and under the threat of massive demonstrations against the law, the political wisdom had so changed that the anti-sleeping law was amended to allow homeless people to sleep on undeveloped public lands and in public byways and some parks.

The victories of the homeless movement are particularly impressive given the barriers it faced. Its volunteer organizations were composed mainly of people struggling to survive:

> S U Z A N N E : Some of these people are in such desperate straits that they're only thinking about themselves right now. They can't even help. I want to initiate action, and it's a little hard to get them all together behind me. . . . When I think of who can I ask to make phone calls and stuff, everyone's just so desperate, and even when they do find a place, I'm not so sure they're still gonna be interested, you know? They're involved in their own lives.

Further, as resource mobilization theorists have noted, social movements require resources.[19] Although the original organization and most of the work of both the SPA and the HPA were done by homeless people, their ability to survive as organizations and make progress required resources from the outside. Financial donations were essential in maintaining an SPA office and retaining the services of the Legal Defense Center to represent the HPA. The efforts of the Homeless Coalition were greatly increased when a housed supporter gave the money to hire a part-time organizer. Additional, the ability to speak with some authority to public officials rested in part on the prestige and political clout of housed people who were already connected with the political establishment.

At the same time, there were tensions within the Coalition between homeless and housed activists. Often the issue appeared to be "efficiency" versus "empowerment":

> FIELD NOTES, 1/7/85: Although many of the professional social service types and housed activist politicos understand how important empowerment is, we constantly slide into doing things ourselves instead of encouraging homeless people to do them. Why? 1) It's hard to reach them because of no phone or fixed address; 2) We're better at it from experience, thus the chance of success is greater.
>
> Why is success so important? 1) That's the main reason we're doing all this work, besides empowerment: to win improvements for homeless people; 2) We're (ironically) afraid that lack of success will drive homeless people away; 3) We have egos and reputations as effective political actors on the line; 4) We need to justify to our superiors and funders that we're doing something; 5) It's demoralizing to us to lose constantly.
>
> In many meetings there's some point when one of the [housed activists] gets annoyed at some homeless person for taking up precious time going on and on about his or her individual problem, how hard it is in the streets, etc. But annoying as these monologues are sometimes (since we all feel we already know their story and

troubles), they always serve in some way to remind us that we are not bearing the brunt of the problem, that giving homeless people the chance to change their lives themselves is what we have to be about.[20]

Nor were tensions limited to interactions between homeless and housed activists. Antipathy between subgroups also hindered Coalition work.

FIELD NOTES, 1 2 / 6 / 8 4 : In discussion with Myra [a Street Person] and a few others after the [Homeless Coalition] meeting, some feelings came across clearly, [among them] . . . animosity toward the "ladies" of the SPA for setting the agenda of the Coalition to their benefit . . . [while] a number of the [Skidders] are annoyed and impatient with [Street People] Demo Dan and Eric the Red for dominating meetings.

Even within the more homogeneous HPA and SPA groups, there was friction. As in most political organizations, resentment toward leaders surfaced from time to time, perhaps enhanced by the fact that leaders often had greater resources than most of those they represented (hence their ability to spend more time on political work). The couple who remained the backbone of the HPA, for example, lived in a camper-trailer of their own. One worked regularly and the other, a skilled housing renovator, worked whenever he needed funds. Another mainstay received SSI payments, which, while insufficient to gain housing, left him with a comparatively good income for the streets.

The split between homeless leaders and the rank-and-file was exacerbated by the pressure on leaders to compromise with the political establishment:

FIELD NOTES, 6 / 1 5 / 8 3 : Meeting between HPA, assistant City Attorney, merchants from the Fig Tree area regarding information booth: Cashier at gas station across from Fig Tree says he calls police when he sees drinking there, and his customers are afraid. HPA say the drinkers aren't their people, they don't like drunks either. City Attorney wants to know how many people the HPA will have at booth. . . . Claims he can make interpretations, including no sign bigger than the table and no more than three people staffing it; threatens (nicely but firmly) legal action if no cooperation.

Agreed: Sign no bigger than table, staffed by three people, city will talk to police about being a greater presence there.

{RR: Note—In order to keep the sign and booth, the HPA is agreeing to discourage people from using the gas station, agreeing cops should come by more, and often disassociating themselves from other street people.}

Despite these problems, gains were won by a number of means. First, and not to be understated, was the specter of chaos that the HPA often invoked. Typically, the HPA would raise hell and be denounced by political officials, who would then look more favorably on requests from the SPA or religious groups. The HPA served as a daily, visible reminder that the problem of homelessness would not simply fade away, as many politicians hoped.

Second, against this backdrop, slow progress was made through rational analysis and argument. For instance, in 1986 the Homeless Coalition persuaded the County Health Department to assign a nurse to provide medical outreach at the shelters, largely by arguing that disease among the homeless population was a public health risk, and that those homeless people not treated early in their illnesses wound up being treated in emergency rooms at County expense.

Third, raising homelessness as a public issue galvanized some "respectable" segments of the community, particularly the religious and mental health communities, who had already become concerned about the issue through their own experiences. In the winter of 1984–85, the Interfaith Task Force on Homelessness (ITFH) was created, composed of religious leaders and representatives of the Homeless Coalition. Its greatest success came in creating what was dubbed the "Church of the Month" program, in which various churches served as shelters for a month. The shelter revolved through five churches twice and eventually attained permanent status at Transition House.

A familiar social movement dynamic operated throughout this history. It might be called the "good cop–bad cop" phenomenon,[21] a constant dialectic in which a militant wing (the "bad cop") pushes the powers that be and a moderate wing (the "good cop") receives some dividends from that action. Although the SPA was disturbed at being linked to the HPA and increasingly divorced itself from the latter's image (eventually leaving the Homeless Coalition), it seems clear in retrospect that the limited support the SPA received from the City was due in large part to its position as a respectable alternative to the HPA. It might well have received nothing at all if the HPA had not constantly raised the issue of homelessness in such a visible fashion.

Similarly, the Homeless Coalition, largely because of its refusal to divorce itself from the HPA, became the bad cop shortly after its founding, while the ITFH was cast in the role of good cop, representing a safer, more responsible option for the City Council, the County Board of Supervisors, and others to support. Even though Coalition members were instrumental in organizing the ITFH and formulating strategy and plans in its early months, their representatives were removed from member status in July 1985. Those sponsoring and supporting the exclusion cited the Coalition's unsavory reputation and HPA connections. "These people," one ITFH member said,

Doonesbury

BY GARRY TRUDEAU

"are not the people we want to help." Over the next few years, the Coalition continued to be a major actor in local politics, supplying reports, lobbying politicians, conducting outreach in the community, and mounting demonstrations. But its proposals were rarely supported by either City or County government. The ITFH, on the other hand, received a number of grants, as did several other religious organizations.

Ironically, the 1986 battle over anti-sleeping laws transformed the Coalition into the good cop and gave it one of its major victories. When the national homeless advocate Mitch Snyder threatened to overrun the city with protesters, political and civic leaders became alarmed that the attendant national publicity (including a week of *Doonesbury* cartoons) would harm the city's image and even disrupt the crucial tourist industry. Additionally, many worried that the costs of jailing huge numbers of demonstrators would break the City budget. On the other hand, many residents were outraged at what they referred to as Snyder's "blackmail" and strongly objected to changing the law in reaction to it. Since direct negotiations with bad cop Snyder were politically unfeasible, prominent politicians began conferring with the Homeless Coalition (which had ties to Snyder) over ways to avert the proposed demonstration. In a compromise settlement, the Coalition and a larger citizens' movement that had joined the fight agreed to substantial amendments in the anti-sleeping laws (rather than outright revocation) and in return "advised" Snyder that his presence would no longer be necessary. At the August 19 and 26 City Council meetings that legislated the changes, the reports and advocacy of the Coalition, which had never before been mentioned approvingly by City Council members, suddenly became the ostensible basis for amending the laws. At the same time, the City/County Task Force on Homelessness was resurrected to begin dealing with homelessness as a social—rather than simply a law enforcement—problem.

The good cop–bad cop dynamic generates results for several reasons. The bad cops alert elites to the existence of a problem. Besieged by issues, and rarely in contact with disadvantaged people, those holding political power are not attuned to the needs of the powerless. Gaining their attention at all often requires going beyond the limits of normal discourse. For example, the City Council received Coalition reports as early as June 1983, but never saw its way to addressing the issue of homelessness until clashes between the HPA and the police began attracting media attention.

Second, the actions of the bad cops change the terms of the debate. The tactics seen as legitimate are altered. Before Snyder threatened to come to Santa Barbara, backroom negotiations between Coalition representatives and City Council members would have been seen as inappropriate—the activists would have been advised simply to petition the Council as any other group would do (and as it had done repeatedly without any results). Similarly, the Coalition lacked the power to demand a public meeting to discuss the anti-sleeping laws before Snyder entered the picture. Once the range of options had been widened by his threat of massive civil disobedience, backroom negotiations and public meetings looked tame by comparison.

The bad cops also frame the issue in a way that makes claims on public officials. Homeless people and their advocates were able to present a different picture of the nature of homelessness (for instance, challenging the label of "transients" applied by elites and the media to all homeless people). These alternative frameworks were then adopted and made more accessible to potential allies by the good cops—the SPA, the ITFH—while the most radical claims contained within them were modified. Sympathetic housed people with greater weight in the community—and thus greater political clout—became supporters of the good cops, which entailed supporting the alternative framing of the issue first introduced by the bad cops.

The reactions of public officials accelerated this shift in framing, since one of the most effective ways of discrediting the bad cops was to contrast them with others who shared their state but not their militancy. As the homeless movement in Santa Barbara gained strength, local officials turned from denying that homelessness was a local problem to declaring that they were ready to aid "women and children" or "our local homeless," but had no sympathy for "Fig Tree types." While invoking the good cops in order to deny benefits to the bad cops, officials legitimated the issues the bad cops had raised as *public* concerns.

A final factor, and one that underlay many of the actions described above, was the threat of chaos. It was clearly of major importance in Santa Barbara, and the Snyder episode was only the most obvious example. The unrelenting presence of the HPA was a daily reminder that the problem of homelessness required governmental action. Further, its constant disruption of other people's daily lives implied the possibility of more serious consequences if no response was forthcoming. By demanding jury trials, HPA members disrupted the smooth functioning of the judicial system, threatening greater costs and the eventual bogging down of the system as a whole. By appearing at City Council meetings (with some members refusing to abide by the generally accepted rules of decorum), they threatened to disrupt the ability of local government to take care of business of any kind. By engaging in standoffs with the police, they threatened the normative respect for law and order that civil peace depends on. By refusing to remain hidden—as Skidders and other subgroups normally do—they threatened the shopping environment of the downtown area, and thus the profits of business owners there. These threats demanded—and received—a governmental response because they threatened the everyday lives of others beyond the "problem population."[22]

Unlike the classic good cop–bad cop interrogation, however, this dynamic in a social movement is not a conscious strategy. Even though the good cops were invariably the beneficiaries of the crisis created by the bad cops, in Santa Barbara as elsewhere, the two wings were often antagonistic. As seems to be the norm in this dynamic, the good cops tended to see the bad cops as impediments to progress, crazies who were discrediting the movement as a whole. Often the good cops disavowed the bad cops: The SPA progressively disassociated itself from the HPA "scuz," and the ITFH eventually excluded Homeless Coalition representatives from voting membership.[23]

Yet it is clear that much of the progress made by the homeless movement in Santa Barbara came through a dialectical process in which the demands and actions of the bad cops were a major factor in the decision of public officials to make resources and rights available to the good cops, while the presence of the good cops enabled officials to distribute some resources rather than fight the whole movement to the death. Without bad cops, it is unlikely that officials would have given anything at all. But without good cops, it would have been much more difficult for officials to make the concessions they eventually did.

The ebb and flow of political events followed a pattern typical of social movements. Activists and advocates would become concerned over an aspect of homeless life, often in reaction to a specific event such as the Jungle raids or the Burr murder. They would then organize themselves for protest and seek to draw in members of the political establishment on their side. If the threat of disruption by homeless people combined with the political clout of their allies was great enough to affect the normal running of the city, public officials would move to rectify the most onerous conditions through negotiations with the more moderate homeless representatives. Once the turmoil had died down, progress on resolving the problems of homeless people would stop or be reversed until a new wave of protest was mounted. For instance, once the uproar over the anti-sleeping law died down, the compromise was weakened by the City both legislatively and administratively. Sections of the amended law prohibiting sleeping in parks, on the beach, or on developed city property were reinstated. Police enforced the amended law in waves, stepping up the pressure whenever homeless encampments became visible.

Yet some victories were achieved. In Santa Barbara, homeless people have established their right to vote and to sleep on unimproved public lands. A County medical outreach program administers health care. Existing shelters have received greater public support, and two additional shelters (Transition House and, in the winter, the National Guard Armory) have been added. Escape had been facilitated for some, and homeless life has been made somewhat easier for many. These are impressive gains for a movement deemed highly improbable, if not impossible, by earlier theorists.[24]

The existence and relative success of the movement call into question the characterization of homeless people—and particularly Street People—as isolated from each other. Although resources (generally from outside the homeless population) were necessary, it succeeded only because the people within it, largely homeless, created and maintained ties characterized by a sense of responsibility and reciprocity. These feelings were intensely powerful within the core groups of activists, but extended beyond to a general loyalty felt by, and acted on, by larger groups of homeless people. Progress required real sacrifices: public identification, collective resistance to police, expenditure of scarce time and energy on organizing tasks. Without a vision that entailed loyalty to homeless people as a group, and daily practical ties to others involved in similar work, such sacrifices could never have been made. "Homeless, not helpless," read the buttons of one homeless organization. The existence and success of a homeless movement, as well as the day-to-day survival strategies of homeless people, suggest that this is more than just a political slogan.

Chapter 6

Getting ahead and the barriers to escape

Getting by is all some homeless people expect, but most hope for much more—they hope to get ahead:

> GLEN: It's a joke—"Wow, isn't it great being a lazy bum, I would hate like hell to be given a job right now." A lot of them will do *anything* for a couple of bucks. It's not like you are out there living on a yacht or something; you're in a jungle that has no mercy. You welcome any opportunity to walk out of it and leave that life in back of you.

While the social category "homeless people" continues to grow, individuals are constantly entering and leaving the state of homelessness. Through personal initiative, mutual aid (such as sharing housing), luck, or a combination of factors, most people eventually escape; few remain homeless for longer than a year to eighteen months.[1]

Escape means finding a place to live and securing the additional resources necessary to afford it. Like getting by, it entails the creation or reestablishment of networks designed to gather resources, primarily economic but also psychological. Those with preexisting networks and a social margin that has not been totally depleted are more likely to succeed. This escape, of course, may be permanent or merely a temporary reprise in a pattern of episodic homelessness.[2]

Resources

A steady and significant income is generally necessary for permanent escape. Public assistance in itself is rarely sufficient:[3]

> CHRISTINE: I couldn't afford a place by myself. A place by yourself is in the neighborhood of four hundred dollars, and that's exactly what I get from welfare to cover everything. So I lived in my van, in a friend's front yard.

Welfare regulations often increase the difficulty of escaping homelessness. Simply being processed for some programs may take two years.[4] Limits on savings thwart efforts to get ahead:

> LYNN: First, last, and deposits add up to quite a lot of money. And when you're living on welfare, you can't have more than a thousand dollars cash in your possession. Then how the hell are you supposed to save up for first, last, and deposit if you can't do that? Nice little circle there.

Limits on earned income are further barriers. For example, Kathie complained that while a SSI check by itself was insufficient to get housing, any income she earned over $60 per month (in 1984) was deductible from her check. Homeless people have also suffered, as have many poor people, from welfare regulations that penalized working or staying together as a family unit. Until 1990 many states barred AFDC payments to two-parent families; many still deny aid to families where one parent is employed.

These problems extend beyond cash assistance programs to other forms of aid. GR housing vouchers are insufficient for renting most units, and are even less often accepted. Public housing, in Santa Barbara as elsewhere, is badly overloaded, with a waiting list several years long. Section 8 rent levels have failed to keep up with the rapidly rising private market.[5]

Permanent escape from homelessness thus almost always means finding more work, more stable work, or better-paying work.[6] Yet some homeless people are unable or unlikely to work. For example, no Church guest with a serious physical disability had a full-time job; similarly, no Church guest with a mental disability had a full-time job, and this holds for Wingnuts generally, who are largely dependent on outside help if they are to escape homelessness. The dearth of available spaces in community board-and-cares makes such escape difficult for those whose families cannot or will not take them back. Occasionally Wingnuts are able to patch together various entitlements and programs: Rachel, for instance, finally began receiving SSI and found a place in a government-subsidized housing project. But a single break in the arrangements—loss or even delay of an entitlement, eviction from subsidized housing because of acting out—often leads back to homelessness.

Homeless children and elderly people cannot find work because of their age; some adults who would otherwise be able to work cannot because they have children and free or affordable day care is in short supply.[7] Disabilities and personal circumstances that prevent escape through employment usually afflict at least a quarter of unemployed homeless people, and often many more, in studies across the nation.[8] Given the great difficulties involved in securing a steady job and a residence for even the most job-ready of homeless people, those with characteristics that make employment or housing more difficult to find are extremely unlikely to escape homelessness for more than the briefest periods without direct and significant intervention by others. Family and friends or some form of social service agency might intervene, but given the finite resources of both private and public caretakers, such arrangements are less dependable than direct improvements in the individual's own financial resources.

Most homeless people without these specific problems, in Santa Barbara as elsewhere, are working or seeking work. As we saw in Chapter 3, Transitory Workers are totally focused on securing employment, expect to make their escape through employment, and do so. Latino Families' typical escape strategy is for the breadwinner to find more work—that is, to work more than forty hours a week.[9] For independent gardeners and landscapers, this means attempting to expand their contacts through their current employers, often individual homeowners. For those working in other occupations, it means attempting to find a second full-time or part-time job. Street People are also likely to be actively looking for work. They have few responsibilities, such as children, to prevent them from doing so, and fewer resources, such as networks of housed friends, to provide alternative ways of getting ahead.

Skidders are considerably less likely to be looking for work for the sake of either getting ahead or getting by. Many, like Lynn, are instead pursuing an education that will facilitate escape from lower-class life, rather than accommodation to near homelessness:

> I want to go into the registered nurses program and possibly be a certified nurse-midwife. I want to get my A.S. degree here and transfer to South Oregon State College for my master's. That's the five-year plan.

Given the difficulty of obtaining work, it is devastating to find that even full-time employment may not lead to housing. Homeless people often complain that the wages paid for the kinds of jobs they can get are a major obstacle to escaping homelessness:[10]

R O G E R : There are jobs out there for three thirty-five or four bucks
an hour that can give you a take-home of five hundred a month,
and if you can get a room for two hundred fifty, you've got two
hundred fifty left over. [But] with me and two, sometimes three
kids, . . . five hundred would not last too long. They won't rent a
one-bedroom apartment to three people. Two bedrooms you are
talking seven hundred dollars. Then you apply for that and they
say, "Well, how much do you make?" You can lie and say, "I
make two hundred fifty a week." Well, they'll say, "We can't take
you because . . . one week of your salary should [equal] the rent."
. . . We are talking twenty-eight hundred a month [to get a
$700-a-month place]. I would love to have a job like that. Not in
Santa Barbara!

Two-thirds of the group I interviewed for the Homeless People's Project
worked (25 percent full-time, 39 percent part-time) yet remained homeless (see Appendix). Those guests working full- or part-time remained in
the Church shelters almost as long on average as those not working.[11]
Direct or indirect evidence of similar difficulties for homeless low-wage
workers appears in many studies.[12]

As Roger discovered and other homeless people repeatedly point out,
their biggest problem in finding housing is not simply their low incomes
but the disparity between their financial resources and rental rates. It
cannot be said often enough that the demise of affordable housing is the
single greatest component in the explosion of homelessness. While lack of
an adequate income is obviously of great importance, homeless people
around the country who have some income remain unable to find any
housing, including the vanishing SRO unit.[13] For some who might have
enough to make the rent, the prospect of paying virtually everything they
have for housing—leaving nothing for "living"—may be more than they
can abide. Even those who have an income sufficient to pay rent may be
unable to overcome the barrier of first, last, and deposit.

Thus rising from little or no income to some income does not
guarantee housing. Escape still requires finding a place with low rent, a
landlord who accepts Section 8 vouchers, and/or no first, last, and deposit
requirement. As in finding substitute housing, discrimination against
children complicates escape for some people, particularly Latino Families
and Skidders; for Latino Families and other people of color, there may be
problems of racial discrimination as well.

In response to these barriers, many homeless people resort to fabricat-
ing stories:

P A T : I decided that I would just mention that I had one child. I would
say that the other one was somewhere else and that he would be

there at a later date, which I didn't like doing. But it was getting to be necessary.

SONJA: He asked what my income was. I said eight hundred. I had to lie a little bit. My experience has been that if you don't make four times what the rent is, they don't want to rent it to you.

Similarly, many people are forced to break the law by offering to pay landlords under the table to supplement the rents allowed under the Section 8 program:

SONJA: They might look at you wrongly if you are offering them money under the table. Like you are going to lie or do something wrong at the drop of a hat. You have to kind of be careful. Yet you've got to survive too.

A few programs in Santa Barbara have helped some homeless people get into new housing. A revolving loan fund administered by Catholic Social Service has helped some households, mainly Latino Families, to pay first, last, and deposit, but it is a comparatively small fund with grants limited to $300 per household and available only to those working steadily. The SPA has achieved some success in matching single-parent families with each other or with prospective landlords.

Flight

Housed Santa Barbarans frequently ask why homeless people remain in town instead of moving somewhere they can live more cheaply. Some *do* in fact leave town. Kids leave in order to lose themselves in larger cities;

Doonesbury

BY GARRY TRUDEAU

DOONESBURY COPYRIGHT 1986 G. B. Trudeau. Reprinted with permission of Universal Press Syndicate. All rights reserved.

Transitory Workers search for greener pastures. Migrants in all subgroups return to families in order to use their resources if available.[14]

Those who stay appear to do so because they believe Santa Barbara is their *home.* Many are long-term residents: Church guests had lived, on average, twenty-seven months in town; SPA callers (housed and homeless) an average of five years; HoPP interviewees, just under six years. Thirty percent of the Church guests had previously had a residence in town, as had 61 percent among the HoPP group and 80 percent among the SPA callers.

Others have found something in town that makes them feel "at home." Almost all of the HoPP interviewees said they planned to stay, and their reasons for doing so—friends and family, homeless activism, school, or job—clearly show that sense of belonging.[15] Aside from the obvious resources of established networks, there is an advantage in knowing the layout of a town:

> K E V I N : The streets aren't that stable, you know. They're not stable to begin with, and to go someplace else and live on the streets is even less stable. Once you know where you are, you really don't want to make the situation worse.

Moving is also beyond the financial capacities of many homeless people:

> L I Z : We can't move. Because you need money to move. You need money to travel, to get your stuff to go where you are going. First and last, and all that kind of stuff. There is worse than here. So you are stuck. . . . You can't stay and you can't go.

Without substantial resources, many people (rationally) anticipate that flight will merely transfer their plight to a new town where they will face many of the same problems, but without the networks and knowledge they have already developed in Santa Barbara. The lure of lower rents or more plentiful jobs may not compensate for such a loss, or for the suspicion with which they would be regarded in a new community. In any case, they know reports of better conditions may turn out to be only rumors.

The Downward Cycles of Homelessness

The barriers to escape I have been discussing are material problems of inadequate income relative to housing costs. In that sense, homelessness is not a problem but the end result of other problems, an extension of poverty across the very thin boundary dividing homeless people from other impoverished people. But in examining the daily lives of homeless people, it has become clear that they face additional barriers that derive from the condition of homelessness itself—the ways in which *homelessness perpetuates homelessness.* Being homeless is qualitatively different from being housed though poor.

To begin with, the lack of a home base makes everything more difficult. The simplest activities, such as "going to the bathroom" when there is no bathroom, become logistical problems. When substantial escape tasks are involved, these problems are large indeed: Staying clean, for example, is especially important when a homeless person is seeking a job or a place to live. The lack of a home phone or a place to get mail may easily lead to missed connections and deadlines that sabotage the escape effort. As we have seen, the lack of a home address may be grounds in itself for denial of employment or assistance; without a place to store documents, few homeless people are able to hold on to valid identification, making welfare workers even less willing or able to grant entitlements. Without a home base, there is often nowhere to leave children while the parent pursues job, entitlement, or housing leads. Many parents miss such leads rather than leave their children unattended on the streets.

Life on the street also means a lack of access to such money-saving conveniences as cooking facilities. Homeless people unwilling or unable to eat at the Rescue Mission or other places offering free food must get their meals at fast food restaurants. Wright similarly notes that, lacking refrigerators, homeless people must buy in the smallest quantities available, minimizing their food dollar.[16]

The most critical extra expense is the need to pay first, last, and deposit to get into new housing. Whereas someone living in an apartment has only to come up with rent each month, homeless people often have to come up with three times the rent in order to get into a place, a total of $1,500 to $2,500 in Santa Barbara in the mid-1980s; and, as noted above, AFDC can be terminated if someone accumulates over $1,000 in savings. Further, as Michael Perez has pointed out, "Due to the large amount of cash-in-hand required to rent even a studio apartment, homeless people who do obtain employment often must remain homeless for long periods, during which they are still risking arrest nightly. Arrest can mean missed hours or days, exposure [as a homeless person], and probable dismissal."[17]

Resources, time, and energy may be used up in simple survival. The extreme deprivation of homeless people may force them to "spend" their entire social margin in getting by, as when Mark reported that he had "just burnt too many friends trying to take care of this situation, waiting things out."

THE LABELING BARRIER

The barriers to escape discussed above would exist regardless of how others felt about homeless people. But homelessness often entails another entire set of barriers, the effects of being labeled homeless. "When a stranger comes into our presence," Goffman has written, "first appearances are likely to enable us to anticipate his category and attributes, his 'social identity' . . . [because] society establishes the means of categorizing persons and the complement of attributes felt to be ordinary and natural for members of each of these categories."[18] When housed people encounter those people they identify as homeless, "ordinary and natural" attributes are clearly lacking: They are unclean, disheveled, perhaps carrying their "home" on their back. But these marks signify more than just "differences": in a society in which home is central to identity, they convey failure, for only failures, it is thought, could lack so universal a possession. Indeed, with the possible exception of the romantic image of the hobo, the terms in which North Americans have defined homeless people have always been negative: animal-like, violent, mentally ill, morally wayward, lazy.[19] As Goffman has observed, "We tend to impute a wide range of imperfections on the basis of the original one."[20]

Thus a subtle but exceedingly critical transformation occurs: "Homeless" evolves from a description of a person's circumstances to "a characteristic . . . internal to that individual."[21] Being labeled "homeless" conjures up the very picture that this book has sought to dispel, an image exemplified by the misnomer "transient." A favorite street story tells of a man who has lived on the streets of Santa Barbara for twenty years: When asked what he likes least about his life, he says, "Being called a transient." Such terms convey all sorts of meanings about homeless people: that they are unstable, irresponsible, or voluntarily in their state because of wanderlust; that they are not our problem; that they are not like the rest of us.

Such perceptions affect resource gathering, as when a homeless jobseeker is unable to fill out an application that asks for a home phone and address. Those blank lines say clearly to the employer that this person is "a risk," as Glen said; "a suspect rather than a prospect," in the words of Jonathan. Thus one of the cruelest ironies of homelessness is the home–job downward cycle: Without a job, you can't get a home; but without a home, you can't get a job.

Other vital resources are cut off by labeling in much the same way. Inability to furnish prospective landlords with references renders homeless people suspect as good tenants; welfare workers resist granting aid to "transients." Labeling, in short, does not simply have a psychological impact on the labeled, but imposes material constraints that make escape harder and harder as time passes and social margin dwindles.

Certainly, the sensitive housed person is capable of rejecting such generalizations when interacting with individual homeless people, but such a rejection requires considerable effort. Housed individuals enter interactions with homeless people "free" to alter their conceptions, but, nonetheless, with preconceptions that are resistant to revision and further influence which revisions are most likely to be made. For example, the common (but inaccurate) view that most homeless people are mentally ill and former mental hospital patients is the starting point for most housed people's interpretations of what an individual homeless person is "like." This framework is solidified by those seen most often on the streets, since mentally ill people are the least able and the least prone to undertake the "passing" strategies that other homeless people often use. Yet it also leads housed people to interpret ambiguous actions of the homeless people they see as signs of mental illness. Michael Sloss observes that a homeless person wearing an overcoat on a warm day will be assumed to be mentally ill, but might actually be using the coat to hide and carry possessions.[22]

This labeling is often described by homeless people as one of the hardest things to bear about their condition. It robs them of rights taken for granted by anyone else.

> CHARLIE: We're human beings too. I think that would be the main thing [I dislike], you know, being treated just like dirt. There's a lot of people have that attitude.

> GLEN: One of the real difficult things about the street is the fact that suddenly now that you are poor, you've lost all your rights to be a person. . . . [For example,] you can't stand in front of the [store] windows too long.

This knowledge erects boundaries to behavior. Homeless people know they cannot enter into casual conversation with housed people. They know asking a police officer for directions may entail all sorts of questions and hassles. They know that very few employers will give them a job if they cannot produce a home phone and address.

Asked what housed people should know about homeless people, many HoPP interviewees stressed that they simply wanted to be seen as valid human beings, similar to other people, and not as worthless, ruined shells of dangerous criminals:

> HENRY: The homeless are the same as they are. They drink about the same amount, some of them have cars just like they do. Some of them actually do work, right next to them in their line of work.

> HANK: [I'm] just the victim of circumstances. Bad luck. . . . You know, I've said to myself, "Why the hell do these things happen to me?" I don't drink, I don't smoke, I don't . . . do anything crazy when I've got money. . . . I'm just a victim of bad luck, I really am. I think people should realize that these things can happen to anybody.

ADAPTATIONS AS BARRIERS

Homelessness is also perpetuated through some of the ways in which homeless people adapt to homelessness. As Elliot Liebow argues of "streetcorner men" in *Tally's Corner,* these adaptations are generally responses to real material conditions rather than values passed on within a subculture:[23]

> GLEN: It doesn't matter what they were before they hit the street.
> ... They can't really clean their clothes, so their clothes get dirty, they keep looking at themselves, then they start referring to themselves as a bum.

Adaptations are selected by homeless people from the menu of what is available, a reflection of macro processes mediated through local contexts as well as one's personal social margin. These adaptations then further limit the possibilities for action that remain. For instance, the mother who evaluates the local job market as unlikely to offer any job that will pay enough to escape homelessness may elect to subsist on an AFDC payment. She is then unlikely to seek or accept work (which would cause her to lose her AFDC payments) and unlikely to find permanent housing (since AFDC regulations keep her from accumulating first, last, and deposit). Similarly, the homeless alcoholic who decides that the Rescue Mission is his best means of obtaining resources loses the ability to participate freely in the job market, since the Mission controls his daily work schedule.

For the most part, especially in the early stages of homelessness, homeless people are merely trying to pursue the same goals as the society at large. When asked what they would like to be doing in a year, HoPP members responded conventionally: studying, working a nine-to-five job, traveling.[24] When asked what they expected to be doing in a year, not one of the forty-four people I collected oral histories from wanted or expected to be homeless. But the options available to better their lives are limited; the strategies they can pursue are limited and shaped by the constraints they face. As they continue to find their way to those goals blocked, they become more willing to adopt means that are seen as deviant by the larger society. For instance, like Pat and Sonja, who lied to landlords, many homeless people report increased lying to friends and authorities. In Goffman's terms, they *must* lie to prevent their "discreditable status" being discovered, thus leading to a "discredited status" with attendant loss of social margin and options for agency.[25] As a result, homeless people spend a great deal of time managing information about themselves. Sometimes this works out, but many must weave an elaborate web of deceit whose unraveling at any time may lead to the loss of job, friends, housing possibilities, and even custody of children.

A more important example of the pressures toward "deviant" adaptations can be found in the criminal and arrest histories of people in the HoPP group. When those homeless more than a year were compared with those homeless less than a year, the longer-term homeless people were found to be over two and a half times as likely to have been arrested for illegal sleeping crimes, over twice as likely to have been arrested for other crimes, and one and a half times as likely to have committed a crime other than illegal sleeping. As Glen explained:

> It's amazing some things that come into your head. You get involved in criminal activity. Suddenly a criminal activity within reason is not criminal any more. It's just basic survival. For instance, me sneaking into the showers [at the local marina] when there's a "no trespassing" sign. That's criminal, but it's something that I am being forced to do.

Clearly, long-term homelessness and a decreasing social margin make criminal activity more likely, including public status crimes: When friends will no longer take you in, you are more likely to use the alleys for your bathroom.[26] But, further, the *likelihood of arrest* for criminal activity increases with time homeless:[27] Simple probability dictates greater police contact over time;[28] increased time homeless weakens the ability to pass as housed, increasing the likelihood of police surveillance and arrest due to stigmatization.[29]

Criminal activity could conceivably lift a person out of homelessness, but the small-time crimes reported are unlikely to provide enough of a financial boost to change one's life materially. More often these acts lead to eventual arrest and further labeling. Illegal or deviant activities may also take their toll in self-labeling and loss of self-esteem, as when Lisa reported that "pulling tricks . . . made me feel like shit. Made me feel like nothing."

The criminal activity of individual homeless people, low-level and nonviolent though it largely is, also contributes to the collective labeling process. The housed population's consequent fear of criminal activity by homeless people may further narrow alternative survival options for homeless people, translating

> into political resistance to much-needed services and facilities. The result can be a set of policies . . . that exacerbate the plight of the homeless and narrow their options for survival. Unfortunately, as those options narrow, the option of more serious criminal activity as a survival strategy may become more viable, thus leading to a self-fulfilling prophecy of sorts.[30]

Another obvious hazard of homelessness is a slide into drink and drugs.[31] While many homeless advocates have questioned the belief that homelessness is frequently the *result* of substance abuse, they often acknowledge that homelessness in some cases leads to increased use or abuse of alcohol or drugs.[32] This is frequently seen as a defensive strategy:

> A relatively small percentage of the homeless are alcoholics, but many drink. One would have to endure the personal experience of life on the street to understand just how necessary a drink can be. . . . A stiff drink makes it possible to absorb a little more cold and harassment and abuse. . . . It is alcohol that enables you to nod off on a heat grate, parboiled on one side, chilled on the other, as uncomfortable as you would expect to be on a steel and concrete mattress.[33]

Less common in the literature on homelessness—but more common in the literature on alcoholism—is a view of alcoholism as the primary escape problem for many homeless people:

> Some shelter workers share such rationalizations as "being homeless is so miserable that the only thing to do is drink." This is not helpful to the guest, in that by sharing their hopelessness you give them no chance for a future. In addition, alcoholics will often say that all they need is a job and to be reunited with their family. Shelter workers often accept this and go along with these sentiments. However, it is important to realize that these are not the solutions to the homeless person's problem at this point.[34]

In this conception, alcoholism is a disease that has a life of its own beyond the social environment in which it developed or flourished.

Subgroups in Santa Barbara differ considerably in substance use and abuse.[35] Latino Family members simply do not use alcohol or drugs, except perhaps to have a drink at a birthday party or a beer on the weekend.[36] Many, however, mentioned that they believed drug and alcohol use was increased by homelessness, although it appeared that such comments were not usually based on personal experience:

> JAVIAR: No, not in my case, I care for my family too much to hurt them doing something like that, but I know about a lot of people who are using drugs or alcohol to cope with homelessness.

Transitory Workers, in keeping with their general devotion to work and keeping out of trouble, also report little use of alcohol or drugs:

> HANK: I drink a little bit. I mean, I'm not a teetotaler. But I don't get myself in trouble because I drink, let's put it that way. Never.

The drinking habits of most Skidders do not appear to be significantly different from those of their friends from their former lives. They certainly do not appear in public drinking situations, although a few report increased private drinking, typically with one or two friends.

But for Kids drinking and especially drugs are an integral part of the street scene. For some, it is their arrival on the streets that begins their routine use of drugs, while others had already begun experimenting before leaving home.[37] The availability of drugs on the street is in some cases the chief lure of that life:

> Q: What do you like most about being in the streets?
>
> LISA: I like the drugs! [laughs] The drugs mainly. The drugs and those kinds of friends. . . . They [her parents and other authority figures] say . . . "You could do something with your life," and I'll sit there and go, "The only thing I want to do with my life is take drugs."

Kids who do not use drugs or alcohol—typically those who have already "gone through that scene"—are extremely rare. Most Kids I met in Santa Barbara do not yet appear to be substance-dependent, but drugs and alcohol are a more routine part of their lifestyle than is true for any other subgroup, as data from other studies suggest.[38]

A number of studies have hypothesized that mentally ill people use street drugs and alcohol as a form of self-medication,[39] and this is evident on the streets of Santa Barbara. Jonathan, an intermittently recovering alcoholic Wingnut, commented:

> Whole controversial thing, marijuana. But I have found it to be very medicinal for me, getting free from all these anger things, and sometimes when I find those little [marijuana] cigarettes, I can go to the park, let this rage and anger, whatever, wear off.

Substance abuse is most connected in the public mind with Street People. Those on the streets of Santa Barbara report widespread use of soft drugs—particularly marijuana—when available, but often report that they use such drugs less than before they were homeless, simply because they lack the money.[40] Joints are the unit of sale on the streets, as opposed to the quantities in which people with money buy such drugs. Marijuana, unlike alcohol, generally seems to lead to few street problems other than those associated with its illegality:

> GLEN: [After breakfast] it's a real scramble to run around and find a joint and get high, which is just part of street survival. . . . Even the winos . . . would much prefer to have some pot, because they realize they are gonna be mellow and everything's all right. If they get into alcohol, they are pretty rowdy and get into trouble.

Alcohol, however, is legal and more easily obtainable, and it provides the sensation of warmth on the cold nights that occur in a beach community, regardless of the season.

The use of alcohol is widespread among Street People, but it is not clear how much more those on the street drink than people with homes (a third of whom are reported to be moderate to heavy drinkers),[41] nor whether the same people drink more when homeless than when housed. Street People's estimates of the percentage of Street People who are alcoholic were very close to that of the County Alcohol Program Director (10 percent), if "alcohol" is taken to mean those whose primary activity each day is drinking and securing funds for drinking.

Street People say they drink for a number of reasons. Many see drinking as a way to fill up empty time and cope with boredom, reinforced by the comforting nature of the social scene that grows up around that time-filling activity:[42]

> MAYOR MAX: It's just because of the everyday doldrums of nothing else to do after you look for a job and you get something to eat, and you sit around for two more hours, just waiting for the next place to get something to eat.

> MARK: [By nighttime] there's absolutely nothing new to do but stay out of trouble, and so Jerry and I will get a small bottle of wine and split it.

Many drink as an escape, both from the actual physical conditions of cold and from the mental fatigue of street life. As Perez says of his own life as a homeless person in Santa Barbara, "It is not pleasant out there, and alcohol is a cheap, readily available escape."[43] Similarly, some drink to dull their physical pains.

Others attribute their drinking to rejection by mainstream society:

> ELI: I came here, to Santa Barbara, to [get] clean, [to get back my] mental health. And I found rejection here. So I went back to drinking. Got a few tickets. Nothing serious. Just open containers, drunk in public. And I did that about six months, and I got tired of that, so I decided to go to the Salvation Army and sober up again. And I stayed sober for eight months. And I went back on that train of drinking again. That's about it. It's a vicious little circle. Because every effort I put forward, there's somebody who's gonna slam the door. They won't leave it open just enough for me to come in.

Finally, some drink to celebrate, especially when a paycheck or an entitlement rescues a Street Person from a period of extreme poverty:

> KEVIN: After I get money, I go out . . . and have a few drinks. . . . And then there's just so many people out on the streets that don't have anything. I don't like to sit there and drink by myself. So I have to go and find somebody else, and we have a party.[44]

Most Street People in Santa Barbara appear to be either casual or moderate drinkers; alcohol abuse is not the primary issue in their homelessness. Many use alcohol as a more or less planned vacation. But there is no doubt, even among many people on the streets, that the continuous drinking of the "winos" and the intermittent drinking and drug use of some Street People can cause serious problems.[45] Sustained alcohol or drug use is detrimental to one's physical and mental health,[46] and heavy drinkers and dopers know it. When I commented to Jack that he didn't seem to show any effects from drinking, he cut me off: "Long-term I do. My face. My kidneys."

Aware that substance abuse may interfere with escape, many Street People adjust their behavior accordingly. Jack stopped drinking while homeless, knowing that it had brought him to the streets:

> I'm not gonna drink. I can save my money if I don't drink. If I drink one beer, I can go, I can stay in that bar and spend fifty, a hundred dollars [laughs]. That's why I can't afford rent sometimes.

Mark believed his escape from homelessness required help from others, necessitating a responsible—sober and drug-free—lifestyle:

> Whether it's the [Rescue] Mission or the Salvation Army or a private citizen [he asks for help], then certainly I've got to be willing to work for it. And I think that includes not getting stoned or drunk or anything on the side. I don't think that would be honest. You know, I really want to make an effort. *I want out of here.* Badly.

But despite this awareness, many oscillate between days, weeks, or months of sobriety and periods of heavy drinking, sometimes a "controlled binge,"[47] but sometimes all-out, continuous drinking that usually ends with them in jail on some alcohol-related charge.

Those suffering from alcoholism on the streets are offered little help. Throughout the 1980s, the county's official detoxification center was the county jail rather than a medical facility.[48] Nor are there many options for indigent would-be recovering alcoholics. While a number of organizations, including Alcoholics Anonymous, are available, few are tailored to the needs of homeless alcoholics, nor do most even welcome these most difficult cases. Throughout most of the 1980s, private hospitals treating alcoholics in the metropolitan Santa Barbara area offered a total of three free beds, and, as a result, an estimated 2 percent of the yearly population in the private programs were "lower State Street alcoholics."[49] The Rescue Mission and the Salvation Army both operate alcoholism programs that are mainly used by low-income people, but admittance requires a period of prior sobriety, and, as we have just seen, there are few places where homeless alcoholics can "dry out" in Santa Barbara other than the county jail. Even those who do manage to get into and complete a treatment program are likely to reenter the same circumstances of poverty and homelessness they came from, making permanent recovery unlikely.

Thus the role of alcoholism and heavy drinking (as well as the less common problem of drug abuse) in perpetuating (or causing) homelessness must be understood contextually, not merely in their etiology but in appreciating the difficulty of a cure.[50] While the treatment of alcohol and drug abuse has seen no dramatic, obvious failure on the scale of deinstitutionalization, funding suffered in the post–Proposition 13 and Reagan administration years.[51] Santa Barbara County funding for alcoholism programs dropped from $389,500 in 1980 to an average of $324,400 from 1981 to 1984 (apart from the loss to inflation). But equally important were the severe cuts in other public assistance programs, particularly housing, for the simple truth is that without stability of some kind, treatment of substance abuse, like treatment of mental illness, is rarely successful.[52]

My experiences in Santa Barbara shed some light on the relationship of substance abuse to homelessness. Although alcohol is a part of street life for many members of the visible homeless population, substance abuse is no longer (if it ever was)[53] the major cause of homelessness, nor is it the major barrier to escape for significant portions of the total homeless population.[54] Its role appears to be exaggerated because most people (and researchers) do not see the hidden homeless populations, who suffer far lower rates of alcohol (or drug) abuse; at the same time, alcoholics (along with mentally ill people) are the most visible of the visible homeless population. While addictive behavior is certainly a problem for some (and this number may be much greater in large cities like New York), for many more alcohol use is in some sense purposive (if not productive): It is used to deal with physical pain, depression, or boredom; to ward off the cold; to momentarily escape a dismal present; and to provide a unifying activity for social interaction. Solitary drinking appears to be rare for most homeless people except Wingnuts. Drinking and drug use instead serve as a way in which homeless people (like housed people) display friendship and engage in sharing. That this may in some cases complicate their escape does not change their intent.

At the same time I do not minimize the devastating impact of alcohol on some homeless people.[55] Eli drank to alleviate his bitterness, yet drinking prolonged his homelessness: A drunk driving accident during a week-long binge led to the loss of his chauffeur's license, rendering employment in his usual line of work impossible. Kevin's "planned drunks" on pay days used much of the income he had left after paying off his many fines and bills, making it more difficult for him to save enough for an apartment. Arrest and labeling as a drinker can lead to self-identification as a street person and drinker.[56] Prolonged drinking makes employment, and thus escape, more difficult at the same time that it makes homeless life appear, to some, more bearable in the immediate present.

Again, these forms of "deviant behavior" are not typical of homeless people. While about a third of those in the HoPP group said crime and alcoholism were effects of homelessness they heard about or saw in others, far fewer felt that homelessness had changed them personally in that way. HoPP group members who reported using drugs or alcohol typically said they used them no more frequently while homeless. For some who use them, drink and drugs become a barrier to escape; for most, drinking and drug use are coping devices that sometimes complicate escape but less often prevent it.

Other adaptive behaviors may lead to a general labeling of homeless people that acts against them individually and collectively. When people "carry the banner" at night and sleep in the parks during the day, when it is legal and safe, housed people may be led to characterize homeless people as bums and loafers who should be out looking for work instead. Some choose to sleep in the streets instead of shelters, finding the former a safer and more "normal" environment, but this choice is interpreted by housed people (and some care-givers) as a preference for street life. Glen argued that other bizarre-appearing behavior is also adaptive and reactive to homeless life:

> A lot of times maybe people just think that street people are crazy when they drive down the road and they see this guy looking at the cars and yelling at them. They think he's berserk, but he's just reacting normally. He's fed up with the fact that after so many days he's walked up and down the street, people staring holes through him all the time. He just has to communicate.

As understandable, even "rational," as this behavior may appear when seen through the lens of homeless life, it nevertheless contributes to the difficulties homeless people have in escape by reinforcing their collective image as insane.

As constraint grows with time and options for agency decrease, various forms of adaptation become more likely. While some may enhance ability to escape, such as a resolve to give up drinking or a stepped-up drive to find work, most at best facilitate survival (such as getting Food Stamps or finding intermittent casual labor jobs); at worst they may make escape more difficult (such as criminal behavior and drinking).[57] The "individual" choice of adaptations and escape strategies, however, is played out against a backdrop of local and national constraints, including employment and housing markets and welfare policies. Personal characteristics over which the individual has no control, including age, health, and race, affect choice of adaptations as well. Among the most important of these factors is social background: Those who have fallen from a middle-class status, such as many Skidders, and those who are part of stronger cultural networks, such as Latino Families, have more options. As a result, members of these groups are unlikely to engage in the more severe and dangerous adaptations, such as crime, that those with less social margin may eventually engage in.

ACCEPTANCE OF THE LIFE

For an extremely small number of people, homelessness breeds homelessness because it becomes an accepted way of life:

> MARK: [Some] people, once they hit, never really get out of it, never really get ahead. It starts to become a pattern. And it starts getting to be just too easy to do. It's like, "I've finally got [the money to get] myself into an apartment, but I can go ahead and just blow it today. . . . I mean, what's the worst thing that can happen? Maybe I can't pay rent. So what? I can take care of myself out there!" You know, it just becomes too much of a pattern.

Yet, here again, many more people attribute this attitude to others than espouse it themselves. Mark, for example, worked two jobs in his desire to escape. Mayor Max told of meeting "professional drifters, as you would call them—they know the spots where the food is at, and that's where they go," but Max worked about thirty hours a week scavenging and recycling metal and cans.

To be sure, some homeless people, virtually always Street People or Kids, enjoy *aspects* of street life, principally a lack of responsibilities or, alternatively phrased, the experience of freedom:

> Q: Is there something you like most about being homeless?
> RAY: You're free. I can go and come as I wish. Talk to, see whoever I want. I can do whatever I want. There's no limits, no bounds, no laws, you understand?
> WENDI: Sometimes I don't feel like working, I just feel like going. . . . It's not an easy life, but it's easy going.

But just as it is rare to find a person who became homeless voluntarily, it is rare to find homeless people who prefer to remain so. Dora's words stand for most people in the HoPP group:

> There is nothing I like about this kind of life. I dislike everything: no privacy, no room, no kitchen, no bathroom, no place to wash clothes, no place to move and breathe freely without fear.[58]

THE TOLL ON HEALTH

Finally, homelessness takes a toll on the physical and mental capabilities of homeless people. The great need for health care found by the Homeless Coalition/County Health medical outreach program demonstrates that physical health is a frequent casualty of homeless life, even in Paradise. Although major disabilities did not show up in the HoPP interviews,[59] many interviewees complained of chronic poor health. Latino Families, generally living in cars and unheated outbuildings, almost unanimously reported constant colds and flu. Those who frequently sleep on the streets—Street People, Kids, and Wingnuts—report high incidences of skin diseases, colds and flu, and occasionally weight loss.

Homelessness further complicates the already fragile lives of those with mental illnesses. Analysts disagree about whether homelessness can *cause* mental illness, but there is little question that homelessness aggravates preexisting mental illness.[60] Kathie's eviction from Section 8 housing touched off another round in a thirteen-year battle against homelessness and mental illness:

> The day after I got my eviction notice, I started making mistakes bookkeeping-wise and stuff. And it was like a regular pattern of things that went wrong as far as—I thought I was under control but I guess not. . . . There was my stability. I think that one of the main reasons I was able to make such progress with my mental health and stuff here was because I had a stable base with that apartment for four years. I didn't have to worry about being out on the street, and selling blood, and god knows what else in order to have some stability.

In addition, homelessness makes it exceedingly difficult for mentally ill people to receive treatment and benefits.[61] Their mobility (complicating contact with social workers and creating residency problems), the unwillingness of institutions to tolerate their behavior, their own distrust of such institutions, and their inability to navigate the entitlement bureaucracies all militate against their receiving ongoing care or public assistance. Given the scarcity of treatment resources, most professionals are not inclined to deal with the most intractable cases, and homeless mentally ill people are the most difficult of all.[62] Especially with the newer laws restricting involuntary commitment, many such people now seem doomed to fall through the cracks, living on the streets with short stops in jail.[63] The same is true of programs for substance abusers: Resources are tight, waiting lists are long, recovery rates are low,[64] and homeless people are the least desired clients.

Homelessness also creates mental stress for those without preexisting mental illnesses:

GLEN: There are some out there that are just absolutely [crazy]. . . .
But I would say that every one of us, every person . . . , you are
definitely walking around in a state of shock. It's the only way that
you can cope.

In the beginning, homelessness is disorienting, especially for those with
no previous experience on the streets:

JULIA: Everything was very, very temporary, very acute, and very
traumatic.

SONJA: I saw a news show. They showed that woman in the bushes
with a stroller. They were living in the bushes! You never think
that you could be joining them. Especially so suddenly.

The homeless person begins to feel "different" within a very short time:

MANUEL: The realization that one is homeless makes a very strong
impact on one's self-esteem and confidence. It's a feeling of not
belonging. It's like a sensation of hanging by a delicate thread
which could break any moment.

LIZ: I'm just very lonely. Very, very lonely. I even drive down the
street and I look at people's houses and at night, I look through
the windows as I'm driving by. I think it feels like everybody in
the world has their own little spot but you. How important it is to
have your own little table and knickknacks around you! It really
makes a difference.

This sense of difference stems from the new role that previously
"normal" people must now occupy: that of outsiders. Every day is a lesson
in their nonstatus. Housed people avert their eyes or look through them
when they pass on the street.[65] Police and merchants treat them as
potential problems rather than as citizens or shoppers. Employers treat
them as unemployables. Welfare workers treat them as freeloaders. The
only people who do not look down on them are others in a similar
position—but, as Goffman has noted of stigmatized people generally, the
newly homeless person is likely to "feel some ambivalence; for those
others will not only be patently stigmatized, and thus not like the normal
person he knows himself to be, but may also have other attributes which
he finds it difficult to associate himself with."[66]

Disorientation is often followed by deep depression as the reality of
the situation sets in:

MARGIE: It gets depressing after about the third month that a
person is homeless, though. Then you begin with your personal
situation. Is it working out? Or should I just give up altogether?

Guilt and shame often accompany depression. Although few explicitly blame themselves for their plight, their doubts are often revealed when they speak of other homeless people:

> RAY: A lot of them are failures, they're sick mentally, emotionally, or physically, or something. They have a demented mood or attitude about their lives. They think, "Well, this is where I belong." And they never get out of the street.

> KATHIE: You know, there are a lot more people that were middle-class that are now sort of sliding down the scale. And everybody sorta puts the blame on themselves, you know, like, "What could I be doing that I could have prevented this situation?" You know, you feel hopeless.

The mental stress of homelessness may be manifested in many ways:

> DULA: My nerves [are affected]. I have spells in which I just sit and cry because I am so depressed. I feel desperate, so now I want to munch into everything in sight. I've gained twenty-five pounds.

> CAMILIA: [It has affected] my sexual life because I worry too much and I can't function. I don't feel free. I don't respond.

> LIZ: My daughter has been sick for the last two months; she has never been sick [before]. She has caught one thing after another. I know a lot of it is stress in not having your own place.

> JUANITA: It was affecting my children. They were not [acting] normal. They aren't destructive, but something was happening with the three of us. We couldn't get along.

Mental stress can turn into bitterness toward other people. Relationships become strained and are frequent casualties of the life, making survival even more difficult when families are torn apart. Some transform bitterness into energy and channel it into escape strategies, either individual or collective and political. But for others, bitterness becomes despair, passivity, and paralysis:[67]

> CHRISTINE: You have *no idea* [what it is really like] until you've been out in the streets. . . . It's humiliating, and the insecurity is just overwhelming. . . . When you don't know where you're going to be next month, or tomorrow night, you can't do anything. *Nothing.*

> JULIA: If you really look at it from a broad perspective, it doesn't matter. You don't have to care, nor should you care. There is no hope. That's what I have experienced, and that's what I'm

perceiving others are experiencing, along with all these other human problems that you have to deal with. I think they believe there is no hope. I understand. I've been there.

This paralysis becomes a barrier to escape:

BRUCE: It's difficult when you don't have a base of operations, it is hard to get out there and push. For a number of reasons. One thing is there is a certain kind of a creeping diminishing of self-confidence that you need to go out and deal with The Man out there. A lot of that comes from the fact that you are very illegal most of the time. Even if there isn't a cop watching you, those feelings are still inside you.

Depression, paranoia, paralysis, loss of self-respect, loss of identity, a sense of isolation—all seem to be characteristics connected with what Howard Bahr, Theodore Caplow, and others called disaffiliation. Yet disaffiliation is not a characteristic: It is a gradual *process*, the result of a chain of events. Margie emphasized, "You don't start losing out from your family and your friends. You lose contact with them."

Some homeless people do, in fact, withdraw from mainstream society from time to time, or otherwise display behavior that looks like disaffiliation, but it is clear that this "individual" adaptation is made in the face of larger structural processes, mediated through individual experiences:

JULIA: You have a little bit of hope one day, you talk to one person who's encouraging. . . . You know there's more in life. Much more. On every level. You might get some temporary encouragement which could give you a little bit of momentum in a very positive direction. It might carry you . . . until your next abusive encounter, which sends you right back down.

While homelessness may lead to periods of alienation and disaffiliation, it is a mistake to think that most homeless people become permanently disaffiliated. Despair and hopelessness appear intermittently, coexisting with more positive feelings as homeless people struggle to envision a different future while managing a desolate present.[68]

Countering Disengagement and Disaffiliation

Despair and alienation can become one more barrier to escaping homelessness. While Goffman is correct to argue that the position of stigmatized individuals is mainly a question of condition rather than will,[69] the loss of will renders escape impossible. Retaining the will to escape requires rejecting the label of "homeless" and all it implies, both through redefining oneself and through maintaining ties with mainstream society.

COPING AND SELF-WORTH

For many people, homelessness seems to be a daily lesson in their own lack of worth, taught by the material conditions they live under and the opinions others hold of them. The need to cry out against this feeling, the need to be seen as *somebody*, is apparent in many of the stories homeless people tell.[70] Skidders, Transitory Workers, and Latino Families dwell on what a mistake it is, what a surprise it is, for someone like themselves to be homeless. Street People's etiquette, on the other hand, usually calls for exaggerating one's Street prowess. Henry describes a run-in with the police: "He swung his billy club. Of course, I do know some martial arts. Out of all the blows he did swing, only about three of them actually landed. The other ones I was able to block with my feet." But Henry in fact knows no martial arts, nor is fighting his strong suit.

Perhaps the most successful coping mechanism is to cast oneself in a helping mode, sometimes only in one's imagination, but often in reality. Zeke describes how he became an aide at the Church shelter:

> It started back at Trinity Episcopal. They knew what they wanted to do, but they didn't know how to set it up. They were asking for volunteers, so me and Greg . . . decided, you know, "Let's give them a hand. . . ." Well, it's shocking working here 'cause we started out the ones volunteering and now they're coming to me, asking all sorts of questions: "How should we do this, how should we do that?"

This helping mode explains in part why the HPA and SPA were able to make the advances they did. A number of homeless people who saw little in life that excited them found a sense of mission and purpose in helping others. At the same time, helping distances the homeless person from his or her state. Those who are active in political or service work often speak of "homeless people" as others, as a group the speaker is familiar with but not a part of.

CONNECTIONS

Most studies that have looked at length of homelessness have focused on individual traits such as gender, age, race, education, or debilitating characteristics such as addiction or mental illness,[71] without regard to context. But to understand who escapes homelessness, when, and how, the important question is what ties homeless people have to other people and mainstream institutions.[72]

A work life keeps some in contact with the housed world. For example, 91 percent of those HoPP group members working full-time had emergency contacts, compared with 63 percent of those not working. Marriage (or having a partner) also seems to hold people in contact with the mainstream world.[73] Although there are few data bearing on *why* marriage impedes disaffiliation, a number of possibilities seem plausible: A sense of responsibility comes from caring for another; more mainstream contacts are available to two people than one; one person can attend to getting-by tasks while the other works on getting ahead. For a couple or a single person, children seem an especially strong bridge to the housed world. Those Church guests with children were three times as likely as those without children (and HoPP parents were more than twice as likely) to have spent the previous night at the home of a friend or relative. A number of studies have also found that alcohol and drug abuse, often signs of disengagement, are considerably less common among homeless parents than among the childless.[74]

Remaining in a town where one had a previous housed and work life is also important for retaining affiliations;[75] certainly one's social margin is linked to remaining in one's hometown. The importance of long-term residency is clearest for Skidders and Latino Families. Skidders and their children, for instance, tend to exist within the same middle-class world they had inhabited before, even though their place within it has changed. The psychological strains of being in this world but not fully of it are profound. But whatever the toll and costs, it cannot be said that they are isolated from mainstream society. Their children usually continue to go to the same schools; those working usually continue to work the same jobs; their peer group usually remains the same (unless they descend into street life).

Finally, political involvement seems to counter disaffiliation. Activists in the HPA, the SPA, or the Homeless Coalition tend to have few periods of despair and paralysis. Politics serves the same function for them that children serve for homeless parents, providing links to mainstream institutions and a sense of responsibility, a mission to perform, a feeling that what one does actually *matters* and can change someone's life.

In short, disengagement is least likely when the homeless person preserves a sense of *efficacy*. A homeless parent who sees her efforts lead to a bed for her child has a sense of her own agency. A homeless person who volunteers to work in a shelter feels a power in aiding others who are powerless. A homeless activist who sees City Council change the anti-sleeping laws feels a sense of individual competence and effectiveness. These are, of course, the very qualities that homelessness attacks, and that are most necessary to avoid paralysis and consequent disengagement leading to disaffiliation.

But the conditions associated with maintaining a sense of efficacy—or even mainstream ties—do not necessarily translate into escape, since both will *and* condition, agency *and* constraint, are important. Affiliations that preserve spirit and allow access to resources, such as a work life or continued ties to housed friends and family,[76] may facilitate escape, but other circumstances and conditions that typically reinforce efficacy and affiliation may not. The most obvious of these is the presence of children. Parents in both the HoPP group and the Church shelters were no more likely to have been homeless less than a year than those without children.[77] The problems of finding child care, the cost of renting a home large enough for children, and anti-child discrimination all impede escape for even the least alienated parent, particularly in tight housing markets.

Sorting out these contradictory effects is complex, yet the basic point remains: Will and agency are not always enough to ensure escape, but without them, escape is not possible. And will and agency seem most likely to survive when the individual has ongoing contacts with institutions and members of mainstream society, particularly contacts where efficacy can be demonstrated.

One of the clearest lessons of the Santa Barbara data, as well as other studies,[78] is that the attenuation of both will and mainstream contacts is in large part a function of the amount of time one is homeless. Compared with those Church guests who were homeless more than six months, those homeless for a shorter period were somewhat more likely to have a regular source of funds and significantly more likely to have an emergency contact; they were at least twice as likely to be married, to be working full-time, and to have slept the previous night in the home of a friend or relative.[79]

The risk of disaffiliation increases with time largely because material constraints increase, making survival and escape, as well as any kind of efficacious agency, more problematic. As we have noted, "passing" as a housed person becomes more difficult, obtaining stable employment becomes less likely. The temptation to flee an area (with its attendant preexisting networks) rises from a wish both to avoid the contacts from one's former life that now bring shame and to find work and housing elsewhere.[80] As these processes reduce ties to mainstream society, another of the downward cycles of homelessness appears: Those who are more removed from mainstream society become progressively less able to gain access to the resources it controls, thus becoming still more removed.

Whether disaffiliation is a permanent or episodic state of (some) homeless people is of crucial importance in designing programs to deal with homelessness. If homeless people are irrevocably disaffiliated, the best we can hope for and do is to provide caretaker programs that make their lives somewhat easier. But if disaffiliation is relative and reactive to immediate conditions, programs that stress empowerment and efficacy are more promising.

Values and Getting Ahead

Some disaffiliation theorists have argued that those who are removed from mainstream affiliations may also be expected to lose contact with—or actively reject—mainstream values, thus becoming *normatively isolated,* a further barrier to escape.[81] There is a clear logic to such an expectation: People's world views reflect their material circumstances. But conversely, if homeless people are not isolated from mainstream society, their values may instead be expected to resemble its values. In fact, tied to mainstream society as they are, most homeless people in Santa Barbara continue to hold most of the same values.[82]

This attachment is evident among all subgroups. As might be expected, the values of those most hidden are generally consistent with those of the groups they are hiding within. But those on the streets also largely adhere to the values of the larger society. Even the emphasis on "freedom," interpreted as anti-social irresponsibility by the greater society, tends to be couched in terms of mainstream values, as when Greg compared his life to that of the bald eagle, which "represents freedom, strength, things like that, what our country . . . was founded on."[83]

Homage is also paid to justice and honesty, as seen in Kevin's assertion that 95 percent of street people have a conscience, Mark's declaration that anything he loses in the park is inevitably found and returned to him by other homeless people, and Mayor Max's confidence that those homeless people who steal from others are dealt with by "street justice."

The rules of the game are also generally respected (even though these are people who have suffered badly in that game), both because homeless people retain a respect for most of those rules on a cultural level, and because they understand that their access to resources depends on respecting those rules. Eli leaves his bench in the bus station coffee shop when things get busy "so that they can take care of their business"; Mark gave up drink and drugs to show those who might help him that he was "willing to work for it."

The prevalence, especially among those on the streets, of trust in God belies reports by the Rescue Mission that homeless people have "fallen from God" or Sara Harris' characterization of homeless people on Skid Row as people who "have lost all semblance of faith in God."[84] While piety might be expected among those who get most of their resources from religious shelters, a belief in God (though not often organized religion) was professed by nearly all Street People and Wingnuts I encountered, often as a result of their homelessness:

HENRY: I was totally away from [religion]. Until I actually came to San Diego, I didn't really believe anything about the Bible. I

couldn't care less. In San Diego, this lady minister told me that
the Lord was actually helping me and following with me, and she
gave me twenty dollars and she said, "The Lord wants me to give
you this 'cause you need it. From here on, people will help you
along the way." [After that] . . . every time, the money was never
there until it ran out. . . .

Q : You think the Lord is looking after you?

H E N R Y : Oh yeah, definitely, because He helped me find something
I needed. I don't have to worry. If I need something, I find it.

Virtually all homeless people once had a housed life that included
socialization into the values of their family, ethnic and racial group,
geographic area, and class, but also familiarized them with what we speak
of as "American values." That socialization into mainstream values,
however, has been followed by a socialization into the outlaw and
devalued status of homeless life. Rights that were taken for granted
become endangered; social interactions with both strangers and friends
have been altered; the material underpinnings of norms and values have
been shaken. What is noteworthy is the degree to which mainstream
values *survive* the extreme deprivation of homeless life. Despite their
outcast and outlaw status, homeless people are still intricately involved in
mainstream society through material ties and therefore, as materialists like
Marx have argued in general and Liebow has shown in the case of
"street-corner men,"[85] through corresponding values and ideas.

Although the general values of the larger society seem to be he-
gemonic for both the hidden homeless population and those on the streets,
these competing socialization processes often produce what Hyman
Rodman called "value stretch": mainstream values are adhered to, but
interpreted in ways that may allow otherwise unacceptable behavior.[86]
Shoplifting, for example, was generally not endorsed by most of the people
I came to know *except* in the stores of merchants known for their hostility to
homeless people. Breaking and entering crimes were rare, yet nearly all
the homeless people I knew condoned breaking into a car for shelter when
the weather was cold.

Such actions conform to Robert Merton's characterization of criminal
deviance as behavior intended to reach the goals established by mainstream society when legitimate avenues are closed.[87] It is precisely this
perceived difference between accepted values and the ability to realize
them that may cause homeless people to feel "drastically out of place,
demoralized by their inability to establish homes, find work and belong."[88]
Boasting, fighting with the cops, sneaking into showers, sleeping in the
day because of a lack of a place to sleep at night, even counterproductive
activities like drinking and drug abuse are all attempts to realize the goals

and values of the larger society: material security, respect from others, the feeling of freedom.

As values may be stretched, new norms may develop in response to the changed material conditions of homeless life. This is naturally less true for those encapsulated in mainstream lifestyles: Skidders, Latino Families, and, to a lesser extent Transitory Workers. For those who live off street resources, however, there are new rules to learn:

> B R E T : When you get out on the street, it's like going to school every day. When you go to school, they teach you a lot. Napoleon and all that bullshit. When you get out in the street, Napoleon don't exist. Napoleon's ways don't exist. You know, you get here and you try to create Napoleon, you gonna wind up dead. It doesn't phase.[89]

Learning the streets involves practical knowledge: where to find food, where to find temporary shelter, where to find clothes, where it is safe to sleep. The rules of relating to housed society must be learned: stay invisible, stay low-key. The norms of each group must be learned: where it is safe to leave your belongings out, what questions may be asked, when food and drink are shared and when not.

As with values, the norms of street life are not produced and reproduced through a cultural conveyor belt but emerge in response to the material constraints and practical dilemmas of day-to-day survival:

> G L E N : It's just fitting in [to your new status]. It's just the same thing as in the army, it's basic training. You take all these different individuals and suddenly they are all wearing green and they are learning a new language and a new programming. . . . You could be sitting with someone that might have two or three years of college [and not know it], and just suddenly at the end of the week, you'll get discussing something and his entire vocabulary changes, his facial expressions. Suddenly you realize that you are looking at the real man this man is.

Visions of the Future

As Liebow has noted concerning streetcorner men, some homeless people may spend their meager resources enjoying the present, not because they do not envision a future, but because they envision a future very much like the present.[90] Eli and Henry both spoke of this as a factor in drinking on the streets: When one has a job that will never produce enough income to afford a place in Santa Barbara, one is likely to spend whatever money one can get on making the present more bearable. If there is no foreseeable escape, the need for future-oriented goals is lost:

> G L E N : [We need] cottage industries. You could say, "We have gardens out here, you can work hours there . . ." That's one thing that maybe people do not realize: we are all goal-setting people, and suddenly on the streets, you have no need for it.

When speaking of the future, the subgroups are influenced by both their backgrounds and the constraints of their present lives. Skidders, largely middle-class in background and surrounded by a middle-class life, do not expect to be homeless, or even poor, for very long, as suggested by the large number pursuing an education instead of working. Latino Families, enduring longer periods of homelessness with less reason for confidence in a better future, rarely think about advancing their skills and education to escape lower-class life entirely, but they are very focused on escaping homelessness:

> G A V I N A : I just want a place with a bedroom, a bathroom, and a kitchen, so we don't have to live like animals in the mountains. A house or apartment so we can keep warm and I could fix meals for my family.

Transitory Workers show a similar orientation, but with a greater confidence, based on experience, that escape is imminent. They rarely have grand plans to become rich but always look to a near future without the aberration of homelessness:

> Q : What would you like to be doing in a year?
>
> H A N K : In a year? Well, I know what I'm gonna be doing *if nothing changes in my lifestyle* [emphasis added]. I'm sure I'll be in a whole lot better shape in a year than I am now. I'm sure I'll have a car again, I'm sure I'll be living somewhere halfway decent, and I'm sure I'll put my wardrobe together.

Kids, like most children, rarely display practical plans for the future. Their focus is generally on day-to-day hustling, but when basic needs are met—as when Lisa spent a few weeks in the KBSAY youth shelter waiting for a custody trial—a realistic appraisal of the future is much more likely:

> Q : What could be the best thing for you that could come out of the court case? What do you want to happen?
>
> L I S A : Placement. Home, a real home, you know, like, people who understand where I'm coming from.

Wingnuts almost invariably envision a future mainstream life of security and normalcy, often harking back to the time when they last felt secure. Julia, whose happiest days were her college years, says she would like to be "studying formally through an accredited institution." Jonathan, a star athlete in college and past newspaper editor, now forty-six, says:

> I would like to have a dormitory room at UCSB, yeah, and a slick little portable electric typewriter, and be involved in a research project. Putting out dynamite graphics. Getting involved in publishing, getting involved in the edification, the education of the young people.

But when Julia is asked what kind of a place she would like to live in, she replies, "I don't even think along those terms right now"; when Jonathan is repeatedly pressed to write an article for a local alternative paper as a way of getting back into newspaper work, he refuses, saying he cannot write without a workspace. For most Wingnuts, beset by problems of maintaining mental balance as well as the insecurities of the streets, the future is more a glowing dream than a destination that can be reached step by step.

Given their more divergent backgrounds, Street People show the largest variation in their visions of the future. Some show a short-term, "cyclical" orientation to time,[91] an unending daily cycle of different feeding and sleeping places, operating within a monthly cycle of Food Stamps and other entitlements (theirs or those of others they are in contact with). With the barest of resources, pressing survival needs, and dismal future possibilities, some Street People, particularly those who have been homeless longer, lose hope, and therefore projections, of escape.

Yet this should not be overstated. Almost all Street People in the HoPP group were immediately able to provide a realistic description of the type of home they might escape to, typically a lower-middle-class apartment or house. A number were carrying out short-range plans for immediate escape (such as Mark's intention to ask one of the missions to put him up for a few months while he saved enough for first, last, and deposit) and longer-range plans to escape lower-class life (such as Jack's goal of getting a college degree). Still, their identification with their homelessness is strong. When asked what should be done about homelessness, Street People tend to suggest short-term solutions: emergency shelters, homeless centers, and so forth.

My interviews and informal discussions with members of all the Santa Barbara subgroups highlight, again, the tremendous influence the feeling of efficacy has on the expectation of escape from homelessness and lower-class life. Homeless people need not only ongoing contacts with mainstream society but relations in which they are not subordinated or treated as children incapable of handling their own affairs, and which hold out the promise of a different life in the foreseeable future:

> H E N R Y : A lot of these shelters are afraid to give these people their freedom. They come in and feed them, shower them, bed them,

and they're out. Now, to get a homeless person off the street, you first of all have to make this person feel like they're welcome, make them feel like they're at home, make them feel like part of society. . . . But the most important thing is to let the people know that there is something to look forward to. By just putting them up for the night, you can do that forever and you're not really going to solve anything except keeping them out [of the elements], getting them dry and warm.[92]

The picture I have drawn of the struggles of homeless people in Santa Barbara to get ahead—like the picture I have drawn of how they get by—differs from that held by much of the housed population and found in much of the literature on homelessness. Homeless people are not, by and large, asocial villains who pursue self-destructive behavior in the face of readily available alternatives. They seldom remain homeless simply because they drink or spurn offered aid or desire to stay on the streets. But neither are they simply passive victims of macro-processes who become permanently alienated, disengaged, and disaffiliated. On the contrary, most homeless people are active agents who spend much of their time striving to find work, to procure entitlements, to locate affordable housing: in short, to do what they need to do in order to get ahead.

Chapter 7

Homelessness
and the
American Paradise

I n the time I spent with homeless people in Santa Barbara, I developed
a very different picture of who they are than the one I began with.
Instead of alcoholic men with wanderlust, I found a wide variety of
people who had become homeless for a wide variety of reasons. I found
large-scale social processes instead of individual proclivities and characteristics as the major causes of homelessness. Instead of disaffiliated isolates
with a preference for homeless life, I found people striving to preserve or
develop roots and to escape the streets.

The more time I spent with homeless people, the more apt the
analogy to musical chairs appeared. Resources are dwindling relative to
need, especially and most importantly the resource of affordable housing.
When the music stops, there are simply not enough chairs for everyone.
Who gets caught without a home depends on personal characteristics, luck,
preparation, background, local environment, and many other factors. But
these processes insure that *someone* will be caught without a home.
Certainly, some of the homeless people in Santa Barbara had personal
problems—Rachel's mental illness, Jonathan's alcoholism, Dula's lack of
job skills—yet these led to homelessness largely because of social processes that determined the decrease in resources. In this sense, the stories
of all those homeless in the Paradise of Santa Barbara are representative of
the stories of homeless people throughout the United States. The growth
in homelessness primarily reflects the intensification of long-term structural problems, including poverty, discrimination, unemployment, the lack
of a comprehensive human service system, and the crisis in affordable
housing.

Arguments Against Aiding "the Homeless"

Given the evidence that homelessness is a social, rather than simply an individual, problem, social intervention might be expected. Given that longer periods of homelessness increase both the danger of disengagement and the material barriers of escaping homelessness, early intervention seems prudent. Yet most communities strongly resist programs to serve "the homeless" arguing that aid is not morally justified, that it will exacerbate the problem on a local basis, or that it is too expensive.[1]

The "moral argument" asserts that homeless people have created their problems themselves or have no desire to escape their condition. Rather than repeat the fundamental arguments of this work, I will refer to the musical chairs analogy and point out that it does us little good to blame those who are eventually caught without a chair.

The "magnet [or Mecca] theory" argues that providing services will attract more homeless people to a locality, thus worsening the problem.[2] This argument seems plausible, yet it has not been confirmed by this or other research. National estimates of the percentage of local homeless populations who come from out of state range from 25 to 50 percent.[3] Census data, however, show that a (highly varied) average of 40 percent of the *housed* population were not born in their present state of residence.[4] Significant portions of Santa Barbara's homeless population were once *housed* residents of the city, including three-fifths of the HoPP interviewees and four-fifths of the SPA callers.[5] Even among the much less rooted Church guests, 30 percent had previously been housed residents, and over half were from California; only 22 percent came from the East or Midwest. While homeless people are certainly more mobile than housed people (and mobility is one rational escape strategy), their migratory pattern is not as far off the scale as one might think.[6]

The more important question is *why* homeless people move. Although the fear of attracting destitute people through generous aid seems reasonable, the data from local studies overwhelmingly demonstrate that homeless people move for the same reasons housed people do—chiefly climate, the presence of friends or family, and perceived job opportunities.[7] There is little evidence that homeless people are drawn to services.[8] It may be that large metropolitan centers magnetically attract some of the homeless population and repel others.[9] *Within* metropolitan areas, homeless people may move from surrounding suburbs into central cities where welfare, shelters, and employment are to be found, a rational coping strategy. But no data collected to date show that social services cause homeless people to undertake *major* relocations. Localities desiring to discourage in-migration of homeless (and other) people would be more successful in doing so by creating high unemployment than by curtailing services.

Finally, the "cost argument" suggests that, whatever the sympathies of local decision-makers, localities simply do not have enough money to fund necessary programs. This argument assumes that local governments are not already spending large amounts of money on homelessness, a false assumption that arises because these costs are often hidden in the budgets of programs that are not specifically or exclusively aimed at homeless people. Some local governments have become aware that they are spending great sums on emergency shelters and other programs. The variation is quite wide: While Dallas reported spending only $200,000 annually on programs for homeless people in 1986, New York City was reported to be spending $274 million in 1987 for emergency shelter alone.[10] But when hidden costs are tabulated, the figures rise substantially. Atlanta, with far fewer direct services for homeless people and a homeless population estimated to be perhaps one-fifteenth the size of New York's, was said to be spending over $20 million (the money coming from private organizations as well as government) as early as 1982, and expenditures for services other than food and shelter were *nine times* as great as emergency food and shelter costs.[11]

Data from Santa Barbara illuminate some of these hidden costs. In 1983 the City and County spent over $100,000 enforcing the seven local statutes that in various ways outlawed sleeping outside of a residence.[12] County Health administrators estimate that $200,000 a year was being spent in the mid-1980s providing medical care for homeless people, much of which could have been saved through earlier intervention.[13] Mental health service costs, while difficult to estimate, are unquestionably significant.[14] Preliminary research also points to substantial hidden costs in programs such as Child Protective Services and alcoholism treatment (or jailings), as have been found in other cities.[15]

The costs of homelessness will be higher in the long run: Philip Clay estimates that almost 19 million Americans will be homeless by the year 2003 if current trends continue;[16] as judicial and political pressures mount to deal with homelessness, the public cost per homeless person will rise as well, as it has in New York and other cities. Moreover, some social costs are beyond quantification, particularly the coming of age of a generation of children brought up in homelessness: Many may be expected to be angry, disturbed, and unemployable at best, and sociopathic at worst.

Calculating the immediate costs of preventing and ending homelessness would be extremely difficult. Part of the calculation would have to deal with what level of help we are prepared to give. Shelters that merely house people, for example, are usually much cheaper than those offering services.[17] But shelters of any kind are not a solution; they merely furnish homeless people with the most basic relief while veiling the problem from the rest of society. Homeless advocates and activists must state plainly that true solutions will be significantly more costly than shelters have been, but also emphasize the tremendous financial and social costs homelessness currently exacts.

The cost argument needs to be further studied and reevaluated. The available data cannot demonstrate conclusively that preventing homelessness would save money, but they certainly suggest that, at the very least, some of the funds spent on such programs would be offset by savings in other areas. While neglect of the homeless population may appear cheaper in the short run, in the long run it may well be more expensive, not only to homeless people, but to the national economy.[18]

The Failure of Recent Policies

THE SOCIAL POLICY BACKGROUND

Failed or misguided social policies have helped to create, aggravate, and perpetuate homelessness; in some cases the results have been so bad that the policies seem irrational. Federal and local policies have often acted to reduce the supply of affordable housing. Federal tax laws have traditionally rewarded practices that led to escalating housing costs;[19] the failure of federal monetary policies to control interest rates was a contributing variable, as financing costs pushed building costs beyond the grasp of median- and below-median-income households, and rendered all but the most luxurious rental housing virtually unprofitable for the builder. On a local level, gentrification has been encouraged and abetted by city governments hungry for higher-income residents—with disastrous consequences for low-income housing (notably the disappearance of half the SRO units in the country during the 1970s).

Although some of these policies pre-date the 1980s, the drastic cuts in housing assistance in the Reagan and Bush years—73 percent by 1990, the largest cuts in any domestic program[20]—dramatically worsened the position of low-income Americans. Thus in the same period in which federal tax and monetary policies further impaired the private market's ability to provide low-income housing, the federal government cut back its own long-standing (albeit incompletely met) commitment. Support for public housing, for example, dwindled to almost nothing in the Reagan years.[21] Because it takes time for federally subsidized housing to make its way through the "pipeline," the worst effects of these cuts are still ahead of us. Even in the late 1980s, only a quarter of all eligible low-income households received any kind of federal housing subsidy.[22]

The federal government also failed to intervene effectively in private market processes that restricted the supply of affordable housing. For example, the Single Room Occupancy Rehabilitation Program of the

McKinney Act, designed to encourage the reclaiming of disappearing SRO rooms, aided the creation of approximately a thousand units in its first three years,[23] compared with the one million units lost in the 1970s. Thousands of federally subsidized units are now becoming eligible for prepayment of the remaining mortgage and removal from rent-level constraints. Although their fate now appears somewhat more promising (see below), a chance of widespread displacement remains.[24]

The situation has been much the same for public assistance. Levels of assistance offered by federal means-tested programs were (and are) insufficient to prevent dire poverty and homelessness, particularly in those programs not indexed to inflation.[25] Welfare regulations actually helped produce homelessness in the 1980s—for instance, the denial in many states of AFDC and Medicaid to two-parent families encouraged desertion by husbands, with a consequent diminishing of potential family income.[26] As with housing, this tattered safety net was further shredded by the Reagan administration cutbacks affecting several million low-income households. Some portion of them, we can assume, became homeless.

Finally, the policy of "deinstitutionalization" was irrationally implemented at both state and national levels. Funding was insufficient, and the system was so decentralized that many of the most troubled fell through the cracks. Community-based facilities were resisted at the local level,[27] federal oversight of existing facilities was minimal,[28] basic survival and social services were not mandated or funded, and the patchwork nature of centers and programs exacerbated a major problem in mental health treatment: the lack of an aggressive outreach program.

THE RESPONSE TO HOMELESSNESS

Once the explosion of homelessness had alerted officials to the problem that public policies had helped to create, federal and local agencies were shamefully slow to respond.[29] As Boston's Emergency Shelter Commission pointed out in the winter of 1987–88, "If the record number of people on America's streets and soup kitchen lines had been driven there by natural catastrophe, many parts of our country would be declared disaster areas. But even though homelessness is a national problem, the Reagan Administration has given only lip service to the issue."[30]

Officials within the Reagan administration, from the top down, were at best ignorant about homelessness. In the early 1980s, the president suggested that homelessness was voluntary; the attorney general declared that people ate at soup kitchens "to save a buck." Clearly, homeless people were not part of the Reagan "majority."

After several years of advocacy work, the federal government responded to the crisis through grants to localities for emergency shelter support, administered through the Federal Emergency Management

Administration (FEMA). Average authorizations from fiscal year (FY) 1983 through FY1986 were $75 million, an annual average of $38 per homeless person, assuming two million homeless people in the country, as Marjorie Hope and James Young point out.[31] (Not all of this amount was targeted exclusively to the homeless population, and not all of it was actually appropriated.) Since 1987, major funding for expanded services has come through enactment and reauthorization of the Stewart B. McKinney Act, which has authorized greater but still insufficient amounts of funding: from about $400 million in FY1987 to $1.136 billion (or $568 per homeless person) in FY1992. Actual appropriations in FY1991 were $682 million ($341 per homeless person).

Implementation of many McKinney Act programs, and subsequent expenditure of funds, has often been slow, while oversight and monitoring have been characterized by the General Accounting Office as "inadequate."[32] As with the FEMA monies, complex application procedures and conflicting regulations have made it difficult for funding actually to reach homeless people.[33]

This sort of bureaucratic intransigence is epidemic within the agencies charged with action on homelessness. A glaring example is the federal government's reluctance to make available more than a minute percentage of the tens of thousands of vacant housing units it owns, despite the 1987 McKinney Act's requirement that federal agencies survey their properties and make "underutilized" ones available to local governments and non-profit organizations to assist homeless people. When HUD resold an estimated 70,000 homes in 1988, only 300 were made available for homeless-related projects. When the Farmers' Home Administration (FmHA) resold 14,000 homes in FY1988, only 3 were made available to homeless projects. The Veterans Administration (VA) sold almost 24,000 homes in the same year without any going for homeless-related projects.[34] Similarly, although the 1989 Savings and Loan "Bailout Bill" explicitly instructed the Resolution Trust Corporation (RTC) to make some of the properties formerly held by bankrupt S&Ls available to low-income families, "the program has fallen far short of expectations due to the failure of the RTC to implement properly its provisions."[35]

The irrationality of federal policies goes further: At the same time that FEMA and McKinney Act funding was being increased to deal with homelessness, other policies continued to perpetuate or promote it. For instance, even as the first FEMA monies were being made available for emergency shelters, an estimated six million low-income tenants who were in need of housing assistance were "unable to receive it because of program limitations." One example is HUD's policy change in the 1970s that raised the tenant's share of rent for federally subsidized housing from 25 to 30 percent of household income,[36] increasing homelessness and blocking escape for those who were already homeless.

Finally, the monies available were often directed not at ending homelessness, but at *managing* it. Far more funding was authorized each year through the McKinney Act for shelters and other emergency services than for providing or stimulating the creation of additional permanent housing.[37] The National Coalition for the Homeless noted in February 1990 that "no homeless housing program is aimed at [providing permanent housing for] homeless families, even as the administration proposes selling off public housing units from the inventory."[38]

The FY1990 appropriations under the McKinney Act took a first, tentative step in the right direction by moving some funding from shelter support to supportive housing demonstration projects. By 1991, localities were required to include prevention strategies and plans for long-term housing in the Comprehensive Homeless Assistance Strategies (CHASs) required to receive federal funding; $150 million was appropriated for transitional and permanent housing demonstration programs (the latter for homeless people with disabilities); and a number of restrictions on funding were loosened.

In general, each reauthorization of the McKinney Act in the 1990s has seen significant improvement. Aside from the greater emphasis on long-term and permanent housing, assistance for those with disabilities, including substance abuse, has been improved; barriers to the education of homeless children have been attacked; surplus properties have been made easier to obtain for homeless people and the groups serving them; social services have been linked to housing for mentally ill homeless people; incentives have been added for treating dual-diagnosis patients; and assistance to families, including child care and "Family Support Centers," has been authorized.

But major problems remain. Funding is still minuscule. For instance, spending on McKinney Act programs that directly assisted homeless people in 1990 "constituted an imperceptible 0.05% of the federal budget"[39]—although homeless people make up perhaps 1 percent of the population. Sudden changes or overly complex regulations keep local organizations from receiving available funding. Coordination between agencies remains weak; in some cases departments are actually in conflict.[40] The narrow definition of "homeless" adopted by HUD excludes the doubled-up from transitional or permanent housing programs. Most importantly, subsidized housing programs receive less funding each year.

Changes in the McKinney Act have also failed to remove some of the more onerous welfare regulations that restrict aid to homeless people. For instance, AFDC funds may not be used for transitional housing; procuring Food Stamps is still problematic for those without a permanent address. Many localities apparently still deny assistance to those who cannot prove a local residence, while outreach efforts for most programs have been minimal—although this seems to be slowly changing.[41]

Those with special problems among the homeless population have fared even worse. The General Accounting Office reports that McKinney funds have not been targeted at their congressionally mandated "special emphasis" groups of elderly and handicapped people, families, Native Americans, and veterans.[42] The Bush administration argued that mental health is a state responsibility, while SSI benefits for unemployable mentally disabled people remain below the poverty level.[43] Despite the administration's proclaimed emphasis on fighting substance abuse, appropriations for McKinney Act Drug and Alcohol Abuse projects have totaled less than a quarter of the funds applied for.[44] Until 1991, the documented conjunction of homelessness with the spread of AIDS was not even addressed by the federal government.[45]

The basic issue is one of spending priorities, most obvious in the contrast between federal spending on housing programs and spending on military programs (three cents for housing for each dollar for "defense"), or between the amount the federal government will spend on housing and the amount it will spend on rescuing the Savings and Loan industry (approximately fifteen cents for housing for every S&L dollar).[46] Similarly, the question of priorities arises when considering the revenue lost to the federal government through homeowner deductions (i.e., the ability of homeowners to deduct from their taxable income the amount paid for mortgage interest and property taxes): Not only is this sum five times greater than the amount spent by the federal government on low-income housing, but it is potential government revenue that instead remains overwhelmingly with upper-middle-class and upper-class households.[47]

The Bush administration's policy of cutting housing programs appeared to change with the passage of the 1990 National Affordable Housing Act (NAHA), generally considered the most significant housing legislation since at least 1974. The Act included some limited support for new construction and support for nonprofits and other forms of "social ownership." Other provisions linked social services to housing programs, decentralized funding and program decisions from HUD to state and local governments, and took steps to preserve housing and avert the threat of massive displacement through prepayment of mortgages on federally subsidized projects.

But many housing advocates argue that the bill falls short. Some of the programs that sound best—for instance the Homeownership Opportunity for People Everywhere (HOPE) program to encourage the purchase of public housing units by current tenants—may be unworkable in view of the gap between available funding and housing costs, but could ultimately undermine existing programs (such as public housing itself).[48] Similarly, while NAHA appears to have solved the prepayment crisis, these units will be saved only if a number of difficult contingencies all work out: a lack of market pressures from gentrification, substantial organization of tenants, adequate technical support, and adequate subsidies.[49] And funding remains far below pre-Reagan levels: Chester Hartman notes that if the current income–housing cost gap gets no worse, "it would take a full 100 years" to solve the housing crisis at current funding levels—"but it's not likely we'll even see that $3–4 billion in new money."[50]

Given this continuing lack of support from Washington, local efforts continue to try to manage homelessness as a public problem rather than eradicate it. Robert Fitch points out, for example, that then New York mayor Edward Koch's much ballyhooed project to get homeless mentally ill people off the streets (Project Help) in reality meant getting them off the streets of the Central Business District.[51] Local shelters, attempting to meet desperate needs on insufficient budgets, preserve social order by excluding those subgroups they feel unable to accommodate, particularly families, substance abusers, and those who are physically or mentally ill. Local governments, under pressure from business and civic groups, attempt to move homeless people out of their jurisdictions as the most cost-effective way of "dealing" with the problem.

Jonathan Kozol has written: "Enlightened policy is not persistent. It is spasmodic. For this reason, it does not prevail."[52] Enlightened policy does not prevail because the eradication of homelessness would require profound changes in our economic and political structures, in our ideology, and in our public planning. Such changes would reverse the privileging of those with resources over those without resources, a change those with resources—regardless of their beliefs about homelessness per se—are going to resist. Given their far greater resources on all levels, basic structural change will be difficult at best, unlikely at worst.

What Is to Be Done?

"Is homelessness the result of our capitalist system?" Hope and Young ask. "Of course it is," they answer.[53] But, as they further argue, the great variation in the extent of homelessness in different countries[54] suggests that even within a capitalist framework, homelessness may be largely prevented by intelligent and humane public policies. Constructing a blueprint for eradicating homelessness—which means eradicating the underlying problems that create homelessness—lies beyond the scope of this work. Recent works (cited in the endnotes) provide detailed discussions in each area addressed below; here I outline some of the more important measures that might be taken.

Policies can best be envisioned by looking separately at prevention, escape, and amelioration (that is, cushioning the lives of homeless people while they remain homeless), though, of course, there will be considerable overlap. I begin with two basic assumptions: Homeless people, by and large, are neither slackers nor crushed disaffiliates, and therefore will respond to programs that remove the structural barriers they face; and the aim is to prevent and eradicate homelessness rather than merely contain it.

PREVENTION

Housing

Creating enough affordable housing to meet actual (not market) need is the key to preventing homelessness.[55] The 1949 Housing Act set as a goal "a decent home and a suitable living environment" for all Americans; the 1968 Kaiser Commission recommended a ten-year national housing goal of building or rehabilitating 26 million units, including 6 million low- and moderate-income units. We have fallen far short of the latter goal, to say nothing of the former one. What would it take to house our nation?

Four principles should guide all housing policy: (1) discouraging displacement; (2) encouraging production; (3) ensuring affordability; and (4) ensuring availability. All of these will require substantial government intervention and activity. Many policy-makers may be expected to reject such an approach, if not on moral or ideological grounds, than on "practical" ones: The history of housing in the United States since World War II, they will argue, has been a triumph of the private market in which "America's middle class was made, in terms of housing, the envy and the bewilderment of the world."[56] Why would we want to entrust the task of providing housing to government, which will do it less efficiently and more expensively?

Three answers are readily available. First, even if this characterization of government were true, the private market is demonstrably no longer able to house even middle-class America at affordable prices. Second, whatever success the private market enjoyed in housing the middle class, it has never been able to house poor people adequately. Finally, the notion that housing in the United States is solely the product of the private market is a myth. The suburban explosion that is said to have bewildered the world would never have occurred on such a scale without the government's multi-billion-dollar highway construction and mortgage subsidy programs. Gentrification in the central cities is a current example of how private investment is aided and essentially made possible through public funding, whether this takes the form of tax breaks or direct outlays on infrastructure and other services. If the homeowner deduction is included as a housing subsidy—as indeed it should be—the percentage of U.S. households living in "subsidized housing" rises from the 5 percent who receive direct subsidies to more than 30 percent. A quarter of all mortgages are guaranteed by the Federal Housing Administration (FHA), the VA, or the FmHA. As Hope and Young argue, "virtually all American housing is subsidized in one way or another."[57] The real question is how we choose to use those subsidies.

Among the policies that should be implemented at the local or state level are developing early warning systems to detect buildings in danger of becoming uninhabitable and initiating an appropriate response; earmarking funds for land-banking and acquisition and rehabilitation of affordable housing or buildings suitable for developing affordable housing; enacting tenants' rights legislation that includes controls on rent, eviction, demolition, and conversion, plus emergency rent assistance (as well as emergency mortgage assistance for homeowners) to prevent displacement; reversing the policies of exclusionary zoning and displacement through gentrification by mandating inclusionary zoning in each locality and linking construction of upper-income housing or nonresidential development with construction of affordable housing.[58]

But the size of the problem, the limits on local resources, and local fears of becoming a magnet for low-income people all point to the importance of a substantial federal role. The very first steps should be to reauthorize all housing programs that create additional units or preserve existing affordable housing at funding levels equal in current dollars to 1980 funding levels,[59] to rescind all restrictive regulations passed since 1980 (such as the requirement that assisted tenants spend 30 percent rather than 25 percent of household income), and to require state enactment of tenant protections as a condition for receiving federal housing funds.

In the immediate short run, it may be desirable to pursue policies that reward private investment in building and maintaining affordable housing. Employer-assisted housing programs could be supported through liberalized corporate tax treatments of such benefits. A variety of local programs have provided below-market loans and outright grants to producers of affordable housing, or combined one-time subsidies with government-owned land, zoning density bonuses, or other inducements. The provision of the 1986 Tax Reform Act that used tax credits to encourage corporate funding of low-income housing has been very successful. These carrots should be balanced by a large stick: strict regulation of lenders to guarantee a supply of credit for builders and buyers of affordable housing.

In the long run, however, eradicating homelessness—or at least its housing component—will require reexamining both our ideological and our programmatic approaches to housing. On an ideological level, we need "a clarification of the status housing holds within our national imagination. Is it 'a gift'—a kindleness, a favor—or is it more properly perceived as an inalienable right?"[60] Clearly I see it as an inalienable right, a form of security a civilized nation should guarantee to all residents. Perhaps the best analogy is to education. We believe that universal free education is necessary both for the good of the individual and for the good of the society. Housing should be seen similarly. As with education, this view does not preclude private housing for those who desire and can afford better facilities than the norm, but it guarantees everyone a decent standard.

Ensuring this standard will require public policy to move away from programs that aim to augment demand through supplementing the housing incomes of poor people and toward programs that directly augment supply. This, in turn, requires moving toward the decommodification of housing. Our only significant current program of this type is public housing, a much-maligned program that, despite significant problems, remains of tremendous worth to many low-income people. Public housing should, for the first time, be realistically funded; adequate operating subsidies should be established and uninhabitable units renovated.

But, further, public policy, and particularly federal policy, must couple an enormous increase in funding for affordable housing with an emphasis on what housing activists call "third stream" housing: community-based, nonprofit, and produced according to policy goals rather than market profitability. The third stream replaces private ownership, production, and financing with social ownership, social production, and public financing.[61]

Although establishing a national right to housing may be a "utopian fantasy," as James Wright and Eleanor Weber suggest, local programs incorporating aspects of third stream housing are already operating in some cities.[62] And there is ample precedent for such plans at the national level: As Gilberbloom and Appelbaum point out, 400,000 units have been built for military personnel under conditions approximating third stream efforts.[63]

In contrast to the United States, which has the lowest percentage of directly subsidized units (about 5 percent) among industrialized nations, a significant portion of the housing created in Europe since World War II has been in the public/social sector. As a result, the populations of most Western European countries are better housed than that of the United States, and at lower cost.[64] The extent of decommodification in the various countries has ebbed and flowed with changes in disposable income, political currents, and leadership. Third stream housing has not proven so attractive to all citizens as to completely replace private housing, as some European proponents expected it would, but the baseline of a right to housing, combined with the creation of a significant amount of nonmarket housing, has never been seriously questioned in most European countries in the postwar period.

Funding such an ambitious program will be difficult; it serves no one's interest for housing advocates to argue otherwise. The Institute for Policy Studies proposals range from a low-cost option of $29 billion in the first year to a highest-cost option of $87 billion;[65] proposals by other proponents of decommodification also involve substantial sums. Yet this should not deter us. Not only is prevention of homelessness a more cost-effective strategy than dealing with its effects (see above), but a social housing program additionally promises to return money to the various levels of government through the creation of independent, self-sufficient taxpayers and increased sales and property taxes. Second, these policies are in the interests of the vast majority of Americans. Affordable housing has become an issue for working- and middle-class people as well as those living in poverty. Further, placed in context, these amounts are not as great as they first appear. Gilderbloom and Appelbaum's total proposed budget would cost $55 billion annually, a considerable amount, but less than is lost through the homeowner deduction (by their calculations); and, as they point out, it is one-fifth of the 1987 defense budget.[66]

Programs involving direct government aid will require substantial outlays to begin with, but some can be operated as revolving funds, such as a National Housing Trust Fund to provide downpayment assistance or finance rental projects. Others, however, will need continuing funding, and therefore new funding sources need to be realistically identified.

Some advocates have argued that a major source of funding already exists: The money going into shelters, they say, should instead be redirected into creating permanent housing.[67] Although public policy should certainly be moving from warehousing to prevention, eliminating shelters would cause such widespread suffering in the interim that it cannot be implemented in good conscience. A compromise suggested by the Manhattan Task Force seems more practical: New shelters should be built so that they can be used as permanent low-income housing in the future.[68]

It is also time to call on the suburbs and other localities that have excluded poor and homeless people through zoning and lack of services to take up their part of the burden. New "linkage" taxes are also a possibility: One in use in New Jersey provides subsidies to builders of affordable apartments under the Urban and Balanced Housing Finance Act through a small increase in taxes on luxury and commercial realty transactions.[69]

Two final funding sources have already been alluded to. The first is the defense budget: The end of the Cold War means little to our population if funds are not diverted into resolving our domestic problems. The second is the homeowner deduction, a glaring target that has drawn attention from both sides of the political spectrum. A total elimination of the deduction is not politically feasible, nor is it necessarily sound public policy, given that the deduction enables many households to own their own home.[70] But a rational tax policy would certainly eliminate it on second homes and would cap deductions at a level that equals the median deduction now taken by the median-income homeowner.[71] The National Housing Institute has suggested that replacing the deduction with a progressive tax credit for homeowners would not only increase federal revenue by approximately $5 billion, but would aid low- and moderate-income households in achieving home ownership.[72]

Welfare and social services

Homelessness can be prevented through the provision of housing, but many of those vulnerable to homelessness have other serious problems that must be addressed if they are to live productive lives. Reform of our welfare and social service systems is badly needed.[73]

As with housing, a humane public assistance system can be achieved only after a national consensus is reached on its goals. And, as with housing, the defense of a true safety net rests on the twin assumptions that such a goal is good for the individual and ultimately beneficial for the society as a whole. Poverty appears to depend on macro-economic trends, but the history of this country and others makes it clear that economic growth in itself will not eliminate poverty, though it may decrease it.[74] The creation of a welfare system that lifts all residents above the poverty line, of course, runs against the contention of conservatives and business ideologists that generous welfare benefits sap people of initiative and hurt productivity.[75] In fact, many Western European countries and Japan have more complete welfare systems than our own while achieving higher productivity.[76]

Welfare programs are currently funded at cynical levels—cynical because policy-makers are well aware that only a fraction of the eligible population is making use of those programs. Welfare reform should insure universal coverage instead of restricting each program to an arbitrarily chosen subgroup of the needy while emphasizing cost containment and the winnowing out of "cheats," a tiny minority in all welfare programs.[77]

But it is not enough to make public assistance *available*; as our examination of public assistance in Santa Barbara made clear, availability must be combined with *active outreach* by caseworkers. Waiting for people who are impoverished, in some cases confused, and in many cases ignorant or terrified of service agencies to approach those agencies and ask for help is absurd. Welfare policies should be proactive, emphasizing early intervention.[78] Targeting "at risk" individuals and families is, of course, far more difficult than responding to stated need when someone applies for welfare, yet an active outreach effort would help such targeting immensely.

To create an all-encompassing safety net, two even more radical changes are necessary. First, at the local service delivery level, all income support and social service programs need to be centralized and administered by a single administrative unit. In a single agency responsible for income maintenance and social services, whatever the particular need or problem of the client, caseworkers would *remain with their clients*. Program specialists might still be required to aid caseworkers in determining the best source of support or other help from available programs, but the essential tie must be between worker and client, not worker and program. Hope and Young have noted that "the most successful actions in reaching those who have fallen through the cracks seem to be the efforts of individual advocates working in the interstices of the system."[79] Under the form of organization I am advocating, caseworkers would be such individual advocates; dedicated, ideally, to ensuring contact with, not control over, their clients.

Such a reorganization at the local level can take place only if a second radical change is adopted: All income maintenance programs should be federally funded and monitored. Problems like political fragmentation, inequitable local standards, and pressures on local politicians to decrease local costs all require such a change.

Centralization, universal coverage, and early intervention could be simultaneously accomplished if individual programs were replaced by a universal aid program, such as a negative income tax,[80] which combines a universal form (everyone would file regardless of income level) with a way to pinpoint those who need aid the most (aid levels would be means-tested). Cost of administration would be low, since the machinery is already present through the Internal Revenue Service. Such a program would provide decent and equitable levels of aid while avoiding stigmitization.[81]

Two additional principles need to be embodied in all welfare reform. First, "family" integrity must be supported, in contrast, for example, with the policy in many states of denying AFDC to two-parent households. Second, welfare policies should encourage transition to employment by providing real financial incentives and a practical support system for those seeking work.[82] Most fundamentally, jobs must be available for those who complete training, whether they are encouraged in the private sector through local and federal tax incentives for employers or created by the federal government itself. (I return to this point in the section on "Employment" below.)

While most of the previous discussion has focused on material support, social service agencies need to go beyond dispensing financial aid to include other forms of intervention and support to *prevent* poverty, including family and job counseling. Thus the institution of a negative income tax (or some other universal income program) would not annul the need for the kind of local organization I am calling for. Aside from the aggressive outreach required to make sure that individuals take part in the negative income tax program, the need for nonmonetary social services will still remain.

Stabilizing vulnerable families
However "family" is defined—and I would argue that any mutually supportive household that calls itself a family should be considered one—the mutual care and responsibility that ties such a group together is

an invaluable asset for preventing homelessness.[83] It should be supported
and strengthened by proactive, rather than reactive, public policies. An
immediate, short-term advance would be to restore the funding of family
programs (including child nutrition, Medicaid, and AFDC in addition to
social services) to pre-1980 levels, and to include currently excluded
children (for instance, older children of poor families) in public assistance
programs such as Medicaid.[84]

Support should begin *before* family creation, in the form of guaranteed
prenatal and delivery care. Existing families in emotional or financial crisis
should have counseling and other supportive services available before the
crisis drives them apart. The expansion of social services I have described
above, particularly in regard to outreach, is of prime importance in this
early intervention stage. Families that have experienced break-up should
be protected against further disintegration. Here, too, the entitlement
policies mentioned above would help divorced or separated women who
find they cannot support their children—or even their child care costs—on
their income alone. The scandalously low percentage of fathers making
child support payments could be raised immediately if law enforcement
agencies were directed to treat nonpayment as a form of robbery.

One last area of family policy that could be strengthened immediately
involves preventing teenaged or unwanted pregnancies. It is clearly in the
interests of both individuals and society to deter children from having
children, yet we have made few inroads into and committed few resources
to the prevention of teen pregnancies. Increased outreach to teens,
education, and protection of the legal right to abortion are all required.

In the long run, the United States needs to move toward the kind of
integrated family policies found in many European countries. Europeans
benefit from family allowances to help cover the costs of child-rearing,
high-quality, state-run child-care centers, family planning services, and
maternity and health benefits. Such a system effectively strengthens
family units and prevents crises instead of responding to them when
vulnerable families begin to break apart.

Mental health

Public policies concerning mental health and homelessness are analogous to
those concerning public assistance: The key issues are coordination and
organization, levels of aid, availability of services, and outreach.[85] Deinstitutionalization has led to a vacuum of responsibility in which there is no
overall direction or coordination from the federal to the local level, although
it was clearly the intent of the 1963 Community Mental Health Centers Act
that the federal government would assume leadership and responsibility.
Thus the first step, and one immediately possible, is to clarify levels and
areas of responsibility within localities, between local, state, and national
governments, and between agencies at the national level.[86]

A crucial current flaw is a lack of continuity of care as individuals move from one type of assistance to another. Follow-up of discharged mental hospital patients, for example, is almost nonexistent.[87] There is clear evidence from Santa Barbara and elsewhere[88] that patients who are guided to entitlement or mental health agencies, in person or through specific referrals and appointments, are considerably more likely to make the transition to a new agency than those simply informed of the alteration in their bureaucratic status. The value of workers remaining with their clients despite program changes applies even more here than in welfare reform, given the enormous potential of the most difficult patients to be shunned by each individual program.

A coordinated system will be expensive. In the short run it appears that mental health care will continue to be provided by a mix of private and public agencies, and therefore the expansion of private insurance and Medicaid to cover community-based services is necessary until mental health costs are fully borne by a national health care program (see below). Public funding needs to be increased and redistributed from institutional care to the greater need (in terms of numbers) for community care. Further, the promise of deinstitutionalization must be kept by building the 60 percent of community mental health facilities that were mandated but not built.[89]

Crucially, funding must be available for basic survival needs as well as mental health treatment. Treatment is difficult, if not impossible, without providing some kind of stability for patients; indeed, it does little good to treat mental illnesses if people's basic survival needs are not met. Beyond this, mentally ill people, like other low-income people, may require help with job training, entry into entitlement programs, family counseling, and so forth.

As with welfare reform, sound mental health policy requires active outreach. Mental health practitioners must venture into the field, investing the time and care required to build a trusting relationship with people who have good reason (as well as behavioral tendencies in some cases) to distrust "the system." Even the pretreatment stage of gaining public assistance to stabilize a mentally ill person financially may require extensive outreach efforts.

Finally, a sound mental health program would encourage independence for those capable of independent living and provide appropriate confinement for those who are not. The legal restrictions surrounding involuntary confinement were a reasonable reaction to the arbitrary abridgement of the rights of mentally ill people in the past. Yet sometimes confinement is as necessary for the individual as it is for the society at large. More restrictive laws, however, must also establish the right to decent and humane conditions for those confined, including the ability to challenge confinement orders, and the right to local care, including outpatient commitment. For those who are gravely disabled, confinement must not become a form of warehousing that robs the patient of initiative or control. As a volunteer in a shelter told Hope and Young, "Nothing is worse on the human spirit than having nothing to do."[90]

Some of these recommendations can be implemented in the short run, but reassigning responsibility from the federal to the local level, assuring linkage between all levels, and committing caseworkers and medical personnel to clients rather than programs all require a complete reorganization of the mental health care delivery system. If we are to avoid the present two-tier system in which high-quality mental health care is available only to those with adequate private resources, a national health care program that fully funds mental (as well as physical) health care is a necessity. In short, as with housing, we must move in the direction of decommodifying mental health care.[91]

The thrust of public policy concerning substance abuse should be much the same: adequate funding, greater coordination, outreach and early intervention, linkage to housing and social services, tying workers to clients rather than programs, "endway" houses for chronic abusers, coverage for treatment through a national health care program, and decommodification of care.[92] Drug abuse and, perhaps to a lesser extent, alcoholism are spurred by the despair of life without a reasonable hope of attaining a meaningful job and a satisfactory standard of living. Drug commerce and violence are spawned by these conditions, coupled with the enormous sums of money commanded by drugs largely because of their illegality. The long-term eradication of substance abuse will require structural changes in life chances that involve housing, entitlements, and employment. In the meantime, given the obvious failure of prohibition to deter drug use (and its large role in promoting drug commerce and violence), public discussion on legalizing and regulating drugs should begin.

Health care
Although researchers have rarely spoken of illness as a major factor *causing* homelessness, it merits attention.[93] Illness can lead to poverty and homelessness through lost earnings or the costs of medical care. In recent years the rise of AIDS has led to increased homelessness among HIV-positive people when these causes are combined with discrimination in housing.

Protection against loss of earnings and medical costs is now possible only through private insurance coverage or government programs. Private insurance, however, is too expensive for most people if it is not part of employment benefits. As a result, "only one in five poor, non-elderly Americans and one in two of the near-poor are covered by private insurance."[94]

Since the mid-1960s the federal government has been the major provider of health care to poor people, particularly through Medicare, Medicaid, Community Mental Health Centers, and the Veterans Administration. Medicare, CMHCs and the VA, for all their problems, have worked well for many patients; Medicaid considerably less so. All health care for poor people faces three major problems: inflation in medical costs (considerably higher than inflation in general), the tendency of poor people to have more (and more severe) medical problems than the general population, and a chaotic, inefficient delivery system. But Medicaid has faced a series of other problems as well: exclusions, varying eligibility by state, and a general failure to reach much of its eligible population.

While short-term improvements are possible,[95] the lack of a national health care system is an embarrassment to a modern industrial nation, as well as a tragedy for its population. Despite conservative claims to the contrary, available data indicate that such systems are no more expensive than private delivery systems and are considerably more efficient.[96]

Employment

Many theorists (including homeless advocates) stress the importance of education and training in fighting unemployment.[97] Yet this emphasis masks a more fundamental problem, the occupational structure of the nation. As long as the number of jobs, and the number of jobs with decent wages, remains the same, education is of little importance on the macro level. It may change the players, but not the number who cannot find a job that pays decent wages. While literacy and other skills are clearly essential for employment, poverty and unemployment cannot be solved through education alone.[98] An employment strategy that will effectively prevent homelessness must ensure job placement as well, through government-created jobs, hiring incentives, or other inducements to the private sector. This is, of course, much easier when the economy is expanding than when it is stagnating or shrinking.

Further, structural supports are needed to ensure that people can take these jobs, chief among them the provision of high-quality, affordable day care and an adequate transportation system. Even if jobs and support are available, wages must be high enough to lift workers out of poverty.[99] Finally, care must be taken that tax policies do not penalize the working poor to such an extent that unemployment is a better option than employment.[100]

In the long run, however, unemployment can only be truly vanquished by a policy of full employment with the government as employer of last resort. While American economic wisdom deems full employment inflationary and political wisdom deems it unfeasible, Michael Harrington has mounted a convincing argument that a policy of full employment would strengthen the economy while benefiting almost everyone.[101] The change in global political alignments in the 1990s suggests that full employment should be accomplished in part by redirecting the military budget to job-intensive peacetime industries. The current status of homemakers as unpaid laborers—and the way in which that status might be changed in a full employment situation—should be the subject of public debate.

ESCAPE FROM HOMELESSNESS

The major components of public policies designed to facilitate escape from homelessness are already contained in policies to prevent homelessness: affordable housing, a complete safety net, an affordable and comprehensive mental health system, a full employment policy. Yet, as I have continually argued, the conditions of homeless life further complicate the problem of escape. The downward cycles of homelessness call for additional policies for those caught in the whirlpool.

Housing
Securing housing for homeless people will not solve all their problems, but it is certainly a necessary step. Aside from ending their literal homelessness—no small thing—housing provides the stability and sense of permanence needed to gather the energy and resources for the journey back to independence. While housing policy in the United States must aim to provide decent housing for all Americans, the immediate need is to provide it for those who lack housing entirely, and housing policy should therefore devote the bulk of its resources in the short run to providing housing specifically for homeless people.

The most obvious way to do this is to help homeless people to use existing resources, providing them with Section 8 vouchers, grants for first, last, and deposit, and priority for public housing units. But this kind of approach recreates the problems I have alluded to with regard to prevention: By failing to create additional amounts of a scarce resource, it only leads to further competition between those who are already homeless and those vulnerable to homelessness, perpetuating the game of musical chairs. When New York City recently fulfilled a 1988 promise to remove homeless families from welfare hotels by giving them priority in vacant public housing units, tenants complained that housing officials were augmenting the problems of public housing by "dumping" homeless families into their projects when overcrowded resident households should have priority.[102]

A compromise that balances speed and greater fairness is to concentrate first on repairing currently uninhabitable units in public housing or government-owned properties, as some localities are already doing.[103] At the same time, construction earmarked for currently homeless people should begin. Support for nonprofits that seek to create such housing should be integral to this effort, as is the current practice in New York City's Capital Budget Homeless Housing Program.

Mechanisms already available for creation and rehabilitation include mortgage bonds, low-income housing tax credits, tax-exempt bonds, and the enforcement of already mandated programs for use of government properties, including HUD homes and Title V of the McKinney Act. A few states have already set up programs to create housing specifically for homeless people, such as New York's Homeless Housing Assistance Program, but many local governments still rely largely on direct or indirect federal funding (e.g., Community Development Block Grants). The establishment of state or federal housing trust funds would greatly aid this emergency program.

Transitional housing is another need. Although many homeless people need little more than housing and a source of income, others have (or have developed) deeper problems that necessitate a transitional period in which their housing is combined with available social services.[104] Although such projects are currently supported by HUD Transitional Housing Grants, applications far exceed available funding.[105] Increased funding is required, and restrictions on the use of funds need to be relaxed. Victor Bach and Renee Steinhagen have proposed subsidies for developers of transitional housing that reverts to private (but low-income) permanent housing after a set period (ten years is their suggestion).[106]

Two principles should guide the development of permanent and transitional housing for homeless people: coordination of programs and funding in a single office, and community involvement. Housed people are apprehensive about homeless people. Their fears need to be assuaged through education, involvement, and plans that do not "dump" large numbers of "homeless units" in concentrated areas.

Public assistance

Homeless people, we have seen, are unlikely to be receiving the public assistance they are entitled to. The suggestions made under "Prevention" would go a long way toward changing this. Three of those suggestions are especially important to reach a particularly vulnerable population: centralization in a higher-level agency that coordinates and supercedes local offices and programs, worker–client ties that supersede worker–program ties, and aggressive outreach. Outreach must extend beyond shelters to the street level, the nooks and crannies where homeless people hide, and to doubled-up households, in ways that will not expose those hidden to the threat of eviction by bringing their presence to the attention of private landlords or public housing authorities.

Escape through the public assistance system would also be facilitated by relaxing proof-of-residency and documentation requirements, and restrictions on savings, a major barrier for Skidders on AFDC, for instance.

As argued above, transitional housing (as well as shelters) should be adequately served by social service workers. But, further, social services should extend for a period *after* permanent housing is obtained to avoid relapse into crisis and homelessness. In general, it is imperative that public assistance officials and lineworkers understand that even though homeless people share some problems with other disadvantaged people, their needs and situation are not identical. When designing and implementing assistance policies, officials need to be sensitive to homeless people's lack of a home base, outlaw lives, and fear of official notice of any kind.

Stabilizing vulnerable families

Supporting family stability is part of escape from homelessness as well as prevention. The same principles apply: Social service policies should never offer incentives for desertion or disintegration, and social services and material aid should remain in place for a period *after* permanent housing has been obtained, to prevent relapse into poverty and homelessness.

One area not previously covered is education. The McKinney Act's Education of Homeless Children/Youth program has been inadequately implemented. As advocates have pointed out, total funding needs to be increased to cover ancillary fees for transportation, textbooks, and tutoring.[107]

Mental health

Reaching the mentally ill homeless population is perhaps the most difficult aspect of facilitating escape. Often disorganized, suspicious, and highly mobile, they are not readily stabilized even when agencies make a great effort to do so. Outreach to such individuals is extremely hard work, and yet more necessary than for any other subgroup among the homeless population. In practical terms, this means that mental health workers will need to spend a great deal of time making contact with mentally ill homeless people on the latter's turf: in shelters, on the streets, in coffee shops and parks. Further, workers must expect even the initial stages of outreach to be extremely time-consuming. Essential to gaining trust and aiding mental health is the guarantee of housing. Aside from its psychic importance, stable housing provides the chance for an ongoing patient–doctor relationship. Especially given the loss of SRO units, homeless mentally ill people cannot be expected to procure housing as equal competitors in the housing market. Merely augmenting their resources through Section 8 vouchers and cash assistance will not solve their housing needs in competitive, low-vacancy areas where they are the last choice of landlords. Thus programs specifically aimed at creating housing for mentally ill people (such as the Section 202 program) and those which create or preserve the type of housing traditionally used by mentally ill people (e.g., SROs) must be protected and expanded.

Other essentials for stability include food, clothing, medical care, and social services. Assuring stability requires that mental health workers double as social workers, getting mentally ill clients enrolled as quickly as possible in public assistance programs such as SSI and SSDI. Again, worker–client ties are essential.

Stabilization will eventually allow many to lead independent or semi-independent lives, but we need to recognize that some percentage of mentally ill (or otherwise disabled) people will need *endway* rather than *halfway* housing, with social services available on a permanent basis. The HOPE proposals of the Bush administration appeared to take a first step in this direction in terms of housing, but actual appropriations in recent years have simultaneously reduced funding for nonhousing programs for homeless mentally ill people.

Finally, it is imperative that local, state, and federal programs be coordinated through one agency. Through both their own difficult characteristics and the reluctance of individual programs to deal with them, the homeless mentally ill population is least likely to be adequately served. Only by the direct assignment of responsibilities for clients from a single, unified agency can we reach those most afflicted with mental problems.

Homeless substance abusers may be considered in this context as a subgroup of the homeless mentally ill population, with similar recommendations: outreach on their home turfs, providing stable housing as a first step, ensuring receipt of assistance, and combining substance abuse treatment with other necessary social services, all within a coordinated system that ties clients to workers and delegates responsibility from a central agency. Substance abuse programs can hardly succeed when those completing a program have no stable housing to return to and therefore no nexus of support services.[108] Therefore, housing linked to postdetoxification services is imperative. At the federal level, the persistent underfunding of substance abuse programs for homeless people, at a time when crack and other hard drugs are apparently becoming more widespread in the larger cities, is not only tragic but obviously detrimental to the health and well-being of both housed and homeless people.

Health care

As Wright and Weber have shown,[109] illness among the homeless population is at near-epidemic levels, making employment impossible in many cases. The greatest preventive health measure would be to assure homeless people food, clothing, and housing; in the meantime, drastic steps are required to alter their present health profile, which resembles that of lower-class populations in some Third World countries.

The two overriding principles are prevention and outreach. As seen in Santa Barbara, homeless people are likely to avoid treatment until their medical condition becomes too serious to ignore, causing distress to themselves and, when they eventually seek treatment, additional costs to taxpayers. As with public assistance and mental health work, outreach must extend to where homeless people are, rather than wait for them to avail themselves of services. Treatment programs must allow easy entry without invasion of privacy or significant monetary costs. Further, health care will never be successful without stable housing that affords protection from the elements as well as the possibility of stable relationship with a health care professional. While expansion of programs like the McKinney Health Care for the Homeless program is essential, it is unlikely that quality health care will become widely available to homeless people until a national health care system is established.

Employment

To overcome the extra barriers that lack of a home base presents to homeless jobseekers, local job centers especially for homeless people are needed. Such centers would provide a home base, combining laundry, storage, and shower facilities with the "home" address and phone needed to find work. (Such a facility was first advocated by Nels Anderson in 1923.) Such centers should additionally be involved in job creation in conjunction with the private sector, and in linking employers with jobseekers, as has been done in a number of localities.[110]

The current federal emphasis on job training is critiqued above. It is instructive to note, however, that total funding for the McKinney Act–authorized Job Training Demonstration Program in its first year was $7.3 million. If half of the homeless population can work, this equaled perhaps $60 per potential enrollee.

AMELIORATION

If we are to end the chronic lack of housing, our approach to homelessness must emphasize prevention and escape. And yet the needs of those already homeless are profound and urgent, and the "long run" has very little meaning for those who are cold and hungry. Both morality and the social and fiscal costs of inaction mandate that we also help those who are now caught in the downward cycles of homelessness.[111]

The immediate goal must be to provide a roof over the head of every person who desires one—that is, to establish a national right to shelter as some cities and states have done on a local basis. Such a right would mandate that the federal government fund enough emergency beds to meet the need.

Some researchers have argued that shelters are best run by religious and other voluntary groups, while others prefer government-run shelters. But there is almost unanimous agreement at this point that the government ought to be responsible for much of the funding. Most shelter support at the federal level comes from the FEMA grants available under the McKinney Act, but two options available to the federal government are badly utilized now and should be implemented and expanded: the designation of underutilized properties and the possibility of issuing Section 8 vouchers to shelter providers (as proposed by a working group of the Department of Health and Human Services).

States, for the most part, have until recently rarely used their own money for funding shelters, relying instead on the various block grant programs (which significantly limit funding and use). While a little over half of the cities surveyed by the U.S. Conference of Mayors in 1989 reported using at least some state grants,[112] such funding should be available in every state and in increased amounts. But the enormous scope of the task suggests that an important role for the states is to put pressure on the federal government to take over the bulk of the funding.

Local governments, given their much smaller resources, were least likely to fund shelters directly in the past, although there were some notable exceptions;[113] recent years have seen a trend toward greater funding (often under the threat of lawsuits). Given the limits on their resources, however, their greatest contributions may come in other ways. In some areas they may be able to make buildings under their control (for instance, those seized for failure to pay property taxes) available as shelter sites. But as with the state governments, their primary role should be to exert pressure on the federal government for greater resources and to clear obstacles such as zoning, red tape delaying permits, or inappropriate health and safety regulations that delay or prevent shelter operations. (These changes should be mandated on a state level if there is not willing compliance at the local level.)

Despite increases, funding for shelters has failed to keep up with the continuing growth in homelessness.[114] If sufficient funding were available, what services and characteristics would it ensure in shelters? Kozol offers a lengthy list that may be summarized: They should be about as comfortable as college dormitories, and feature many of the same services.[115]

Critics will undoubtedly argue that providing such amenities will encourage homeless people to remain in the shelters, yet Kozol notes that average stays in New York City "model shelters" are typically *shorter* than those in poorer shelters.[116] The American Dream of a home of one's own, it appears, is a potent force in itself. But the greater point is that if stability is indeed essential for escape, we can hardly expect unsafe, unattractive shelters to help end homelessness.

Manageable shelters are small and personal. The lessons of public housing should be taken to heart when designing shelters: Large-scale shelters will rarely provide a sense of security and belonging, as the New York barracks shelter experience clearly shows. No shelter should separate families (of any composition) or supportive friends, as is currently the practice in shelters housing women and young children that exclude males over the age of ten.

Two last requirements lie outside the shelters themselves. Extensive outreach must assure all those who desire shelter that safe and decent lodging is available. And until sufficient permanent, affordable housing is available, no shelter can avoid "encouraging" people to remain permanent shelter residents.

For amelioration to be successful, services beyond housing must be furnished, either in conjunction with shelters or otherwise: social services, mental and physical health services, employment training and linkages, entitlements, and child care. Some cities have provided "hotlines" that direct homeless people to appropriate services, but centralizing would be still more efficient.

Providing shelters and other services will bring benefits beyond amelioration. As Wright and Weber have said of health care,[117] shelters and services can provide a wedge, a point of reentry into mainstream society for those who have been displaced and, in some cases, become more or less disaffiliated. Further, by providing a more stable existence in which basic survival needs are not in question, such aid creates the breathing space that homeless people need before they embark on the difficult journey back to independence.

Finally, all laws that criminalize homeless people on the basis of their status—notably "illegal sleeping" laws—need to be repealed. On the one hand, they make homeless people's lives much harder; on the other, they present mainstream society as a separate world that denies homeless people entrance and as an enemy to be avoided.

GENERAL STRATEGIES AND PRINCIPLES

The specifics of the detailed suggestions in this chapter are less important than the general principle underlying all of them: Programs to fight homelessness must be designed with specific *problems, not lifestyle groupings*, in mind. Doing so will not only focus programs but will help eliminate needless duplication of efforts. Of course, lifestyle groupings will still matter: There may be instances in which mixing groups is ill-advised because of mutual animosity or differences in what sorts of approaches can work. But programs must consciously address a particular level of the problem (prevention, amelioration, or escape) and specific issues within that level. A program aimed at helping "bag ladies," or even "Latino Families," for instance, will be less successful than one aimed at preventing homelessness through first/last/deposit loans to displaced households, or one facilitating escape through outreach to homeless people by entitlement program workers. This is not to say that creating a slew of uncoordinated programs is the way to attack homelessness.

Coordination is essential, but planners must understand that each component of a coordinated overall plan must tackle a defined problem within a defined stage of homelessness.

Some programs will affect all or nearly all subgroups among the homeless and potentially homeless population. Most obviously, prevention would be greatly aided by a governmental and societal commitment to building affordable housing. Many subgroups would be helped by such prevention strategies as guaranteeing full employment and indexing entitlement levels to the cost of living; by such amelioration strategies as health care outreach and increased funding of shelters; and by such escape strategies as centralization of entitlement programs. Other approaches will be aimed at problems that affect parts of the homeless population, such as low-cost, high visibility, substance abuse programs.

All programs should share certain characteristics. The first is easy entry and minimal screening at entry levels. Excessive regimentation drives away those who cherish their freedom, such as Wingnuts, Kids, and Street People. Excessive means tests scare away those who cherish their housed image, such as Skidders and Latino Families. High visibility and easy geographic access encourage homeless people of all subgroups to enter a program.

Second, services should be centralized. Time is precious to many homeless people, particularly those who are employed or have children. Programs that require people to travel all over town will not be used.

Third, shelter and food needs must be met before escape strategies are launched. Both materially and psychologically, emergency, transitional, and then permanent housing is essential for fighting homelessness.

Fourth, programs must convey a sense of stability; only if they are likely to be there tomorrow can they coax people into making that first, difficult step of using a service today. When the first Church shelter was opened in Santa Barbara, its availability was tied to weather conditions. Weeks later, virtually no one had used the shelter. Few were willing to walk fifteen blocks from the downtown area to find out whether the church had deemed it cold or rainy enough that night to warrant opening; nor were they willing to move belongings from their sleeping places to the church since good weather on the following night would mean having to move everything back again. When the church abandoned the weather test and merely announced that it would be open for a month (and then replaced by another church), the shelter filled immediately.

Fifth, programs that seek to encourage independence and renewed (or greater) affiliation must encourage a sense of efficacy. The desire to resume a mainstream life is strong among most of the homeless population, and it should be used and encouraged.[118]

Finally, there must be coordination between programs, both to avert duplication and to insure that eligible people are being reached. A single directing agency with ultimate responsibility for overseeing the various programs can ensure that programs mesh well with each other and the researched needs of homeless and potentially homeless people.

Shelter and service agency personnel find it challenging to provide help beyond the basic necessities to individuals and subgroups with extremely disparate characteristics and needs. Many providers argue that unattached children, families, those with mental illnesses, and so forth, ought to be separated. Yet how can such separation be reconciled with the importance of centralization and easy entry stressed here?

The National Coalition for the Homeless has advocated a three-tiered approach to the problem: a first stage of emergency shelters, open to anyone who needs help; a second stage of "transitional" housing, segregated by groups' differing needs, with auxiliary linkages to work, entitlement, counseling, and housing programs; and a third stage of "long-term" nonprofit homes, including appropriate in-house services for special populations such as those with chronic mental or physical disabilities.[119] Such a plan incorporates the desirable characteristics mentioned above: easy entry, centralization, meeting of basic needs, stability, and coordination. Massachusetts adopted this approach on a statewide basis in the early 1980s, and similar models are operated by organizations across the country.[120]

The three-tiered approach clearly presents some financial problems. Since specialized services in the second and third stages raise costs above the minimal services required in the first stage, there is always the danger that resources will run out before later stages are developed, thereby creating a permanent shelter population. Funding decisions often reflect a prior conceptual problem: The emphasis on providing emergency shelter can divert policy-makers from dealing with long-range solutions involving prevention and escape, as was often the case in the early 1980s. Whether deliberate or not, finding "the way to operate a better poorhouse"[121] clearly diverts public attention (and funding) from escape and prevention strategies. If permanent solutions are not simultaneously implemented, particularly the provision of affordable housing, temporary solutions become *de facto* long-term solutions, a problem increasingly encountered in low-vacancy areas. This problem is irresolvable without massive additional funding and a commitment to housing the nation. Two simultaneous challenges—temporary amelioration and long-term solutions—demand significant resources and claim our moral (as well as practical) attention.

The Role of the Federal Government

For a number of reasons, real progress in eradicating homelessness depends on leadership from the federal government. To begin with, despite the paucity of evidence in its favor, the magnet theory remains a potent obstacle to progress at the local level. Unless services are mandated and funded at the national level, each community is hampered in its own progressive efforts by the fear that generosity will bring ruin.[122]

Similarly, however cost estimates turn out, it is clear that local communities will not be willing or able to spend the lump sums needed to eradicate homelessness, even if convinced of an eventual financial payoff. Social service agencies dealing with every social problem have argued over the years: "Give us money now to prevent this problem and you will spend less in the future on the effects." But such initial outlays are invariably more than even the most receptive local government can afford. Homelessness is clearly a national problem with national causes. It is unreasonable and unrealistic to expect local communities to pick up the tab for a national problem. If we expected local communities to build Army bases with their own funds, Army bases would never be built. There is simply no substitute for federal funding.

Additionally, if the safety net of social services and mental health care is to be restructured in the ways I have outlined above, the initiative must come from the federal government. As the highest and wealthiest level of government, it is the only one that can structure compliance among lower levels. For the same reason, the change from exclusionary to inclusionary zoning at the local level can only be mandated at the state or federal level, and only the latter can guarantee equitable results by mandating it for all states.

Further, the federal government has great power to frame the terms of the public discussion about homelessness. Homeless advocates in Santa Barbara noted a marked change in the political atmosphere after the City and County committed themselves to social solutions through the creation of an activist Task Force on Homelessness, not because of any specific actions taken by the Task Force but because of the aura of legitimacy it conferred on their efforts. Public opinion polls examining social (as opposed to "blaming the victim") approaches to homelessness suggest that support for progressive solutions is available but "soft."[123] A simple declaration by the federal government of the right of all people to housing would have profound effects on public discourse that would extend far beyond the obvious legal advantages.[124]

Finally, the federal government should take the lead in combating homelessness because in many ways it *created* homelessness. The withdrawal of commitment to public and affordable housing and a national mental health system, the cutbacks in social services, and the rise in entitlement eligibility reviews helped trigger the explosion of homelessness in the United States. Some of these trends were already in motion when Ronald Reagan took office, but that administration greatly exacerbated them. The Bush administration neither restored the Reagan cuts nor demonstrated a clear intention to return the federal government to the role of leading provider of affordable housing.

The growth of homelessness is the most visible sign of the increasing split in the country between the haves and the have-nots,[125] a manifestation of the deterioration of the American Dream. We pride ourselves on being a middle-class nation that takes care of our poorer citizens; now our middle class is embattled and declining, while those living in poverty face a bleaker future every day. Faced with our personal difficulties, we can fall back on comforting notions of homeless people as different, separate, adrift "out there" in a world other than that of housed people. But this is an illusion: Homeless people are tied to the rest of us in the ways they live, the goals they seek, and the reasons they are homeless.

Homelessness is a political question. Studies continue to be useful, but programs will come only when the political forces supporting homeless people are strong enough to back up their studies with political muscle. This, in turn, requires coalitions with the many groups who are also adversely affected by current policies concerning housing, health, employment, welfare, and social services. The problem now is not primarily a lack of information. It is a lack of political will and political power.

Appendix

Researching
homelessness:
A case history

F or many years Kit Tremaine has begun her day with a walk along
the Santa Barbara beach with her dog, Max. In the winter of
1982–83, she noticed something new and distressing: Each morning, as she made her way along Cabrillo Boulevard, men would appear
along the beach and nearby bushes, rolling up bedding and otherwise
acting as if they had spent the night there. There had always been such
men around, to be sure, but there now seemed to be so many that she felt
something new was happening in her town. Tremaine, a long-time
supporter and funder of progressive causes, called a friend in the sociology
department at the local campus of the University of California to see about
having the phenomenon researched: "I didn't know what I wanted done,"
she later told me. "I just thought if we could get someone to study this, we
might have some idea of what to do about it."

Through Tremaine's contact at the sociology department, a friend of
mine, I was approached in December 1982 to draw up a research proposal.[1]
Despite my background in studying social problems and my experience as
a housing organizer, I had no special knowledge of homelessness and had
never even thought of it as a pressing social problem. Yet the chance to get
paid to work on something meaningful to people's lives seemed an
unexpected privilege. And so I drew up a proposal for a study, based on a
few quick interviews with social service workers with first-hand knowledge of the problem and some background reading. By January 1983 I was
funded and beginning a four-and-a-half-year odyssey.

Tremaine's desire that something be done defined my work from the
beginning as a piece of applied sociology. Aside from the form of research

173

to be created, the nature of my employment had further repercussions, for, as William Friendland and Robert Marotto point out, "the making of recommendations constitutes not only an important task of the applied research but, in fact, indicates that the researcher is embedded in distinctive social relationships."[2] Three relationships shaped my research agenda: relations with my sponsor, the political leaders of Santa Barbara, and the homeless people I would seek to gain information from and about. While Tremaine's desires were loosely stated and flexible (beyond a desire to see programmatic suggestions), and those of homeless people were not yet known to me, early discussions with political leaders made their research agenda fairly clear. They were interested in "nuts and bolts" questions: How many, who are they, why are they homeless, and what—if anything—should be done about it?

I began, of course, with some methodological predilections of my own. I had been very impressed with the anthropologically informed works of Elliot Liebow and James Spradley.[3] Following their leads, I wanted to present homeless life in a way that remained faithful to the experiences of homeless people themselves and minimized the presence of a narrator who assumes a higher objectivity than the characters in the story, at least until the subjective experience had been fully presented. Yet I also wanted to assume that narrator's role later in order to tie these separate subjective stories to underlying social roots.

My expectation—indeed, my aim—was not to quantify the dimensions of the problem or population but to explore the experience. In short, I wanted to draw a map of the terrain. Unfortunately, other people were more interested in a census.

Counting the Homeless Population

Government officials were (and are) interested in "head counts" for a number of reasons. Some did not believe that there were enough homeless people to merit the government's attention. (City officials, it will be recalled, at first believed the homeless population to be "thirty drunks on State Street.") Others wanted to know the relative proportions of subgroups in order to determine whether the problem was in fact "their" problem. If the homeless population turned out to be mainly people passing through (other localities' problem) or mentally ill (the county's or state's problem), City officials would not need to react. Many were inclined to believe that the great bulk of homeless people were "transients" and stressed that it would be necessary to show that local women and children—the deserving poor—were involved before government would act. Even officials who were sincerely interested in addressing the problem(s) felt that they needed to know more facts in order to do so.

As long ago as 1923, Nels Anderson observed that "any attempt to state the numbers of the different types of homeless men can be little more than a guess."[4] The counts made in the early 1980s were notoriously inaccurate, and the methods employed were obviously flawed.[5] Many researchers concluded that accurate total counts of local homeless populations were impossible or unfeasible, although recent years have seen many more attempts.[6] But even the most famous of these—the 1984 HUD report—was widely challenged, and its methodology convincingly critiqued.[7]

Given the difficulty, why bother? As the U.S. Conference of Mayors has argued, "The last thing the Congress, the Administration, mayors and community groups need to do is to argue about the size of the homeless population."[8] Yet the first question asked of any researcher by government officials is always, "How many?" The researcher knows that an accurate census is impossible, and that any estimate made will be duly noted as just an estimate but then nevertheless treated as fact. But there is no other choice if one wishes to deal with public officials.

And so it was that I found myself, in mid-1983, trying to get a handle on the number of homeless people in the Santa Barbara metropolitan area. I began by interviewing those whose daily lives made them experts on the homeless population: the police, service providers, and homeless people themselves. Homeless informants estimated that there were three to four hundred homeless people in the immediate downtown area alone. The estimates of police and service providers for the metropolitan area varied from two hundred to two thousand.[9]

Two conversations revealed to me that these estimates largely ignored two groups. First, Suzanne Riordan, founder of the Single Parent Alliance, pointed out that women living with their children in a variety of makeshift arrangements, including cars, campgrounds, and friends' homes, were not generally perceived to be homeless, yet "they're just as displaced as anyone else." When the SPA began a housing location service several months later, approximately seventy people a month were being placed, many of them from such situations.

Through Riordan, I met Guadalupe Kennedy, who later became my interviewer in the Spanish-speaking community. My interest in that population was activated by her comments in an interview:

KENNEDY: I am working now on a new program, employment and assistance for [displaced] people. . . .

Q: Do you have any idea in the whole Latino community how many homeless people there are? Is it possible to guess?

KENNEDY: With [my work at the] schools, and like the ones I know, it's about eight hundred at least.

Q: You think eight hundred in the Latino community alone?

KENNEDY:Yes, and I think that is very low, it could be more.

Subsequent interviews for the Homeless People's Project and analyses of the shelter populations indeed made it clear that homeless Latinos, families, and women were largely hidden and unlikely to come to the attention of most service providers.

The picture that emerged seemed to suggest that there were at least several hundred homeless people in the immediate downtown area, perhaps another seventy-five in the suburb of Isla Vista,[10] and some unknown hundreds hidden throughout the city and surrounding areas. These numbers were quite astounding, considering most estimates of the homeless population at that time. I then compared the Santa Barbara figures to estimates made elsewhere to see if they were reflective of what other cities were finding.[11] Extrapolating from these also led to a wide range of estimates, from two hundred to sixteen hundred homeless people in Santa Barbara City, and from three hundred to twenty-two hundred homeless people in the greater metropolitan area.

Finally, I attempted to use local entitlement program records. Since housing status was not recorded by any program, I was forced to rely on estimates from agency personnel. Combining their estimates of the percentage of homeless people using their programs with total use figures yielded estimates ranging between one thousand and almost ten thousand.[12] The lack of reliable indices of use by homeless people and quantitative data on the proportion of applicants who were repeaters or had moved on made these numbers extremely problematic.

These very loose estimates suggested a homeless population in the metropolitan area of somewhere between one thousand and two thousand individuals. Extrapolations from other cities' counts seemed to confirm this as a ballpark figure. In June 1983, in the first of a series of "Interim Reports," I presented these numbers to the local government and the community generally. Within several days, the homeless population of Santa Barbara was being routinely estimated at fifteen hundred, by the media and some political leaders, as well as by advocates. Rarely were methodological reservations expressed concerning these numbers, except by those wishing to argue that there was no homeless problem at all. The figure became the starting point for all subsequent debate.

The literature warns, and my experience confirms that it is virtually impossible to create an accurate census of the homeless population. The use made of my estimate further bothered me. First, the speed with which it was accepted as truth was clearly inappropriate, a case of seeking refuge from complex issues in "hard" data. Moreover, I felt that the widespread acceptance of the estimate had done little to change perceptions about homeless people. Housed people still spoke of homeless people in the same terms. Most disturbing was the persistent use of "transient" as synonymous with "homeless," a term carrying a load of implicit beliefs, including the voluntary nature of their homelessness and an aversion to work. Homeless people were now perceived to be a larger—but still homogeneous—group, defined by public perceptions formed by encounters with, or observation of, those most visible on the streets.

Hanging Out

My two immediate methodological concerns were to obtain data from a wider range of homeless people and to obtain it in a way that minimized distortions due to informants' fear of public identification, disruption of their lives, or power differentials between interviewer and interviewee. Although most recent data on homeless people have come from shelter surveys,[13] shelter residents are only a portion of the total homeless population, and an unrepresentative one at that. Further, the data obtained from people interviewed in a "captive environment" such as a shelter may be greatly affected by their perceived vulnerability.[14] "Street" surveys designed to interview on their own turf those not residing in shelters may expand diversity and reduce situational bias, but they still miss most of the hidden homeless population and remain highly vulnerable to validity problems.[15] There is little reason to believe that homeless people attempting to remain invisible will reply candidly to the questions of someone who has invaded their privacy and who may mean them no good. And, as with shelter surveys, the data are almost impossible to verify. Because of these methodological concerns and my desire to perceive homelessness as homeless people themselves perceive and experience it, I resolved instead to make extensive use of oral histories, to be collected from the widest range of homeless people in their "native" environments.

In my experience, informants (on any subject) are most forthcoming and truthful when they feel themselves to be in the position of teacher, with the researcher in the position of student.[16] At a minimum, the informant must feel that he or she is on equal footing with the researcher. This, of course, is impossible when interviews are conducted in settings such as shelters in which the informant is in some sense a captive but the interviewer is free to escape following the interview. (This holds even more when the interviewer has power over the interviewee, as when data are obtained from intake interviews conducted by shelter or service program staff members who control admission.) I sought to conduct interviews in which homeless people would become teachers, free to convey the reality of homelessness as they experienced it rather than as conceptualized by the investigator or constrained by (real or imagined) institutional pressures. I was hopeful that oral histories would reveal the diversity of homeless people, and do so in their own terms.

Oral history gathering, however, is suspect, as are all data based on self-reporting, insofar as there is no check on the validity of what interviewees say. Intuitively one might expect homeless informants to embellish, if not completely distort, their accounts in reaction to the vulnerability of their situations.[17] But most investigators agree with Howard Bahr and Kathleen Houts, who argued that "homeless men who consent to be interviewed are no more likely to be consciously untruthful in replying to interviewer questions than are members of most other disadvantaged populations."[18]

Since all researchers agree that establishing trust is essential to obtain truthful interviews,[19] I decided first simply to hang out with homeless people where I found them. In this way I hoped to become a familiar and trusted person, learn the terrain and vocabulary, and locate those homeless people ordinarily hidden from the view of housed people. In this, I was following the path pioneered by Bronislaw Malinowski and traveled by James Spradley, Elliot Liebow, Douglas Harper, Elijah Anderson, and others whose anthropologically influenced goal was to understand the "native's" vision of the world, to discover their order rather than creating one's own. In such a conception, detailing the fabric of daily life is the main job of the researcher, while establishing causes and consequences is a subsequent, and highly tentative, operation.[20]

I began this process by attending a meeting of homeless people I had heard about through my housing advocate contacts. It turned out to be the inaugural meeting of the Homeless People's Association. Although I had not identified myself at the meeting (as no one else had), I remained behind afterward with that hard core of people who always linger after a meeting, the people most interested in the effort at hand, and there I explained my project informally to a few of the homeless people who had led the meeting. Their reaction was uniformly positive, especially since I stressed my desire to collect the stories of homeless people in their own words. One homeless woman, Linda Shriver, invited me to the Fig Tree and the Jungle, where she promised to introduce me around.

As a result of that invitation, I began spending several hours a day with Shriver and the group that revolved around her and the camper in which she lived with several other people. I would ride my bicycle down to the areas of town where she usually parked (changing her location from time to time to avoid police notice and consequent ticketing or arrest for illegal camping), and within a few weeks I was familiar with the places to look: an old boat yard, an alley near where she worked in the mornings, the Fig Tree and other parks. Activities in and around the camper consisted mainly of endless talking and smoking cigarettes. People would come by to talk, or perhaps seek advice from Shriver, who was generally perceived as mother hen of the street people, stay for a while, leave to do errands, and return. Once I felt fairly comfortable with some of the people I met through Shriver, I would go to some of these locations on my own, particularly the Fig Tree, and just hang around. Doing so was easier when I already knew someone there, and this was generally the case. I always brought cigarettes, a valuable tool of entry since, most people rolled their own and store-bought cigarettes were a luxury.

I dressed casually, as I would in my own home, in jeans, a sweatshirt, and a down vest. My appearance was not jarringly different from that of the people I hung out with, but it is unlikely that anyone on the streets who was curious would have missed the signs of my housed status: I was recently showered, had no sleeping gear in my pack, wore relatively new and clean clothing. I made no pretense of being homeless, and was open to discussing what I was doing with anyone who wanted to know, although I rarely volunteered this information except to avoid subterfuge.

In the beginning, Shriver would often introduce me to a group of people by saying, "This guy's from the university, he wants to study you," an introduction whose directness made me cringe, although it was quite true. As I began going out on my own, I sometimes made my own introductions, but my general practice was to hang out with a group only when I saw someone there whom I already knew and who could provide me with an introduction to the others. Although I believed I followed this policy out of a courteous desire not to intrude, in retrospect it seems clear that I was also acting on the common aversion to making conversation with strangers who might reject me for my presumption.

Acceptance, in fact, was generally far easier than I had expected:[21]

FIELD NOTES, 4/4/83: Went down to the Fig Tree. Linda not there. Ran into Virginia Bruce, some other young guys. He introduced me, they accepted me without question, offered me the joint they were smoking. {Later it appeared that one guy, at least, didn't understand I wasn't a homeless person myself, which makes me think that introduction by an in-group member is enough, it doesn't matter what they actually say.}

As I became better known through my presence and advocacy work (described below), acceptance became still easier. However, there were always times when I did not recognize anyone at a location and then, for the conscious and unconscious reasons given above, I generally did not join a group.

During these early months of hanging out, I became acquainted with thirty or forty homeless people who used the Fig Tree as their social base, perhaps fifteen of whom I knew more than casually. Through them I learned of other areas where homeless people hung out, and I would occasionally go there. More often, however, I would meet one of my homeless acquaintances or friends at the Fig Tree and simply accompany him or her through the rounds of the day:

> FIELD NOTES, 5/18/83: Met Bret and Wendi. They were on their way to the 7–11 so I ditched my bike and walked with them. Walking to the store isn't a simple act in their world. There are constant stops to talk with other homeless people along the way, especially since we were going along the tracks, past the Fig Tree. . . .
> Hung around at the [Fig] Tree afterwards, Bret making sarcastic remarks about the people who were drinking. Bret says he never drinks, and said he'd gotten a few people to stop by getting them to stay sober for a few days and check out how ridiculous other people look when they're drunk.
> Walked them over to the Sally [the Salvation Army] where they were eating dinner.

My stance was almost always that of interested listener, rarely saying anything except when necessary to keep a conversation going. The people I hung out with were, by and large, eager to talk. As I had previously learned in collecting oral histories from elderly people, those who occupy low-status roles are as eager as anyone to be listened to: Having less chance to be heard (since who wants to listen to those who have no social standing?), they often jump at the chance to talk to a sympathetic ear.[22]

Thus a process of snowballing began. I gained entree to a group through people I knew, came to know others, and through them gained entree to new circles. At night I would return home and write up my field notes (taking notes while hanging out, I felt, was too obtrusive).

Along the way, I encountered problems typically noted by fieldwork texts.[23] The first is the researcher's emotional resistance to contact with those being researched, including, in my case, some initial fear and a persistent unwillingness to do away with some props of my housed life that distanced me from homeless people:

> FIELD NOTES, 5/20/83: I never go down [to the Fig Tree] as defenseless as they are. I always have some money, keys, a bike. This keeps me from knowing their life.
> FIELD NOTES, 6/19–20/85: It bothers me to find myself sleeping in the hosts' room [at the Church shelter] instead of in the big room with the men. It's an escape.

Second, John Lofland has noted that all social groups tend to have cliques, and identification with one clique may inhibit access to others.

This was true of my alliance with Linda Shriver. Although she was probably the most popular person on the street, she was sometimes out of favor, and some people never liked her:

FIELD NOTES, 3/28/83: Sat around with Linda down at the Tree. Other people come by, are friendly, but some regulars, especially the tougher men, don't sit with her. Am I making a mistake by tying myself too closely to her? She lectures them a lot, and she introduces me as someone who "has a grant to study you." Have to talk to her about that.

FIELD NOTES, 5/23/83: Drove down with Bret and Wendi to pick up Kerry. On the way, Bret rapped it down. He's pissed at Linda for turning over that gun last week, says people at the Fig Tree are looking different at her now. She'll never be in on the inside info again, he said. . . . This makes me nervous, for Linda and me. . . . It also makes me think again that I should cut loose more from Linda, or I'll end up only connecting with the goody-goodies.

There was also suspicion of my motives. At times this was hardly more than the awkwardness new acquaintances often feel, a low-level problem that could be overcome with little time and effort:

FIELD NOTES, 5/13/83: Went by Linda's trailer when I didn't see anyone I knew at the Fig Tree. Linda there, hanging out with Demo Dan and a few people I didn't know. Bret and Wendi came in, asked Linda for a cigarette, which she didn't have, so I gave them some, which loosened them up for the first time since I met them. . . . I felt like they were still feeling me out, but getting friendlier. Finally told them I'd like to interview them at some future date. At first they just said okay, no big deal, but after we talked about it for a while, they started to get excited, started telling me about all the old winos I should talk to, and that they'd line it up. A major breakthrough?

Those who were wounded in some way, especially those whose mental problems included paranoia, were more difficult to deal with. A few months after I met Jonathan and developed a cordial relationship that included some interaction about once a week, he began going out to the university and leaving notes in my mailbox, irate that I could not be reached during business hours to answer what he sardonically called his "impertinent questions."[24] In July 1983 he left this note:

Who are you serving?
Money, Power, Prestige?
The Homeless Peoples' Project?
SELF?

Several weeks later he left me a voluminous collection of notes he had taken over the last few months, with these questions: "Are you a Communist? Are you a Jew?"

Suspicion seemed most prevalent when other factors made homeless life more insecure. In April 1983 a new acting police chief took office. A few days later, forty people, mainly homeless, were arrested on State Street, the city's main drag, on minor offenses ranging from panhandling to possession of marijuana. It seemed to be the new chief's warning to street people that their hanging out on State Street would not be tolerated. Such a bust, huge by Santa Barbara standards, resulted in widespread fear of outsiders and "snitches":

> FIELD NOTES, 4/15/83: 40 people were busted on State Street in drug/vagrancy/alcohol arrests yesterday.... I was standing around with Sandman, Mayor Max, another guy or two, when a guy in a football jersey came up and stood next to me. He was real fried, had been drinking a couple of hours and now was doing acid. I kidded him a little about being still standing up. He seemed to get it, but it was hard to tell since he was so fried. He started talking about his background, German, Irish, and Swedish. Then he said, "You're a Jew." I agreed, asked him how he'd guessed. "Oh, I know," he said, still pretty light. He said that was cool that I was Jewish. He went on for a while about how it was cool, then switched to how Jews own all the pawn shops everywhere in the country, how he didn't like Jews, but I was okay. The he started shoving me and telling me he was going to kick my ass.
>
> Sandman, Max and a few others moved in right away, putting their bodies between us and telling him to cool off. He started getting more and more irate, screaming about Begin being a cocksucker, and why didn't I go back to where I came from, and he was a Vietnam Vet and trained to kill, with something dead inside, and if he ever saw my face again, he was gonna blow it off with a shotgun he had. The whole time he's weaving around, every so often trying to make a move toward me, but Sandman's staying in between us. At one point he started screaming that I was a snitch, but people just laughed at him and Sandman said, "Hey, I *know* the dude, man."

Fieldwork manuals also often warn against "seduction" into the group one is studying. I discuss below the extent to which my sympathies and personal ties to homeless people presented a danger to my "objectivity." But homeless life is so hard, so barren, so unattractive, that at no point did I want to become homeless. A far greater problem was dealing with the differences between my life and that of the homeless people I knew:

FIELD NOTES, 6/26–27/85: It's a very strange feeling to go to the Y[MCA], play hoops, take a jacuzzi, and then head to the shelter. A headfuck. But I feel like without these pleasures, I'd go crazy and burn out. Is this simply rationalization?

While I spent most of the first few months hanging out with those on the streets, I also wanted to make contact with the single parents represented by the SPA, the Latino families Guadalupe Kennedy had mentioned, and runaway/throwaway children. Hanging out with these groups was much more difficult. Unlike the street population, single parents and Latino families did not have hanging-out places where they socialized with other homeless people. In the case of the single parents, I tried to meet potential interviewees through SPA gatherings and snowball from there. I would arrive early and stay late at meetings and social events, trying to strike up relationships with those attending and then work out times I could hang out with them, usually in a neutral site such as a park or coffee shop, but occasionally on their daily rounds.

My friendship with the SPA organizer provided me with as strong a guarantee of legitimacy as an outsider could get. Further, since many of this group were formerly middle-class and still saw themselves as middle-class, there were fewer differences in clothes, speech, or other trappings to divide us. On the other hand, in part because of their background, they were much less willing to acknowledge their homeless situation publicly, even by allowing an investigator to accompany them in their daily routine. Although many agreed to be interviewed, a much higher proportion of the single parents declined than did those at the Fig Tree and similar street settings.

Latino Families presented a different problem. As a non-Spanish-speaker, I was unable to communicate with many, perhaps most, of those Kennedy indicated were homeless (usually first-generation immigrants rather than Chicanos). My solution was to hire Kennedy—a prominent Latina activist involved with many homeless families through her work with social service programs and political organizations—to find potential interviewees and collect their oral histories, using a set schedule of questions I provided.[25]

Unlike single parents and Latino Families, Kids do a great deal of hanging out, but my age (mid-thirties) hampered interaction with them. I spent some time with Kids who turned up at the Klein Bottle/Social Advocates for Youth shelter, with several counselors there, and with a local mother whose house had become a kind of meeting place for displaced Kids. But Kids remained one of the most difficult groups to obtain information about.

As time went on, I also began spending time at shelters, social service agencies, and other institutions where homeless people gathered. The

most important of these were the Church shelters, where I would
periodically serve as a volunteer proctor overnight. Being a proctor usually
involved little more than staying up half the night "on watch" and
preparing the morning meal sometime before sun-up. As a result, I had
hours to sit with shelter guests, a form of hanging out that was more
formally shaped (by the shelters' rules) than my other contacts, but mainly
consisted of the same two activities: talking and sharing/bumming/smok-
ing cigarettes. I also spent some time at the Salvation Army Hospitality
House shelter and the Catholic Social Service sandwich programs, though
these visits were far less frequent and I had no official position or easy
point of entree at either.

As I circulated through these various institutions, hung out, conducted
interviews, and involved myself in advocacy work, many homeless people
became familiar to me and I to them. An acquaintance begun at the
Church shelter might be renewed on the Catholic Social Service sandwich
line, and furthered by a chance meeting in a park. Relationships begun in
one setting would carry over into other settings, and my roles as acquaintance, researcher, and advocate flowed into one another:

> FIELD NOTES, 6/19–20/85 : Most of my evening [at the
> Church shelter] was spent listening to John, 35ish, biker-looking guy
> from Detroit, on a non-stop manic rap. . . . He *desperately* wants a job to
> get together enough money to get back to Detroit where his kids are
> with his aunt and grandmother. . . . Without promising him anything,
> I told him I'd try to see about job leads.
>
> 6/25/86 : Last night I ran into Linda at the Solstice parade,
> asked her about a job for Biker John. She gave me the card of
> someone who wanted gardening work done. Perfect!
>
> I found Biker John with Jose and a few other guys in Alameda Park
> today, lying in his bag. But he seemed stoned, and his reaction was
> much lower key than I'd expected or hoped. Just a hustler? Too
> crushed to get it together?
>
> 6/26–27/86 : On the way up to the shelter, I ran into Biker
> John, laying out his sleeping bag in the park. He was very hot, had
> been refused admittance to the shelter for being on drugs and/or
> alcohol, due, he said, to the screener not understanding he had a
> speech impediment. . . . He eventually mellowed out pretty much,
> said he wasn't going to hurt anyone, he was just pissed. I gave him
> some info on CSS and SA's traveler aid programs for getting a bus
> ticket back to Detroit. I didn't push him on the job lead I gave him
> yesterday, since he seemed enough under siege as it was.

A chance spin-off from an early interview resulted in another sort of
hanging out. In late 1984 I was contacted by the local Department of Social
Service and the Social Security Administration (SSA). One of my inter-

viewees—Rachel—had been determined by these offices to be incapable (because of her mental illness) of managing the money she was to receive in the form of SSI and SSA checks. When asked who could serve as a "protective payee" to administer her money, she had suggested me (a good indicator of her isolation). In light of my debt to her as an interviewee, and assured that not much work was involved, I agreed.

In fact, considerable work was involved. Rachel's life turned out to be a classic example of falling through the cracks, as she was handed from one program to the next without ever becoming permanently attached to a social worker who could help her navigate the system. As soon as I became her protective payee, those workers who had been looking out for her at all saw a chance to lighten their overcrowded case loads and ceased most contact with her.

As a result, I spent a fair amount of time over the next two years with Rachel. This turned out to be tremendously instructive: I learned first-hand what it is like to sit for hours in the Social Security Office, waiting for your turn to speak to a caseworker, only to be told that you lack the correct form and will have to go through the same process the following week; what it is like to journey on foot all over town collecting the documentation needed for this or that agency; what it is like to receive a notice of an appointment you must attend to protect your benefits—but to receive it two weeks after the appointment because you have no stable mailing address. I did not experience these things as Rachel did: I was, after all, going home to a secure residence no matter what the Social Security officials said or did. But through my dealings with Rachel, I was better able to know and understand the world of entitlements as seen by those who seek help.

My friendship (as it eventually became) with Rachel led me to other areas as well. Her periodic acting-out episodes—in which her behavior appeared threatening to those around her—often ended with her arrest, and so I became used to looking in the jail when she was missing. As a result, I became more familiar with the jail and justice system, and with a few of the homeless people who regularly revolve through it. Her periodic episodes also lent me a greater understanding of the plight of homeless mentally ill people: their lack of supports, their loneliness, their despair. At the same time, I became familiar with some of the programs and organizations they can turn to.

What was perhaps most important about my relationship with Rachel was its ongoing nature. Whereas I could hide from the suffering of the homeless people I interviewed when it became too intense, my relationship with Rachel could not be turned on and off so easily. When she disappeared, it was my responsibility to find her. When her SSI check did not arrive, I had to help her find out why. When she finally found a place to live, it was a great moment for me as well. But through good times and bad, our relationship would continue, as the problems and lives of homeless people continue out of sight and mind of the investigator who returns to his or her home each night.

Through the weeks, then months, then years of hanging out, I was involved in an acculturation experience similar to that of someone moving to a new country or a child growing up. As fieldwork manuals often point out, this new culture was learned by observation and then inference. Hanging out largely involved observation, while subsequent review of field notes and the process of shaping the interviews called for more inference. Observation and analysis, of course, were not discrete acts. As Lofland has argued, they occur simultaneously, but the mix of the two changes.[26] In my first few months observation predominated as I struggled to learn the language and terrain. By the last few months and into the writing of this work, analysis prevailed.

Hanging out offered the best opportunity for observation because I was usually free to sit back and observe rather than act. This was not the case with my participation in the homeless movement.

Movement Participation

My hanging out was almost immediately affected by an unforeseen development. In April 1983 a series of articles appeared in the local daily newspaper chronicling the lives of "the homeless," which, in effect, meant the homeless people whose lives revolve around the Fig Tree. As a result of those articles, an officer of a national corporation located in Santa Barbara contacted leaders of the HPA and promised to fund a homeless shelter if the City and/or County would guarantee funding for staff. At this point, the HPA membership was largely devoid of political skills and knowledge. Leaders (who a year later would be able to hold sophisticated discussions on strategies to deal with City Council subcommittees) were largely ignorant of such vital details of local political life as the difference between the City Council and the County Board of Supervisors.

Much as Liebow was recognized as a middle-class resource for a street corner man in trouble and asked to intercede in his judicial affairs,[27] HPA members recognized that my academic and organizing background might be useful in dealing with the City, the County, and the potential benefactor. I was therefore approached to go with them for an initial meeting with the potential donor, whom I will call Mr. Smith, in June 1983. Bound by ties of developing friendships and recognizing my reciprocal obligation to those helping me with my research, I agreed.

Smith, it turned out once we had met, had little idea of what he wanted and less interest in discussing the fine points of the sort of program he would fund. He simply gave the group a deadline of two months in which to draw up a program and secure City and/or County funding. When we met afterward, it was clear that no one in the HPA had any idea of how to proceed, since none had been involved in this sort of political effort before. Largely at my suggestion, a plan was made to organize a series of meetings of homeless people and outside experts (in areas of alcoholism, counseling, and so forth) to draw up a blueprint. At the same time, as the only member of the group with a personal relationship with any elected officials, I was asked to talk to City Council members about funding.

The series of meetings that followed solidified my position as "point person." Six years as a member of the core group of the local Tenants Union had taught me how to run a short and coherent meeting, and although the homeless group tried hard to minimize my role by rotating the chair and dividing up tasks, in the beginning I was the only one aware of such organizer's tricks as writing up notes to serve as minutes and agenda for the following meeting. This is not to say that I did most of the work in this period, or even that many of the ideas that came out of these first meetings were mine. Homeless people, of course, knew far better what they needed and wanted in a shelter. But the organizational role I played fixed me at the hub of the wheel.

Eventually this project broke down, abandoned by Smith in favor of another pet project and shunned by elected officials. But my role as a movement member had been established. My status was no longer simply one of interested outsider but, on at least levels, a member of the group of "homeless" activists.

As my research began to take form under my sponsor's instructions to produce program-oriented data, the HPA began to see uses for my data in their political efforts. Much of the second interim report on my work (presented in January 1984) touched on concerns of the HPA that had been conveyed to me informally over the months. A major section estimating the costs of arresting and jailing people for "illegal sleeping" had been shaped by the HPA's needs and expedited by members' volunteer help in recording and analyzing court and jail records. Although this report was intended to represent the views of many of those working on homelessness, it was quickly dubbed "the Rosenthal report" by City staff and publicly linked with the concurrent activist efforts of the HPA.

My role crystallized when Ms. Tremaine offered to send a leader of the HPA, a leader of the SPA, and me to the national convention of the National Coalition for the Homeless in October 1983. Although I went principally in order to pursue my research, political organizing far over-shadowed research in convention discussions. On the way back from Chicago, the three of us conferred on what we had learned. We agreed that virtually every group that had secured a shelter and other services for their homeless populations had done so through a political effort beginning with a coalition that drew together religious, political, activist, social service, and homeless sectors of the community. We agreed to try to do likewise, and the Santa Barbara Homeless Coalition was born a month later.

Movement participation was in a sense another kind of hanging out. In degree of structure it lay somewhere between the homeless population's own turf of the parks and streets and the shelters, where the rules made by social service and church volunteers informed, if they did not actually shape, interactions. In meetings and other activities, political imperatives framed our interactions. To some extent this meant that homeless people, largely newcomers to political work, were operating on my turf. But the degree to which the turf was mine or theirs depended on the kind of meeting, the homeless and housed composition of the group, the gradual growth of the political sophistication among the homeless activists, and the tasks at hand.

In the early days of the Homeless Coalition, housed people like me were central figures. My field notes were then likely to be filled with tasks I had to do rather than observations. As time went on, and in situations where homeless people had knowledge the housed people did not, there was more of a cooperative spirit. In other meetings, such as those of the HPA, I was strictly an observer with little or no role and influence, and thus more able to remain largely invisible and merely trace what was happening in my notes (as in the meeting between HPA members and the City Attorney recounted in Chapter 5).

Some meetings were devoid of homeless people, the domain of social service workers or interested housed citizens. In the latter case my role was usually that of Homeless Coalition representative and thus full-time advocate; in the former I usually acted strictly as an observer:

> FIELD NOTES, 10/7/85 : Monday morning homeless
> mentally ill information sharing meeting. Discussion of Julia flipping
> out {RR: evidence seems to be she gave herself a punk haircut}. {RR:
> Note how people use "nice" when they really mean "educated" in
> their comments about Julia.}
>   Discussion of Arnie Chase, vet, long time homeless. Lost weight.
> Drunk. "Babbling" about Vietnam War, cutting people's arms off.
> ... They'll try to intervene the next time he's in jail on a 647(f) [drunk
> in public], then send him to the new Vietnam Vets group. This guy
> hangs alone, hides in a bush. {RR: Is there a pattern to where the vets
> are hanging? They don't seem to have a group on the streets. Missing
> it?}

At the height of my activity, a typical week would include a meeting of the Homeless Coalition's Steering Committee, a meeting of the Coalition's Outreach Committee, a meeting of the HPA (as an observer), and perhaps meetings of the SPA, the Emergency Services Committee, the Monday Morning Homeless Mentally Ill meeting, and the Interfaith Task Force on Homelessness. These meetings gave me contact with homeless people in a variety of political situations and power arrangements. The homeless people who regularly attended the meetings were not, of course, "typical" of their subgroups, as the core group of any political movement differs from its constituency. But others would drop by for a meeting or two, or show up at a demonstration or City Council meeting, or otherwise interact the homeless and housed activists.

For four-and-a-half years, much of my time was spent hanging out with homeless people, working with them on political matters, or interviewing them. In short, I sought to become what Goffman calls one of "the wise," individuals who are not stigmatized themselves but who attain almost in-group status by their experiences with, and thus understanding of, the stigmatized group.[28] Two key questions naturally arise. The first is whether my presence changed the behavior of those I studied. Perhaps it did, occasionally, but I would argue that my constant presence eventually eradicated the tendency (and ability) of homeless people to alter their behavior around me. I became a part of the landscape of daily life.

The second question is whether my stance as an activist biased my work as researcher, whether the friendships I made interfered with my objectivity. I have tried to be sensitive to such dangers, but I assume that some bias does inform my work. I made a tradeoff: greater immersion into the world of homeless people in return for a possible loss of objectivity. This tradeoff afforded a number of advantages. I gained much deeper knowledge of the core group of activists, who often, in turn, provided leads to other research possibilities. In addition, the pressures of political work drew us closer as a group than homeless and housed people become in other situations and engendered a feeling of comradeship. The friends I made through these political efforts became my best informants, not simply in reporting their own lives, but in directing me to others (often more hidden) who might shed light on areas of homeless life I had not seen before.

Interviews

The heart of the HoPP data consists of the in-depth interviews I conducted with forty-four homeless people over a three-year period. Since one of my goals was to discover the diversity of the homeless population, I chose my subjects partly on the basis of the apparent novelty of their stories as I had come to understand them before the interview process began.[29] No claim, obviously, is made for the representativeness of those interviewed. My purpose in selecting interviewees was to discover the elements of that universe, not to simulate it. The result was akin to early attempts at mapmaking: I could not say precisely how large a landmass we were about to run into, but I would at least know that one existed and have some idea of its more important characteristics.

Interviewees were found in three ways. First, I simply approached some of those I had come to know through hanging out and my participation in the movement. In particular, interviews of those frequenting the Fig Tree or living at the Church shelter were arranged in this way. Of the twenty potential interviewees I located in this manner, only one declined to be interviewed.

Other homeless people were suggested or directed to me by homeless acquaintances. This was especially true of Skidders and Kids. Generally we set up an introductory meeting to discuss a possible interview, and, if both parties agreed, an interview was scheduled. I attempted to spend some time before the interview hanging out with the interviewee. Fifteen of the final interviews were arranged in this manner, with a rejection rate of about a third.

Gaps in my interviewee group were pointed out to me through the interview process. I routinely asked what groups of homeless people the interviewee saw in Santa Barbara. Those who pointed out missing subgroups were also usually able to advise me where I might find such people, or to line up the interviews themselves. I also attempted to make sure that I was not encapsulated in a closed subuniverse, and thus missing whole groups, by recruiting at places where homeless people were known or suspected to hang out but where I had not previously made contacts or spent time. This recruitment was done through small flyers, reading:

> Interviewers from the University of California at Santa Barbara are interested in talking to people who are homeless or having trouble finding housing in Santa Barbara. The interviews pay $5.00 and last between thirty minutes and an hour. If you would like to tell your story, please leave a message for Rob Rosenthal at. . . . All interviews are confidential. Your name will not be used in any connection with this study.

When interested parties called, arrangements were worked out as in the second case above. Ten interviews were arranged in this way.

Interviews took place wherever the interviewee suggested, usually in parks or coffee shops, but also in cars, shelters, and boxcars. Interviewees were guaranteed five dollars whether they answered all of the questions or not. The voluntary and confidential nature of the interview was stressed. A standard University of California Santa Barbara "Research Subjects'

Information Sheet" was handed out, restating the voluntary nature of participation, and signed or oral consent forms were used. Both explained their rights; the latter required only their spoken agreement to be interviewed and was the choice of virtually all interviewees. Interviews were usually conducted in one or two hour-long sessions.

Except for obtaining factual background information, my intention was to conduct what Lofland calls an "unstructured interview":

> Its object is not to elicit choices between alternative answers to pre-formed questions but, rather, to elicit from the interviewee what he considers to be important questions relative to a given topic, his descriptions of some situation being explored. Its object is to carry on a guided conversation.[30]

My original interview schedule bore the marks of the various forces shaping the research. It contained questions suggested by my interests in paths to homelessness and in social movements, questions common in the literature, and questions suggested by my interviews with potentially important political actors, including merchants, the police, and City officials. This schedule was constantly revised in light of the ongoing interview and hanging-out processes, including explicit critiques I occasionally requested from some of my closer homeless acquaintances.

The major topics covered were: coming to Santa Barbara, background, income and employment, daily activities, interfaces with housed society, friends, health, crime, political activity, and general opinions on the causes of and solutions to homelessness. At any time, however, I was willing to sacrifice complete coverage of my schedule to pursue a topic that appeared to be of interest. As suggested by Lofland, I adopted an attitude of sympathetic understanding and, as he predicted, occasionally had "to live with giving at least some people the impression that you agree with them when in fact you do not."[31]

What I was getting out of the interviews was very clear, but why anyone should agree to be interviewed was less obvious. The five-dollar fee (to equal what I was making per hour on my grant as I calculated it) was a consideration for the poorest. But their cooperation would do little directly to change their lives, a point I went to great lengths to make clear.

In fact, however, most found the interview to be a positive experience.[32] As Demo Dan said during his interview, "[You] do these interviews or whatever, and when it's all over you say, 'That's okay, I'm glad we got that out,' " It is hardly surprising that homeless people, so long denied a hearing by most housed people, were glad for the chance to tell their story to a representative of housed society, whatever their evaluations of his power to do anything about their situation.

Other Data Sets

The strengths of the HoPP data are their depth and scope. But I was also eager to look at other local data sets as a check on the information I was receiving. These included logs of telephone calls to the SPA and intake forms filled out at the Church shelters. Each produced a different snapshot of the homeless population than the one produced by the HoPP data. The SPA callers were parents, overwhelming mothers, often long-term housed residents of Santa Barbara. The Church guests, in contrast, were largely single men, newer arrivals in town, and those with the fewest local ties (hence their need to seek refuge in a shelter rather than with friends or family). The differences can be illustrated by a few sample comparisons.

Children: 7 percent of Church guests had children with them, compared with 43 percent of the HoPP group and all of the SPA call-ins (except those who were pregnant).

Employment: 15 percent of the Church guests were working, compared with 42 percent of the SPA callers and 52 percent of the HoPP group.

Public Assistance: 15 percent of the Church guests were receiving some form of public assistance other than Food Stamps, compared with a quarter of the HoPP group and over a third of the SPA callers.

Local Residence: 27 of 43 HoPP respondents (63 percent) had homes in Santa Barbara at some previous time, with the median length of Santa Barbara residency being 5.8 years; 50 percent of the SPA callers had lived in Santa Barbara more than 5 years, virtually all in a conventional residence at some point. Among the Church group, however, the median length of time in Santa Barbara was 2.2 years, and only 30 percent had lived in Santa Barbara longer than they had been homeless, indicating that they had once had a residence there.

Local Ties: While almost half of homeless SPA callers reported temporarily staying with relatives or friends (48 percent), only 7 percent of Church guests reported having spent the previous night with friends or family, while 62 percent reported having spent the previous night on the streets or in their cars. While only 65 percent of Church guests could give screeners a number or address of a friend or relative as an "emergency contact," 80 percent of HoPP group could name at least one friend or relative who would help them in time of need.

Despite (or perhaps because of) these differences, the data sets tended to complement each other. The HoPP data (both interviews and field observations) remain the heart of my work, but the availability of the SPA and Church data allowed me to have another (and sometimes a better) look at some of the hypotheses that the HoPP data suggested, and to fill some of the gaps in the original HoPP work. While analysis of the three sets together in no way assured that all homeless people in Santa Barbara had been "covered,"[33] the tendency of each data set to emphasize a different slice of the homeless population considerably strengthened my ability to map the terrain.

The Social Roots of Homelessness

Finally, I was mindful of my original intention to explore the underlying social roots of homelessness, recalling Harper's complaint that "all of these studies isolate the culture and study it as though it exists in a vacuum."[34] Some of the data necessary in this stage were readily available, especially on the state and national level. Obtaining local Santa Barbara information, however, proved far more difficult. For example, the exact number of board-and-care facilities housing mentally ill people was unavailable, while confidentiality precluded using the records of the Medically Indigent Adult program. Especially in the first few years, local officials saw no reason to spend time and effort aiding my research:

> FIELD NOTES, 3/17/83: Met today with [deleted], head of [deleted]. Doesn't know how many homeless people use the program.
> No idea of how to figure it out. Won't allow me to look at records due to confidentiality. Says staff doesn't have time to look for me. Referred to line workers.

As homelessness became a bigger political issue, however, and especially as some of my earlier estimates of service use (generated from lineworker estimates) began appearing in print, top officials became more interested in working out ways to get the information I was looking for. In those cases where information was simply not available, I was sometimes able to create the data—for example, gauging the disappearance of SRO units by looking at ten years of hotel listings in the telephone yellow pages and then tracing the records of each through the City's Building Department.

I have argued throughout this work that homelessness is basically the result of a game of musical chairs in which structural factors mandate that some people will be homeless. In the Introduction I said that I wanted "to describe the lives of particular homeless people without forgetting to ask why there are any homeless people at all." By combining intensive ethnographic work with structural data, I have attempted to cover both sides of that question.

A *Postscript on the Study of "Problem Populations"*

It is my hope that this study of homelessness will be of use to researchers looking at "problem populations" generally. First, the downward cycles of such populations need to be closely attended to: the ways in which becoming a member of a problem population leads to further problems that make escape difficult. I take it as axiomatic that prevention is generally a better strategy then attempting to aid escape at a later date.

Once one becomes a member of a problem population, the labeling process is a major hurdle. Even the term "problem population" is a construction from the point of view of those who wish to see daily life as given proceed as smoothly as possible, regardless of the power relations that frame that daily life. Some Transitory Workers, for instance, saw no problem in their situation: They merely wanted to be left alone to work and move on when they felt like it. But the ability of those with power to define their situation as a problem made them part of a group that needed to "be dealt with," whether the ensuing programs were intended to run them out of town or to find them jobs. Such power relations cannot be taken as given or divorced from "the problem" as it arises and takes form in public discourse. Construction of the problem is itself an ongoing struggle between the guardians of daily life and those who are labeled problems, as the HPA came to recognize.

I have also argued that labeling (as a transient, a flasher, a burglar, etc.) has individual consequences beyond the merely psychological. A person's ability to gather the resources to maintain membership within "straight" society wanes as the labeling process is applied to him or her. Treated as part of a problem population, they will begin to act as if that is true, not simply because they have bought into the labeling process, but because their material ability to act otherwise has been crippled. Once material conditions necessitate looking outside mainstream society to meet their needs, their world view will also begin to reflect those changes.

Related to this process is the question of classifications, the experts' version of labeling. Classifying people by their "end-state" is likely to lead to obfuscation. People with a common predicament do not necessarily have a common path, a common lifestyle, a common vision. In the case of homeless people, I have suggested that classifications by path, lifestyle, and barriers to escape are fruitful, and this may prove true for other groups as well. But the greater point is that we must look at the total life context of individual caught in a common predicament rather than ascribe similar attributes to people on all dimensions simply because they share attributes on one dimension.

This study will, I hope, encourage other researchers to make greater use of oral histories to get at the multi-dimensionality of people's lives.

When triangulated with participant observation and structural data, oral histories can be used with considerably less danger of "subjectivity" than most social scientists seem to fear.[35] They can be a door into the real world of the people we are concerned with. We minimize their worth, however, if we use them only to illustrate theories constructed in advance, rather than as the building blocks of theory itself.

As social scientists, we are used to going to the populations we are interested in to find answers to our questions. In that way, we remain locked within a world we have created ourselves, since the answers are, indeed, pegged to *our* questions. On the most basic level, the only experts on the daily experience of homelessness are homeless people themselves, as the people who best understand the world of the junkie, the flasher, the burglar—or the banker—are the people who live those lives and carry those labels. It is not enough to go to them for our answers. We must first go to them for our questions.[36]

Notes

Introduction: W h y   a r e   t h e y   h o m e l e s s ?

1. I address myself to housed people in this work; homeless people are already familiar with the tale I am telling.
2. Ben Reitman, quoted in Nels Anderson, *The Hobo* (Chicago, 1923), p. 87.
3. Anderson, *The Hobo*, p. 86. While stressing personal characteristics, Anderson also looked at the social roots of homelessness, including racial and national discrimination and the need of industrial capitalism for a mobile workforce.
4. See Theodore Caplow, Howard M. Bahr, and David Sternberg, "Homelessness," *International Encyclopedia of the Social Sciences* 6 (New York, 1968), pp. 494–499; Howard M. Bahr, *Skid Row* (New York, 1973). Summarizing the disaffiliation perspective is somewhat difficult, in part because its various strains were sometimes in disagreement, but largely because many of its central terms were vaguely defined. I return to this question in Chapter 4.
5. Carl I. Cohen and Jay Sokolovsky, *Old Men of the Bowery* (New York, 1989), p. 112. Some of the works employing this perspective are David J. Pittman and C. Wayne Gordon, *Revolving Door* (Glencoe, Ill., 1958); Robert Straus, "Alcohol and the Homeless Man," *Quarterly Journal of Studies on Alcohol* 7 (1946): 360–404; Boris M. Levinson, "Some Aspects of the Personality of the Native-Born White Homeless Man as Revealed by the Rorschach," *Psychiatric Quarterly Supplement* 32 (1958): 278–286; Alexandre Vexliard, "The Hobo: Myths and Realities," *Diogenes* 16 (1956): 59–67; Sara Harris, *Skid Row, U.S.A.* (Garden City, N.Y., 1956).
6. See Samuel Wallace, "The Road to Skid Row," *Social Problems* 16 (1968): 92–105; James F. Rooney, "Group Processes Among Skid Row Winos," *Quarterly Journal of Studies on Alcohol* 22 (1961): 444–460; Jack W. Peterson

and Milton A. Maxwell, "The Skid Row 'Wino,' " *Social Problems* 5 (1958): 308–316; Jacqueline P. Wiseman, *Stations of the Lost* (Englewood Cliffs, N.J., 1970).

7. See Bahr, *Skid Row*, p. 284.

8. See Theodore Caplow, "The Sociologist and the Homeless Man," in Howard M. Bahr, ed., *Disaffiliated Man* (Toronto, 1970), pp. 3–12.

9. Michael R. Sosin calls such a perspective the "deficit model" in "Homeless and Vulnerable Meal Program Users," *Social Problems* 39 (1992): 170–188. Among the works he places in this category are Stephen Crystal, Mervyn Goldstein, and Rosanne Levitt, *Chronic and Situation Dependence* (New York, 1982); Roger K. Farr, Paul Koegel, and Audrey Burnham, *A Study of Homelessness and Mental Health in the Skid Row Area of Los Angeles* (Los Angeles, 1986); Gary Morse, Nancy M. Shields, and Christina R. Hanneke, *Homeless People in St. Louis* (Jefferson City, Mo., 1985); Dee Roth, Jerry Bean, Nancy Lust, and Traian Saveanu, *Homelessness in Ohio* (Columbus, 1985).

10. For instance, after at least fifteen years of relative stability, use of the Santa Barbara Salvation Army's emergency shelter increased 500 percent between 1980 and 1985. In 1950 Donald Bogue estimated that there were a hundred thousand "homeless" people in the United States, most of whom were actually living in Single Room Occupancy (SRO) hotels on Skid Row: cited in Peter Rossi, *Down and Out in America* (Chicago, 1989), p. 29. Estimates of the national homeless population in the 1980s ran from about two hundred thousand to three million: (See U.S. Department of Housing and Urban Development, *A Report to the Secretary on the Homeless and Emergency Shelters* (Washington, D.C., 1984); U.S. Conference of Mayors [hereafter USCM], *Status Report on Hunger and Homelessness in America's Cities: 1989* (Washington, D.C., 1989); National Coalition for the Homeless [hereafter NCH], *Homelessness in the United States: Background and Federal Response* (New York, 1987); Martha R. Burt and Barbara E. Cohen, "Differences Among Homeless Single Women, Women with Children, and Single Men," *Social Problems* 36 (1989): 508–524.

11. See Charles Hoch and Robert A. Slayton, *New Homeless and Old* (Philadelphia, 1989); Marta Elliott and Laura J. Krivo, "Structural Determinants of Homelessness in the United States," *Social Problems* 38 (1991): 113–131; Richard Ropers, *The Invisible Homeless* (New York, 1988); Kim Hopper and Jill Hamberg, *The Making of America's Homeless* (New York, 1984); Mary Ellen Hombs and Mitch Snyder, *Homelessness in America* (Washington, D.C., 1983).

12. Given the lack of chairs, of course, those with severe personal problems are most likely to lose out in the competition for scarce resources. See Jim Baumohl, "Alcohol, Homelessness, and Public Policy," *Contemporary Drug Problems* 16 (1989): 281–300; Rossi, *Down and Out*, pp. 45–46.

13. For a discussion of the continued use of disaffiliation theory by some social scientists studying alcohol problems of homeless people, see Gerald R. Garrett, "Alcohol Problems and Homelessness," *Contemporary Drug Problems* 16 (1989): 301–332.

14. See Leona L. Bachrach, "Interpreting Research on the Homeless Mentally Ill," *Hospital and Community Psychiatry* 35 (1984): 914–916; Ellen L. Bassuk,

"The Homelessness Problem," *Scientific American* 251 (July 1984): 40–45; Rossi, *Down and Out;* James D. Wright, *Address Unknown* (New York, 1989).

15. See Peter Rossi, James D. Wright, Gene A. Fisher, and Georgianna Willis, "The Urban Homeless," *Science* 235 (1987): 1336–1341.

16. "To be without a home is to be cut off from the rest of the world:" Kai Erickson, "The Chronic Calamity," *The Nation* 246 (1988): 465.

17. Interviews with Spanish-speaking homeless people were collected by a research assistant, Guadalupe Kennedy, a well-known activist in the Santa Barbara Latino community, using the same interview schedule. See the Appendix for further discussion.

18. For discussions of why I (and other researchers) believe homeless people to be generally reliable informants (given certain conditions), see the Appendix, and Rob Rosenthal, "Straighter from the Source," *Urban Anthropology* 20 (Summer 1991): 109–126.

19. For a narrow definition see Rossi et al., "Urban Homeless"; David A. Snow, Susan G. Barker, and Leon Anderson, "Criminality and Homeless Men," *Social Problems* 36 (1989): 532–549. For a broader one, see James S. Cleghorn, "Residents Without Residences" (M.A. thesis, University of Alabama, 1983), reprinted, pp. 1104–1233, in U.S. Congress, Subcommittee on Housing and Community Development, *Homelessness in America—II* (Washington, D.C., 1984), p. 1139 (original emphasis).

20. Although I believe that a period of thirty days, typical for those living in rental units on a monthly lease, is a more appropriate cutoff point, I have shortened the time limit in recognition of the fact that many nearly homeless people live under weekly or bi-weekly arrangements in hotels and boarding homes. Even though they may (and often do) become homeless from time to time, while they live in such arrangements they are in a qualitatively different situation than those who are truly homeless. For alternative definitions see Roth et al., *Homelessness in Ohio;* Richard Ropers and Marjorie Robertson, *The Inner-City Homeless of Los Angeles* (Los Angeles, 1984); Rossi, *Down and Out.*

21. See Jonathan Kozol, *Rachel and Her Children* (New York, 1988); Cleghorn, "Residents Without Residences." For an overview of methodological issues in research on homelessness, including definitions, see Norweeta G. Millburn and Roderick J. Watts, "Methodological Issues in Research on the Homeless and the Homeless Mentally Ill," *International Journal of Mental Health* 14 (1985–86): 42–60.

Chapter 1: P a r a d i s e

1. The area looked at in this study, described as "greater Santa Barbara City" in census materials, lies within what is known as the "South County" or "South Coast," an area extending from Carpenteria (about eleven miles south of Santa Barbara City) through Isla Vista (twelve miles north), bordered by the ocean and, six miles away, the Santa Ynez Mountains. This area includes more than the city but far less than the county. When "greater Santa Barbara City" or "South Coast" data were not available, I generally

preferred to use city, rather than county, figures, since the city is characterized by "slow growth" restrictions, a high concentration of social service and
governmental agencies, and other factors that were typical of the metropolitan area I was looking at but not of the county as a whole.

2. The comparatively few manufacturing jobs tend to be in nonunion, low-
paying industries such as electronic equipment (31.8 percent of manufacturing jobs), with few jobs in the extensively unionized and higher-paying
industries such as primary and fabricated metals (3.6 percent). The average
weekly wage in manufacturing in the Santa Barbara–Santa Maria–Lompoc
area in 1985 was only 85 percent of the state average. The recent decision to
greatly expand oil drilling in Santa Barbara Channel, however, may fundamentally alter the local industrial structure and thus the workforce.

3. See Chapter 5 for additional discussion of these developments.

4. Consider this letter to the editor of the *Santa Barbara News-Press* in August
1983:

> The recent plea of the "Homeless People's Association" for aid in
> providing shelter here in our fair city reeks with gall. Why should these
> drifters and bums (from all parts of the country) be treated to free
> lodging so they can prey on the innocent citizenry and businesses here,
> to provide for their needed food, and their depraved appetites for
> drugs, liquor or tobacco? . . . The vast majority of the drifters are bums
> because they choose to be bums—to escape responsibility for their
> own support or that of their families. To have their own fling and do
> their own thing—regardless of who was hurt by it. To avoid the
> military, perhaps, but certainly to avoid *work* at all costs.

5. See Robert Fitch, "Put 'em Where We Ain't," *The Nation* 246 (1986):
466–469; Philip Kasinitz, "Gentrification and Homelessness," *Urban and
Social Change Review* 17 (1984): 9–14, Chester Hartman, Dennis Keating, and
Richard LeGates, with Steve Turner, *Displacement* (Berkeley, 1982).

6. Sar A. Levitan, *Programs in Aid of the Poor* (Baltimore, 1990), p. 91; NCH,
Pushed Out: America's Homeless, Thanksgiving, 1987 (Washington, D.C., 1987),
p. 76. For an argument that the effects of these cutbacks have been
exaggerated, see John J. DiIulio, Jr., "There but for Fortune," *New Republic*,
June 24, 1991, pp. 27–36.

7. This figure is rough guideline. As Michael Stone as argued, a concept of
"shelter poverty" that subtracts the costs of nonhousing necessities from
income is a better indicator of what is affordable for the individual
household. See Michael E. Stone, "Housing and the Economic Crisis," in
Chester Hartman, ed., *America's Housing Crisis* (Boston, 1983), pp. 101–106.

8. Cost of a new house: Boston All City Housing Organization, cited in
Hartman et al., *Displacement*, p. 13. Rent: John I. Gilderbloom and Richard
Appelbaum, *Rethinking Rental Housing* (Philadelphia, 1988), p. 21, based on
data from U.S. Department of Housing and Urban Development, *Annual
Housing Survey* (Washington, D.C., 1983). For more drastic estimates, see
USCM, *Housing Needs and Conditions in America's Cities* (Washington, D.C.,
1984); Jonathan Alter et al., "Homeless in America," *Newsweek*, January 2,
1984, pp. 20–29.

9. Institute for Policy Studies, Working Group on Housing, with Dick Cluster [hereafter IPS], *The Right to Housing* (Oakland, Calif., 1989), p. 6.

10. Center on Budget and Policy Priorities and the Low Income Housing Information Service, *A Place to Call Home* (Washington, D.C., 1989). Census figures for 1990 indicate that "almost half of all poor families in the U.S. pay more than 70% of their income on housing": *In Just Times* 2 (October 1991): 1.

11. Santa Barbara Rental Housing Task Force [hereafter SBRHTF], "Rental Housing Task Force Report to the City Council" (Santa Barbara, 1985).

12. Displacement: Chester Hartman, "A Radical Perspective on Housing Reform," in Hartman, ed., *America's Housing Crisis*, p. 21. Loss of units: National Housing Law Project, cited in Kim Hopper and Ellen Baxter, "The Experiment Continues," in U.S. Congress, Subcommittee on Housing and Community Development, *Homelessness in America—II* (Washington, D.C., 1984), p. 511.

13. Cynthia B. Green, "Housing Single Low-income Individuals" (paper prepared for the Conference on New York State Social Welfare Policy, New York, October 1–2, 1982), pp. 5–7, cited in U.S. General Accounting Office [hereafter GAO], *Homelessness* [GAO-HRD-85-40] (Washington, D.C., 1985), p. 25. For an argument that this in itself created the explosion in homelessness, see Charles Hoch and Robert A. Slayton, *New Homeless and Old* (Philadelphia, 1989).

14. Santa Barbara City, *Housing Element Addendum, 1985 Update* (Santa Barbara, 1986), p. 119.

15. See Barry Bluestone and Bennett Harrison, *The Deindustrialization of America* (New York, 1982); U.S. Department of Labor, "Displaced Workers, 1979–83" (Bureau of Labor Statistics, Bulletin No. 2240) (Washington, D.C., 1985); U.S. Congress, Committee on Government Operations, *The Federal Response to the Homeless Crisis* (99th Congress, 1st Session, House Report 99-47) (Washington, D.C., 1985), p. 5.

16. See Bennett Harrison and Barry Bluestone, *The Great U-Turn* (New York, 1988), pp. 63–64.

17. See Fitch, "Where We Ain't," p. 468; USCM, *The Growth of Hunger, Homelessness and Poverty in America's Cities in 1985* (Washington, D.C., 1986), pp. 24, 30.

18. USCM, *Human Services in Fiscal Year 1982* (Washington, D.C., 1982), pp. i, 10.

19. Statement of Mario M. Cuomo, Governor of New York, in U.S. Congress, *Homelessness in America—II*, p. 28.

20. See American Federation of State, County, and Municipal Employees [hereafter AFSCME], *The States, the People, and the Reagan Years* (Washington, D.C., 1984), pp. 1–3; GAO, *Homelessness*, pp. 23–24; California State Senate Office of Research, *Shelter and Services* (Sacramento, 1985); Tom Joe and Cheryl Rogers, *By the Few for the Few* (Lexington, Mass., 1985).

21. Mario Cuomo, *1933/1983—Never Again* (Washington, D.C., 1983), reprinted, pp. 353–443, in U.S. Congress, *Homelessness in America—II*, p. 396; U.S. Department of Housing and Urban Development, *A Report to the Secretary on*

the Homeless and Emergency Shelters (Washington, D.C., 1984). Deinstitution-alization was first proposed in the late 1940s and early 1950s by the burgeoning "community mental health movement," which argued that large, isolated state hospitals were inappropriate environments for treatment; it became theoretically possible in the mid-1950s with the development of medications that reduced affective psychotic behavior. But its adoption by most states and the federal government by the mid-1960s was largely motivated by the growing belief that such a policy would save tax dollars: see Joan Walsh, "The Homeless Mentally Ill," *In These Times* 9 (January 23–29, 1985): 22. Howard H. Goldman, Neal H. Adams, and Carl A. Traube, "Deinstitutionalization," *Hospital and Community Psychiatry* 34 (1983): 129–134, argue that much of the "savings" merely involved a shift from state and local to federal expenses in the form of increased Medicaid, Social Security, and Supplemental Security Income payments.

22. GAO, *Homelessness*, p. 20, citing data in National Institute of Mental Health, *History of the Community Mental Health Centers Program* (Rockville, Md., 1980); Jack Zusman, "The Philosophic Basis for a Community and Social Psychiatry," in Walter E. Barton and Charlotte J. Sanborn, eds., *An Assessment of the Community Mental Health Movement* (Lexington, Mass., 1977).

23. See Goldman et al., "Deinstitutionalization"; Leona L. Bachrach, "A Conceptual Approach to Deinstitutionalization," *Hospital and Community Psychiatry* 29 (1978): 573–578; Bert Pepper and Hilary Ryglewicz, "Testimony for the Neglected," *American Journal of Orthopsychiatry* 52 (1982): 388–392. About half a million people were refused voluntary hospitalization nationally from 1960 to 1980: Patricia Cayo Sexton, "The Life of the Homeless," *Dissent* 30 (1983): 79–84.

24. Leona L. Bachrach, "The Homeless Mentally Ill and Mental Health Services," in Richard H. Lamb, ed., *The Homeless Mentally Ill* (Washington, D.C., 1984), p. 16.

25. In the early days of deinstitutionalization, fewer than a fifth of discharged patients were said to be continuing in regular aftercare programs: R. W. Redick, "Referral of Discontinuations from Inpatient Services of State and County Mental Hospitals, United States, 1969," *Mental Health Statistical Note* No. 57 (Rockville, Md., 1971). As late as the early 1980s, it was estimated that over a third of those discharged received no aftercare referrals of any kind: John A. Talbott, *The Chronic Mentally Ill* (New York, 1982), cited in Marjorie Hope and James Young, "From Back Wards to Back Alleys," *Urban and Social Change Review* 17 (Summer 1984): 7.

26. Hope and Young, "Back Alleys," p. 10.

27. Corliss Porter, "Deinstitutionalization and the Homeless Mentally Ill" (address to the South Coast Coordinating Council, Santa Barbara, California, January 14, 1985); Santa Barbara City, "Senior Housing Study" (Santa Barbara, 1986), p. 5.

28. Arnie Schildhaus, internal memo to Patrick LaCommare, Santa Barbara County Mental Health Administrator, March 16, 1984.

29. Porter, "Deinstitutionalization."

30. South Coast Coordinating Council, "Stress and Distress" (Santa Barbara, 1982), p. 5.

31. Porter, "Deinstitutionalization."
32. See Mary Ellen Hombs and Mitch Snyder, *Homelessness in America* (Washington, D.C., 1983), p. 7.
33. U.S. Department of Commerce, Bureau of the Census [hereafter Bureau of the Census], *Statistical Abstract of the United States, 1986* (Washington, D.C., 1986), p. 56 (table 81).
34. Ibid., p. 62 (table 94).
35. Diana Pearce and Harriette McAdoo, *Women and Children* (Washington, D.C., 1981), p. 7.
36. Ruth Sidel, *Women and Children Last* (New York, 1986), p. 3.
37. Reported in the *New York Times*, June 3, 1983, p. D-15.
38. Klein Bottle/Social Advocates for Youth (internal records, 1982–84, Santa Barbara).
39. The ways in which Santa Barbara differs from other cities experiencing homelessness do not appear to present great drawbacks for this study. In the first place, Santa Barbara has a strong "no growth" ethic, based on a limited availability of water and the desire to prevent the city from becoming "another Los Angeles," as local residents say. While this ethic has doubtless restricted construction of housing, it is unlikely to have led to atypical levels of homelessness, since rents have increased as quickly in Sunbelt cities where growth is promoted as in those with growth restrictions: see Gilderbloom and Appelbaum, *Rethinking Rental Housing*, pp. 94–107.

Second, Santa Barbara enjoys a beautiful climate and a small town ambiance, which, it might be argued, have encouraged people who become homeless elsewhere to migrate to the area. Local shelter records and my own experiences, however, suggest that a majority of Santa Barbara's homeless population comes from the immediate tri-county area, and most are from the Western states. Nevertheless, in-migration generally has been heavy in Santa Barbara as elsewhere in California: Santa Barbara City, *Housing Element of the General Plan* (Santa Barbara, 1979). In this regard, Santa Barbara is perhaps more typical of Sunbelt cities than those in the Northeast and Midwest: (see James D. Wright and Eleanor Weber, *Homelessness and Health* (Washington, D.C., 1987), pp. 51–52.

Chapter 2: B e c o m i n g   h o m e l e s s

1. Some theorists might argue for irresponsibility as a likely trait of poor people, since they supposedly lack "future orientation": see, e.g., Edward C. Banfield, *The Unheavenly City Revisited* (Toronto, 1974). For arguments that implicitly or explicitly oppose this view, see Elliot Liebow, *Tally's Corner* (Boston, 1967); Hylan Lewis, "Culture, Class and the Behavior of Low Income Families" (paper presented at the National Conference on Social Welfare, New York City, May 29, 1962); Lillian B. Rubin, *Worlds of Pain* (New York, 1976). Mental illness, while disproportionately found—or at least diagnosed—among poor people (see August Hollingshead and Frederick Redlich, *Social Class and Mental Illness* [New York, 1958]; Ronald C. Kessler, "A Disaggregation of the Relationship Between Socioeconomic

Status and Psychological Distress," *American Sociological Review* 47 [1982]: 752–764), is found in all income levels, as is substance abuse.

2. Michael E. Stone, "Housing and the Dynamics of U.S. Capitalism," in Rachel G. Bratt, Chester Hartman, and Ann Meyerson, eds., *Critical Perspectives on Housing* (Philadelphia, 1986), p. 46.

3. This pattern of unemployment is not simply due to the lack of heavy industry in Santa Barbara. See Richard Ropers, *The Invisible Homeless* (New York, 1988), p. 44; Dan Salerno, Kim Hopper, and Ellen Baxter, *Hardship in the Heartland* (New York, 1984); USCM, *A Status Report on Homeless Families in America's Cities* (Washington, D.C., 1987).

4. For similar findings elsewhere see Peter Rossi, James D. Wright, Gene A. Fisher, and Georgianna Willis, "The Urban Homeless," *Science* 235 (1987): 1337; *Safety Network* (newsletter of the National Coalition for the Homeless; hereafter *SN*) 9 (January 1990): 1; James D. Wright, *Address Unknown* (New York, 1989), pp. 67–68. Among the few local studies that do not show a majority of homeless people to be high school graduates are Vijaya L. Melnick and Charles S. Williams, *Homelessness in the District of Columbia* (Washington, D.C., 1987); Carol Mowbray, Andrea Solarz, V. Sue Johnson, Emile Phillips-Smith, and Claudia J. Combs, *Mental Health and Homelessness in Detroit* (Lansing, Mich., 1986); Martha R. Burt and Barbara E. Cohen, "Differences Among Homeless Single Women, Women with Children, and Single Men," *Social Problems* 36 (1989): 508–524.

5. For evidence of the disporportionate impact of falling real wages and unemployment on workers aged thirty-five and less, see Richard A. Easterlin, "The New Age Structure of Poverty in America," *Population and Development Review* 13 (1987): 195–208. On primary and secondary labor markets see Michael Piore, "Jobs and Training," in Samuel H. Beer and Richard E. Barringer, eds., *The State and the Poor* (Cambridge, Mass., 1970), pp. 53–83. Piore cities racial discrimination as one major barrier to obtaining secure, well-paying jobs in what he calls the primary labor market, and the disproportionate percentage of people of color in poor and homeless populations provides powerful circumstantial evidence of this. See James D. Wright and Eleanor Weber, *Homelessness and Health* (Washington, D.C., 1987); USCM, *Homelessness in America's Cities* (Washington, D.C., 1984); Ropers, *Invisible Homeless*. Presumably sex discrimination operates as well.

6. For an argument that the first full-time job held by a person is a powerful determinant of future jobs, see Peter M. Blau and Otis Dudley Duncan, *The American Occupational Structure* (New York, 1967).

7. A similar situation holds in communities dominated by agriculture. See Sherry Lantz, "Homelessness and Low Income Housing in Chautauqua County, New York" (Dunkirk, N.Y., 1986); NCH, *Homelessness in the United States* (New York, 1987), p. 21.

8. For instance, only one of twenty-nine Church guests over the age of sixty was working, and that person held a part-time job; no Church guest who had serious physical or mental problems was working full-time; parents of children aged six or less were less than half as likely to be employed as those without children.

9. See Michael Harrington, *The New American Poverty* (New York, 1984), pp. 28,

114, 198. Michael R. Sosin, "Homeless and Vulnerable Meal Program Users," *Social Problems* 39 (1992): 170–188, argues that failure to receive entitlements largely determines which members of the vulnerable group actually become homeless.

10. I have generally separated Food Stamps from other entitlements. Because of their small total worth and mandated use for food, they are of little use in *preventing* or *escaping* homelessness, though often very important in coping with homeless life from day to day. The Church of the Month shelter program is described in Chapter 5.

11. Tom Joe and Cheryl Rogers, *By the Few for the Few* (Lexington, Mass., 1985), p. 27.

12. Nick Kotz, "The Politics of Hunger," *New Republic*, April 30, 1984, p. 23.

13. Estimates of the proportion of the homeless population with serious mental problems and/or previous hospitalizations for mental illness vary widely in local studies. Estimates of those who are mentally ill range from 11 to 84 percent: King County Housing and Community Development Division [hereafter King County], *Homelessness Revisited* (Seattle, 1986); Anthony Arce, Marilyn Tadlock, Michael Vergare, and Stuart Shapiro, "A Psychiatric Profile of Street People Admitted to an Emergency Shelter," *Hospital and Community Psychiatry* 34 (1983): 812–817. Pamela J. Fischer, "Estimating the Prevalence of Alcohol, Drug and Mental Health Problems in the Contemporary Homeless Population," *Contemporary Drug Problems* 16 (1989): 333–390, compares eighty local studies whose estimates average about 33 percent, compared with estimates of 10 to 20 percent of the housed population. Local estimates of past psychiatric hospitalization run from 13 to 34 percent and average about 23 percent: G. Lumsden, "Issues Associated with Housing the Indigent" (Dallas, 1983); Stephen Crystal, "Homeless Men and Homeless Women," *Urban and Social Change Review* 17 (Summer 1984): 2–6; see Fischer, "Estimating the Prevalence" for an overview. The acknowledged expert among Santa Barbara County welfare workers estimated in 1985 that there were between 230 and 525 homeless mentally ill people in south Santa Barbara County, or between 15 and 35 percent of an estimated 1,500 homeless people in the area. For interesting critiques of the methodological assumptions that underlie the higher estimates made by mental health experts, see Wright and Weber, *Homelessness and Health*, p. 91; David A. Snow, Susan G. Barker, and Leon Anderson, "On the Precariousness of Measuring Insanity in Insane Contexts," *Social Problems* 35 (1988): 192–196; and particularly Ropers, *Invisible Homeless*, pp. 146–168. For arguments that mental illness is not in itself a significant variable predicting homelessness, see Sosin, "Homeless and Vulnerable," p. 182; Ropers, *Invisible Homeless*, pp. 155–157.

14. Local estimates of the percentage of homeless people who are alcohol abusers vary from 2 to 86 percent (Fischer, "Estimating the Prevalence," p. 358), averaging about a third (Peter Rossi, *Down and Out in America* [Chicago, 1989], p. 156). Most studies, however, were conducted almost exclusively among *visible* populations, who by all accounts have significantly higher levels of substance abuse than hidden homeless groups (See Wright and Weber, *Homelessness and Health*, pp. 70, 74; and for hidden and visible

subgroups, Chapter 3 in this volume.) Local estimates for hard drug abusers vary from 1 to 70 percent (Fischer, "Estimating the Prevalence," p. 358). Alcoholism experts in Santa Barbara estimate that alcoholics account for "probably less than 10 percent of the [primarily homeless] people on lower State Street": Garland Bradley, Santa Barbara County Alcohol Program, *Keynotes* (newsletter of the Santa Barbara chapter of the National Council on Alcoholism), May 1983, p. 2.

Few researchers have been able to obtain reliable data regarding substance abuse *prior* to homelessness—that is, as a factor increasing vulnerability. The classic post–World War II work arguing that a substantial majority of Skid Row men had drinking problems prior to homelessness is Robert Straus, "Alcohol and the Homeless Man," *Quarterly Journal of Studies on Alcohol* 7 (1946): 360–404. For recent assertions (based on ongoing contact with homeless people) that substance abuse is more likely to be a result of homelessness than a primary cause, see Mary Ellen Hombs and Mitch Snyder, *Homelessness in America* (Washington, D.C., 1983); Jonathan Kozol, *Rachel and Her Children* (New York, 1988); Michael Perez, "Homelessness in Isla Vista" (pamphlet, Isla Vista, Calif., 1984); Ellen Baxter and Kim Hopper, "The New Mendicancy," *American Journal of Orthopsychiatry* 52 (1982): 393–408. More mixed recent discussions are Paul Koegel and M. Audrey Burnham, "Traditional and Nontraditional Alcoholics," *Alcohol Health and Research World* 11 (1987): 28–33; Marjorie Robertson, Paul Koegel, and Linda Ferguson, "Alcohol Use and Abuse Among Homeless Adolescents in Hollywood," *Contemporary Drug Problems* 16 (1989): 415–452. For a thorough survey of estimates of substance abuse using different methods and sites, see Fischer, "Estimating the Prevalence." Howard M. Bahr, *Skid Row* (New York, 1973), pp. 103, 289; Carl I. Cohen and Jay Sokolovsky, *Old Men of the Bowery* (New York, 1989), pp. 195–196; and Charles Hoch and Robert A. Slayton, *New Homeless and Old* (Philadelphia, 1989) contend that the image of Skid Row residents as largely alcoholic was (or remains) inaccurate.

15. See Samuel Wallace, *Skid Row as a Way of Life* (Totawa, N.J., 1965); Jacqueline P. Wiseman, *Stations of the Lost* (Englewood Cliffs, N.J., 1970); James F. Rooney, "Group Processes Among Skid Row Winos," *Quarterly Journal of Studies on Alcohol* 22 (1961): 444–460.

16. See Wright and Weber, *Homelessness and Health*, p. 100. Their data, however, are for those who are already homeless, somewhat clouding their application for purposes of establishing vulnerability.

17. See Kim Hopper, "Deviance and Dwelling Spaces," *Contemporary Drug Problems* (Fall 1989): 391–414.

18. See John Irwin, *The Jail* (Berkeley, 1985).

19. Wright, *Address Unknown*, p. 71.

20. See Howard H. Goldman, Neal H. Adams, and Carl A. Traube, "Deinstitutionalization," *Hospital and Community Psychiatry* 34 (1983): 129–134, particularly p. 132.

21. Leona L. Bachrach, "The Homeless Mentally Ill and Mental Health Services," in Richard H. Lamb, ed., *The Homeless Mentally Ill* (Washington, D.C., 1984), p. 34; Roger K. Farr, "Skid Row Mental Health Project" (New

County Achievement Award entry form, submitted January 29, 1982, to the National Association of Counties, Washington, D.C.). But see Roger K. Farr, Paul Koegel, and Audrey Burnham, *A Study of Homelessness and Mental Illness in the Skid Row Area of Los Angeles* (Los Angeles, 1986), p. 269, for a reconsideration minimizing this.

22. Plans: Marjorie Hope and James Young, *The Faces of Homelessness* (Lexington, Mass., 1986), p. 165. Discharge without plans: Dee Roth, Jerry Bean, Nancy Lust, and Traian Saveanu, *Homelessness in Ohio* (Columbus, 1985), p. 44; *SN* 8 (January 1989): 1. Resources: John A. Talbott, "The Chronic Mentally Ill," in John A. Talbott, ed., *The Chronic Mentally Ill* (New York, 1982), p. 372; Phyllis Solomon, Joseph M. Davis, Barry Gordon, Paula Fishbein, and Anne Mason, *The Aftercare Mosaic* (Cleveland, 1983), pp. 9–15; Hope and Young, *Faces of Homelessness*, p. 166. Structural impediments make it difficult for even the most conscientious of mental health facility workers to ensure that discharged patients will have financial resources available. Processing of applications for most assistance programs takes a minimum of several weeks, longer than the average stay in mental health facilities. Many local welfare agencies require proof of residency, an impossibility for those without the resources to obtain a residence immediately upon discharge.

23. See Stuart R. Schwartz, Stephen M. Goldfinger, Michael Ratener, and David L. Cutler, "The Young Adult Chronic Patient and the Care System," in David L. Cutler, ed., *Effective Aftercare for the 1980s* (San Francisco, 1983), pp. 23–35.

24. A substantial percentage of homeless people in Santa Barbara are recent arrivals, but the figure varies considerably among data sets: 62 percent of the Church shelter guests but only 7 percent of the HoPP interviewees had been in Santa Barbara less than two months; four-fifths of the Church group but only a third of the HoPP group and the SPA callers had lived in Santa Barbara less than a year.

25. Sometimes migration appears to be a move away from an undesirable situation rather than toward a desirable one. These cases typically involve mentally ill people or those experiencing emotional trauma from the breakup of a marriage or relationship. See Knoxville Coalition for the Homeless [hereafter Knoxville Coalition], *Homelessness in Knox County* (Knoxville, Ohio, 1986), p. 25; Bachrach, "Homeless Mentally Ill," p. 15; Richard H. Lamb, "Deinstitutionalization and the Homeless Mentally Ill," in Lamb, *Homeless Mentally Ill*, pp. 64–65.

26. For instance, only 6 percent of those Church guests who had lived in Santa Barbara less than two months were employed, compared with 28 percent of those in town for more than a year.

27. See Burt and Cohen, "Differences," p. 514, for striking evidence of this pattern of dependency among women who become homeless.

28. It has been estimated, for instance, that three-quarters of the women who go on AFDC do so "because their living relationship changes (a husband or lover leaves or dies)": Harrington, *New American Poverty*, pp. 193–194, based on an uncited study by Mary Jo Bane and David Ellwood.

29. Joe and Rogers, *By the Few for the Few*, p. 13. In absolute numbers, however, two-parent families still constitute the largest poverty group: Harrington,

New American Poverty, p. 46. Most families who become homeless are single-parent families, and it is nearly always the woman who keeps the children when couples split up. For example, 18 percent of the single women (including divorced, separated, etc.) at the Church shelters had children with them; another 6 percent were pregnant. Only one percent of the single men guests had children with them. This pattern has been found in local studies across the nation: See Research Atlanta, *The Impact of Homelessness on Atlanta* (Atlanta, 1984), p. 39; King County, *Homelessness Revisited;* Ellen L. Bassuk, Alison Lauriati, and Lenore Rubin, "Homeless Families," in The Boston Foundation, *Homelessness* (Boston, 1987), p. 21.

30. U.S. Department of Commerce, Bureau of the Census [hereafter Bureau of the Census], *Child Support 1981* (Washington, D.C., 1981), cited in Lenore J. Weitzman, *The Divorce Revolution* (New York, 1985), p. 283. The 1990 census figures are only marginally higher: *Hunger Action Forum* (October 1990), pp. 1–2. Thirty percent of responding SPA callers, three of the eleven single mothers in the HoPP group, and none of the single mothers in the Church shelters reported receiving child support.

31. The prevalence of mate abuse reported is highly dependent on the methodology used in a study and the subpopulations surveyed; estimates range from 16 to 45 percent of homeless women surveyed. Cf. King County, *Homelessness Revisited,* pp. 18–19; Emergency Services Network of Alameda County [hereafter Alameda County], *Homelessness in Alameda County* (Oakland, Calif., 1987), pp. 3, 7; Lantz, "Chautauqua County"; William K. Woods and Edward Lee Burdell, *Homelessness in Cincinnati* (Cincinnati, 1987), pp. 35–42. Victims of domestic violence were unquestionably under-represented in the Santa Barbara data sets, largely because such women rarely used the Church shelters and I could not conduct interviews with those in the battered women's shelter.

32. Diana Pearce and Harriette McAdoo, *Women and Children* (Washington, D.C., 1981), p. 17. Weitzman's study in California indicates that in the first year after a divorce, the standard of living of the average ex-wife declined 73 percent, while her ex-husband's standard of living rose 42 percent: *Divorce Revolution*, p. 323.

33. Some theorists emphasize child abuse as a major factor in both vulnerability and precipitating incidents (see Virginia Price, "Runaways and Homeless Street Youth," in Boston Foundation, *Homelessness*, pp. 24–28); I had insufficient data to assess this as a problem in Santa Barbara.

34. *Address Unknown*, p. xi.

35. See Marjorie Robertson, "Homeless Veterans," in Richard D. Bingham, Roy E. Green, and Sammis B. White, eds., *The Homeless in Contemporary Society* (Newbury Park, Calif., 1987), pp. 64–81, for an overview. Thirty-one of 64 respondents at the only Santa Barbara Church shelter where veteran status was systematically noted said they were veterans. This included 57 percent of the responding men, nearly twice the proportion of male veterans in the county. Veterans staying at the Church shelters were twice as likely to be from the Vietnam era as housed veterans.

Ray, homeless almost continuously since his discharge from the army, says, "The thirteen years I was in the service, I was homeless. I never had a barracks hall, I was always on the move." But the high number of Vietnam-era vets suggests that the effects of being a soldier in an unpopular war may well have left some veterans too psychologically wounded to reestablish a conventional life. See Robert Reich and Lloyd Siegel, "The Emergence of the Bowery as a Psychiatric Dumping Grounds," *Psychiatric Quarterly* 50 (1978): 191–201; Sosin, "Homeless and Vulnerable," p. 182, challenges this view. The disproportionate showing of Vietnam-era veterans may also be in part an artifact of the age of homeless people generally, found in virtually all studies to average under forty. Other linkages may exist between military services and homelessness. Perhaps current recruitment advertising that stresses learning job skills is misleading, and the armed forces do not, in fact, teach skills that can be used in civilian life. Perhaps military service is tied to other variables that create vulnerability to homelessness, such as lower-class or unstable family backgrounds, so that military service is an intervening or contributing factor, rather than the main causal variable.

36. United States: Mario Cuomo, *1933/1983—Never Again* (Washington, D.C., 1983), reprinted in U.S. Congress, Subcommittee on Housing and Community Development, *Homelessness in America—II* (Washington, D.C., 1984), p. 366. Santa Barbara: Santa Barbara Hunger Coalition, "Survey of Hunger in Santa Barbara, 1984" (Santa Barbara, 1984) p. 2, based on U.S. Census and Annual Planning Information figures.

37. Rossi et al., "Urban Homeless," p. 1340. While my definition of homelessness would increase this figure, the point remains the same.

38. *Rachel and Her Children*, pp. 12–13.

39. Even within the boundaries set by those macro trends, individual characteristics alone do not determine who is unemployed. Where local areas are stagnating or declining economically, workers will be laid off. Where local economies are seasonal, workers will be laid off seasonally. The structural nature of layoffs tied to macro-economic trends is supported by the employment histories of homeless people. While some have never worked steadily, many studies note that significant portions of local homeless populations are *recently* unemployed: USCM, *Homelessness in America's Cities*, p. 6; Salerno et al., *Hardship in the Heartland*, p. 133; Hope and Young, *Faces of Homelessness*. Even natural factors such as weather may play a role: Shelter workers in Santa Barbara in 1990 reported increasing numbers of Latino families requesting emergency shelter as a result of a prolonged drought that led to widespread layoffs among gardeners and agricultural workers.

40. Unemployment is much more likely to be the precipitating incident for men than women: Eric Goplerud, *Homelessness in Fairfax County* (Fairfax, Va., 1987), p. 20; King County, *Homelessness Revisited*, p. 19; Burt and Cohen, "Differences," p. 514; Rossi, *Down and Out*, p. 187. This fact reflects the persistence of the sexual division of labor.

41. I once asked Michael, another teenager I met at the Klein Bottle Youth Shelter, about the relative proportion of runaways and throwaways on the street. His reply: "When you get to that, what's the difference? You know, does it really matter who makes the last move, you or your parents? . . .

Whenever your parents are pissed off, you're pissed off, and then it just starts."

42. Santa Barbara Rental Housing Task Force [hereafter SBRHTF], "Rental Housing Task Force Report to the City Council" (Santa Barbara, 1985). Again, this is not simply the case in Paradise. Nationally the proportion of renters paying more than 25–30 percent of their income on rent rose from 32 percent in 1950 to 51 percent in 1984: Harrington, *New American Poverty*, p. 118. In just three years (1978 to 1980), households making $3,000 or less saw their rents rise 30 percent: Salerno et al., *Hardship in the Heartland*, p. 7. In colder climates, rises in utility rates may also lead to significant increases in housing expenses: See NCH, *Mid-America in Crisis* (New York, 1986), pp. 2, 23–24.

43. In a novel twist, William Tucker proposes that it is not rising rents, but the attempt to deal with them through rent control, that is the single greatest cause of homelessness: "Where Do the Homeless Come From?" *National Review*, September 25, 1987, pp. 32–43; see the *Wall Street Journal's* editorial of August 23, 1985, for a similar argument. For a thorough critique of Tucker's thesis, see Richard P. Appelbaum, John Atlas, and Peter Dreier, "Scapegoating Rent Control," *Shelterforce* 12 (March/April 1990): 10–12.

44. The Church data, for instance, suggest that about 15 percent of the Church shelter guests became homeless upon migration to Santa Barbara.

45. Although undocumented workers are most prevalent in border cities, they can be found throughout the country. See Goplerud, *Homelessness in Fairfax County*, p. 33.

46. Of course, when a mother becomes homeless, her children do as well. The Children's Defense Fund has estimated that one in five children in the United States, *excluding* runaways, is or will become homeless at some time: *Children in Poverty* (Washington, D.C., 1985), cited in Melnick and Williams, *Homelessness in the District of Columbia*, p. 37.

47. I exclude military discharge here because the paths from discharge to homelessness described by veterans generally do not show the kind of steep decline that characterizes an event as truly "precipitating." Instead there is typically a period following discharge in which the vet is plainly troubled, setting the groundwork for a more jarring precipitating event.

48. On release as a precipitating incident, see Wright and Weber, *Homelessness and Health*, p. 60; Knoxville Coalition, *Homelessness in Knox County*, p. 26. On previous hospitalization, see Mowbray et al., *Mental Health*, p. 14; "Tracking the Homeless," *Focus* 10 (1987–88): 14; Greg Owen, Judy Williams, and June Heineman, *Emergency Shelter Survey* (St. Paul, 1986), tables 114, 116. Unfortunately, few studies differentiate between hospital stays that predate and postdate the beginning of homelessness.

49. Hope and Young, *Faces of Homelessness*, p. 93.

50. Cf. Lamb, "Deinstitutionalization"; Bachrach, "Homeless Mentally Ill."

51. Sara Colm reports that when 14,000 people were shifted from General Assistance to a new employment program in Los Angeles, "we lost 5,000 people in the shuffle, many of them ending up on the streets": in U.S. Congress, *Homelessness in America—II*, p. 239.

52. Manhattan Borough President's Task Force on Housing for Homeless

Families [hereafter Manhattan Task Force], *A Shelter Is Not a Home* (New York, 1984), p. 34. See also USCM, *Status Report*, p. ii; Wright and Weber, *Health and Homelessness*, p. 60; Greg Owen, Paul Mattessich, and Judy Williams, *Results of the Twin City Survey of Emergency Shelter Residents* (St. Paul, 1987); King County, *Homelessness Revisited*, p. 18. Changes in regulations, as well as terminations, may increase vulnerability and serve as precipitating events. For example, HUD's decision in the early 1970s to raise the amount low-income families receiving rent supplements must contribute to their rent (from 25 percent to 30 percent of income) rendered millions of previously eligible tenants unable to receive federal housing assistance: President's Commission on Housing, *Report of the President's Commission on Housing* (Washington, D.C., 1982), cited in NCH, *Pushed Out: America's Homeless, Thanksgiving, 1987* (Washington, D.C., 1987), p. 80.

53. Cutbacks: Harrington, *New American Poverty*, p. 110; and see Joe and Rogers, *By the Few for the Few*, for a detailed account of this process. CETA: NCH, *Malign Neglect* (New York, 1986), p. 20.

54. SBRHTF, "Task Force Report," p. 24. Recently, for example, "aggressive sweeps by the Immigration and Naturalization Service have caused some landlords to evict undocumented workers": Ronald W. Powell, "Tempest Intensifies in De la Guerra Triangle," *Santa Barbara News-Press*, June 3, 1990, p. A1.

55. *New York Times*, February 24, 1983, cited in Salerno et al., *Hardship in the Heartland*, p. 24; cf. Henry B. Schechter, "Closing the Gap Between Need and Provision," *Society* 21 (1984): 40–47, for a larger estimated jump. All twenty-nine cities surveyed by the U.S. Conference of Mayors in 1987 reported more families temporarily living with friends or family members, "and every city considers these families to be at high risk of becoming homeless in the near future" (USCM, "Status Report," p. ii). For example, staggering estimates of overcrowding in New York are reported in Coalition for the Homeless, Community Action for Legal Services, and New York Lawyers for the Public Interest, *Stemming the Tide of Displacement* (New York, 1986), p. iii; Victor Bach and Renee Steinhagen, *Alternatives to the Welfare Hotel* (New York, 1987), p. 8; Manhattan Task Force, *A Shelter Is Not a Home*, p. 48; and John Tierney, "Using Housing Projects for Welfare Angers Tenants," *New York Times*, June 28, 1990, p. B6. NCH, *Rural Homelessness in America* (New York, 1987), p. 8, gives similarly startling figures for rural areas.

56. For instance, studies indicate that over half of the homeless families coming to New York shelters do so from a doubled-up situation: Manhattan Task Force, *A Shelter Is Not a Home*, p. 48.

57. Santa Barbara City, *Housing Element Addendum, 1985 Update* (Santa Barbara, 1986), p. 6.

58. See John R. Logan and Harvey L. Molotch, *Urban Fortunes* (Berkeley, 1987), pp. 111–124. The precariousness of people of color in particular has been intensified by government housing policies. Minorities were largely excluded from the post–World War II suburban boom by racist restrictions in the FHA and VA mortgage insurance programs, while urban renewal was aptly referred to as "Negro removal" by civil rights activists in the 1960s.

See Citizens Commission on Civil Rights, "The Federal Government and Equal Housing Opportunity," reprinted in Bratt et al., *Critical Perspectives on Housing*, pp. 296–324; Dennis R. Judd, *The Politics of American Cities* (Glenview, Ill., 1988), pp. 255–300.

59. Ben Reitman, *Sister of the Road* (New York, 1937), pp. 16–17.

60. Even the grossest estimates of voluntary homelessness, represented by the category "transient" in a number of studies, rarely reach 20 percent (and actual choice may account for only a fraction of these). See Salerno et al., *Hardship in the Heartland*, p. 123; Woods and Burdell, *Homelessness in Cincinnati*, p. 36.

61. Owen, Mattessich, and Williams report that even emergency shelter residents expected to be in conventional housing shortly, with about two-thirds predicting they would be without housing for less than three months: *Results of the Twin City Survey*, p. 9. The few studies reporting contrary results appear to have been conducted in shelters catering to long-term homeless people: Cf. Merv Goldstein, Stephen Levine, and Robert Lipkins, *Characteristics of Shelter Users* (New York, 1986).

62. Chester Hartman, "Introduction," in Chester Hartman, ed., *America's Housing Crisis* (Washington, D.C., 1985), p. 21.

63. International Association of Psychosocial Rehabilitation Services [hereafter IAPRS], *Homeless Mentally Ill and Backlash Against Deinstitutionalization* (McClean, Va., 1985), p. 4.

64. Steven P. Segal, Jim Baumohl, and Elise Johnson, "Falling Through the Cracks," *Social Problems* 24 (1977): 387. See also Wiseman, *Stations of the Lost*.

65. Rossi et al., "Urban Homeless," p. 1340; see Focus, "Tracking the Homeless," for supporting data.

66. Wright, *Address Unknown*, p. 88.

67. SBRHTF, "Task Force Report," p. 26.

68. Bureau of the Census, *Detailed Housing Characteristics, California* [HC80-1-B6] (Washington, D.C., 1983), pp. 41, 53.

69. See Focus, "Tracking the Homeless," p. 23; Leanne G. Rivlin, "A New Look at the Homeless," *Social Policy* 16 (Spring 1986): 5; Manhattan Task Force, *A Shelter Is Not a Home*, p. 34. A significant exception is found in Goldstein et al., *Characteristics of Shelter Users*, p. 24.

70. Vacancy rates: Santa Barbara Hunger Coalition, "Survey of Hunger," p. 10; Santa Barbara City, *Housing Element Addendum, 1985 Update*, p. 6. Total residential units grew less than three-quarters as quickly as population during this period, and this gap was most pronounced for rentals. Although an average of 153 rental units (including available single-family houses) were built annually in the early 1980s, about half that number were lost each year through demolitions and conversions. This phenomenon is typical of many areas: see USCM, *Homelessness in America's Cities*, p. 16; NCH, *Pushed Out*, p. 9; Kozol, *Rachel and Her Children*, p. 202; Hope and Young, *Faces of Homelessness*, p. 98.

71. Rent inflation at SROs has also been significant. By the mid-1980s, fewer than ninety units were available citywide for less than $300 a month. Rossi et al. similarly note that in Chicago in 1985, the average SRO room cost $27

more than the average monthly income of the homeless people they interviewed: "Urban Homeless," p. 1337.

72. Santa Barbara Housing Authority, "Annual Report, 1982" (Santa Barbara, 1982).

73. Interview with Robert Foreman, director of Santa Barbara Public Housing, November 3, 1985.

74. "Task Force Report," appendix B.

75. The Reagan administration's sole contribution to affordable housing policy, nevertheless, was to expand a voucher program similar to the Section 8 program, but allowing tenants to supplement payments to equal market rents. The massive cutbacks in federal housing programs also crippled the construction of additional public housing. Budget authority for additional commitments dropped from $6.5 billion in 1980 to $2.2 billion in 1989; 6,947 new units were added in 1989, compared with 36,727 in 1980: Sar A. Levitan, *Programs in Aid of the Poor* (Baltimore, 1990), pp. 92–93. Although the number of public housing units brought "on line" peaked during the Reagan years through completion of projects already in the pipeline (see Tucker, "Where Do the Homeless Come From?"; John J. DiIulio, Jr., "There But for Fortune," *New Republic*, June 24, 1991, pp. 27–36), the relevant comparison is with need, not past levels.

76. *The Continued Growth of Hunger, Homelessness, and Poverty in America's Cities: 1986* (Washington, D.C., 1986).

77. Manhattan Task Force, *A Shelter Is Not a Home*, p. 41. As housing units built with government loans become twenty years old, owners can be freed from their legal obligation to serve lower-income groups by "prepaying" the remainder of their mortgages. Owners who leave the program are free to convert their properties to serve wealthier tenants and condominium buyers. As many as 900,000 affordable units may be in imminent danger of prepayment by the year 2000: Teresa Riordan, "Housekeeping at HUD," *Common Cause Magazine*, March/April 1987, pp. 26–31. Although the 1990 National Affordable Housing Act provided mechanisms for reducing the number of threatened units, it remains to be seen how many of these will actually be saved. See National Housing Law Project, "Summary of the 'Low-Income Housing Preservation and Resident Homeownership Act of 1990' " (Berkeley, 1990); *Shutting the Back Door* 10 (November 1990), 12 (May 1991); Barry Zigas, *Briefing Materials on the National Affordable Housing Act of 1990* (Washington, D.C., 1991). Although "subsidized housing" is generally taken to mean rental units, the cutbacks in aid to low- and moderate-income homeowners were also significant in the Reagan years: see NCH, *Rural Homelessness in America*, p. 54.

78. Hope and Young, *Faces of Homelessness*, p. 160; Peter Dreier and John Atlas, "Eliminate the Mansion Subsidy," *Shelterforce* 12 (May/June 1990): 21.

79. John I. Gilderbloom and Richard Appelbaum, *Rethinking Rental Housing* (Philadelphia, 1988).

80. "Task Force Report," p. 8.

81. A national study conducted in the early 1980s found that 25 percent of rental units excluded children, and an additional 50 percent restricted families with children: Robert W. Marans and Mary Ellen Colten, "U.S. Rental

Housing Policies Affecting Families with Children," in Willem van Vliet, Elizabeth Huttman, and Sylvia Fava, eds., *Housing Needs and Policy Approaches* (Durham, N.C., 1985), pp. 41–58. Although the 1988 Federal Fair Housing Act outlawed most forms of anti-child discrimination, its effectiveness "remains yet to be demonstrated": Willem van Vliet, "Cross-national Housing Research," in Willem van Vliet, ed., *International Handbook of Housing Policies and Practices* (New York, 1990), p. 61.

82. "Task Force Report," p. 21.
83. Bachrach, "Homeless Mentally Ill," p. 16. Available data suggest that the number of chronically mentally ill people in the United States grew 17 percent from the mid-1970s to the mid-1980s: Howard H. Goldman and Ronald W. Manderscheid, "Chronic Mental Disorder in the United States," in National Institute of Mental Health, *Mental Health, United States, 1987* (R. W. Manderscheid and S. A. Barrett, eds.), DHHS Pub. No. (ADM) 87-1518 (Washington, D.C., 1987), p. 12; telephone interview with Ronald W. Manderscheid, October 11, 1990.
84. See Steven P. Segal and Jim Baumohl, "Engaging the Disengaged," *Social Work* 25 (1980): 358–365; Ellen Baxter and Kim Hopper, *Private Lives/Public Spaces* (New York, 1981); Philip Kasinitz, "Gentrification and Homelessness," *Urban and Social Change Review* 17 (Winter 1984): 9–14; Michael J. Dear and Jennifer R. Wolch, *Landscapes of Despair* (Princeton, 1987).
85. U.S. National Institute on Drug Abuse data from *National Household Survey on Drug Abuse*, 1974 and 1985, summarized in Bureau of the Census, *Statistical Abstract of the United States, 1989* (Washington, D.C., 1989), p. 118.
86. Kasinitz, "Gentrification and Homelessness"; Jim Baumohl, "Alcohol, Homelessness, and Public Policy," *Contemporary Drug Problems* 16 (1989): 281–300.

Chapter 3: Being homeless

1. George Orwell, *Down and Out in Paris and London* (New York, 1950), quoted in Kim Hopper, "A Quiet Violence," in Mary Ellen Hombs and Mitch Snyder, *Homelessness in America* (Washington, D.C., 1983), p. 66.
2. Hombs and Snyder, *Homelessness in America*, p. 9.
3. Ibid., p. 110.
4. For a discussion of how the search for resources frames each day's routine, see Harry Murray, "Time in the Streets," *Human Organization* 43 (1984): 154–161.
5. Kim Hopper and Jill Hamberg, *The Making of America's Homeless* (New York, 1984), p. 2.
6. These classifications, of course, are conceptual lenses rather than impermeable boundaries. The status of homeless people is extremely fluid, with people moving within and between subgroups (as well as into and out of homelessness), often in response to the material resources available at a given time. People may also use up the resources of one network and thus join another subgroup: A Skidder who remains homeless for an extended period may wear out her welcome at friends' homes and become a Street

Person; Mayor Max began as a Transitory Worker and became a Street Person when he ceased to be perceived as an able worker because of the time elapsed since his last job.

I have created no separate lifestyle category for alcoholics. Instead, they are found principally among the Wingnuts, to some extent among Street People, and, to a lesser degree, in other subgroups, as determined by the criteria of relationships and resources. Their escape needs are certainly different.

7. See Santa Barbara County Department of Mental Health, "Preliminary Report: Santa Barbara Homeless Mentally Ill Survey" (Santa Barbara, 1986), p. 3; Marjorie Robertson, Richard Ropers, and Richard Boyer, *The Homeless of Los Angeles County* (Los Angeles, 1985), p. 58; Marjorie Hope and James Young, *The Faces of Homelessness* (Lexington, Mass., 1986), p. 109. Totals are even higher when those already working are added: Cf. Research Atlanta, *The Impact of Homelessness on Atlanta* (Atlanta, 1984), p. 21; Louisa R. Stark, Kathleen E. MacDonald-Evoy, and Arthur J. Sage, "A Day in June" (report, Phoenix, 1983), p. 9; Richard Ropers, *The Invisible Homeless* (New York, 1988), pp. 37, 43. Lower estimates inevitably come from studies restricted to sheltered and highly visible homeless people, including those with mental illnesses and other disabilities preventing them from working.

8. Studies across the nation generally show between 20 and 40 percent of local homeless populations working. The wide variation in estimates is due in part to such methodological and definitional issues as whether only shelter populations are surveyed and how "work" is defined. Obviously, some areas have lower unemployment rates than others; less obviously, joblessness among homeless people is more reflective of the *kinds* of jobs available than the total number. Areas with more casual, temporary, and un- or semiskilled jobs will be better employment markets for homeless people than areas with job opportunities that require higher skills, better references, and so forth: See Marta Elliott and Laura J. Krivo, "Structural Determinants of Homelessness in the United States," *Social Problems* 38 (1991): 126–127.

9. I occasionally heard from people staying in the Church shelters that job offers had been withdrawn when their prospective employer found out they were staying at a shelter. Others complained that they lost jobs when they were arrested for illegal sleeping and thus missed work.

10. The unemployment office itself was of little use to Street People. Through most of the 1980s those who could not prove local residence were barred by federal regulations from job training programs. A local representative stressed to me in 1984 that "neither a car nor cotton field is a residence."

11. For a discussion of possible psychological bases for quitting or not seeking work, see David Snow and Leon Anderson, "Identity Work Among the Homeless," *American Journal of Sociology* 92 (1987): 1351.

12. For direct and indirect evidence of similar totals elsewhere see Hope and Young, *Faces of Homelessness*, pp. 31–32, 109, 282; Stark et al., "A Day in June," p. 9; Ropers, *Invisible Homeless*, pp. 37, 43.

13. Only 15 percent of Church guests, predominantly Street People in the early months, arrived at their first shelter receiving public assistance (24 percent including Food Stamps). Studies across the nation report similarly low

percentages: Cf. James D. Wright and Eleanor Weber, *Homelessness and Health* (Washington, D.C., 1987), p. 144; GAO, *Homelessness* (Washington, D.C., 1985); USCM, *Homelessness in America's Cities* (Washington, D.C., 1984), pp. 25, 56). Most studies indicate a large percentage of homeless people who are eligible for some form of aid but are not receiving it. For a rare argument that this is not so (and that the problem instead lies in excessively stringent regulations in some states), see Wright and Weber, *Homelessness and Health*, p. 144.

Food Stamps, more easily obtained, are an integral part of street life. Beyond their most important function of securing food, Food Stamps are the currency of the streets, where money is scarce.

14. Ann Marie Rousseau, *Shopping Bag Ladies* (New York, 1981).
15. Similar residency barriers are cited across the country: See Jonathan Alter et al., "Homeless in America," *Newsweek*, January 2, 1984, pp. 20–29; Hope and Young, *Faces of Homelessness*.
16. For arguments that denial of welfare in the 1980s was often the result of a deliberate Benthamite strategy by the Reagan administration to impose discipline on workers in general, see Frances Fox Piven and Richard Cloward, *The New Class War* (New York, 1982); Kim Hopper and Ellen Baxter, "The Experiment Continues," in U.S. Congress, Subcommittee on Housing and Community Development, *Homelessness in America—II* (Washington, D.C., 1984), pp. 505–526.
17. For instance, 35 percent of those Church guests receiving entitlements (55 percent if one includes Food Stamps) had slept on "the street" the night before, while only 7 percent reported spending the previous night in a hotel or motel.
18. Blood donation: See Greg Owen, Paul Mattessich, and Judy Williams, *Results of the Twin City Survey of Emergency Shelter Residents* (St. Paul, 1987), p. 7. Panhandling: See Greg Owen, Judy Williams, and June Heineman, *Emergency Shelter Survey* (St. Paul, 1986), table 64.
19. Studies in other localities show a wide range of estimates of criminal involvement: from about one-fifth to one-half of the total homeless population. Interpretation of these figures is complicated by important methodological and definitional issues: type of offense, how long ago the offense was committed, whether the individual was homeless at the time, demographic (particularly sex and age) and subgroup differences, the validity of arrest figures as indicators of actual criminal activity, and the absence of control groups.
20. The most methodologically sophisticated and extensive study of recent years is David A. Snow, Susan G. Barker, and Leon Anderson, "Criminality and Homeless Men," *Social Problems* 36 (1989): 532–549. They conclude that "while the homeless show a higher arrest rate, the majority of their arrests are for non-violent, relatively minor, and victimless crimes" (p. 546). Arrest rates for homeless males for the major crimes of murder, rape, robbery, and aggravated assaults were *half* the rates for housed males in the surveyed city of Austin. For similar findings, see Carl Brown, Steven MacFarlane, Ron Paredes, and Louisa Stark, *The Homeless of Phoenix*

(Phoenix, 1983); Robertson et al., *Los Angeles County;* Kenneth Winograd, "Street People and Other Homeless," in U.S. Congress, *Homelessness in America—II*, pp. 1343–1401.

21. Hope and Young, *Faces of Homelessness*, pp. 251–252.
22. Similarly, Snow et al. report that less than a third of their Austin sample of Street Men had been arrested ("Criminality," p. 540), with criminal activity, especially felony offenses, concentrated among those under thirty-five, those with mental illnesses, and those homeless for longer periods.
23. Cf. Knoxville Coalition, *Homelessness in Knox County* (Knoxville, Ohio, 1986), pp. 21, 28; Ropers, *Invisible Homeless*, p. 43; Carol Mowbray, Andrea Solarz, V. Sue Johnson, Emile Phillips-Smith, and Claudia J. Combs, *Mental Health and Homelessness in Detroit* (Lansing, Mich., 1986), p. 16. Those I interviewed in Santa Barbara who had not been victims were overwhelmingly from the hidden subgroups, whose routine lifestyle kept them off the streets.
24. Local estimates of beds available in relation to the number of homeless people start as low as 4 percent in Miami (NCH, *National Neglect/National Shame* [Washington, D.C., 1986], p. 5), and rarely reached higher than 50 percent until the late 1980s. Admittance rates at shelters are higher, since not all homeless people—even those visible enough to be counted in homeless estimates—seek shelter. Although these rarely reached even 50 percent until the late 1980s, by 1990 the admittance rate in thirty cities surveyed by the U.S. Conference of Mayors had risen to about 80 percent: *Status Report on Hunger and Homelessness in America's Cities: 1990* (Washington, D.C., 1990).
25. Ronald W. Powell, "Tempest Intensifies in De la Guerra Triangle," *Santa Barbara News-Press*, June 3, 1990, p. A-6.
26. The median length of stay in the shelter was three days; strict screening procedures ensured fairness (within the guidelines adopted) in admissions. But in large part the lack of problems at the Church shelters came at the price of excluding those in the most desperate need: alcoholics, mentally ill people, and the most disaffiliated.
27. Although this was true at the time of my fieldwork and for several years after it, service agency workers reported in 1990 that violence, often drug-related, had substantially increased at one of the five Santa Barbara shelters.
28. Declaration of William Clem, M.D., in *Ross v. Los Angeles County Supervisors* (1984), cited in Ropers, *Invisible Homeless*, p. 30. Those in colder climates understand that they must find a place indoors, while some in milder climates feel that they can survive outside during the warmer months. Public officials may also feel more obligation to provide shelter in colder areas.
29. See Chapter 5 for details of the struggle to rescind the illegal sleeping laws. "Illegal camping" laws are still on the books, and so arrests continue.
30. Violence against homeless people is not unique to Santa Barbara, of course. Wright and Weber's national study found that deaths of homeless people were more than twenty times as likely to be from homicides as deaths among the general population: *Homelessness and Health*, p. 128.
31. Although Margie illustrates the plight of Street People here, she is a good

example of how hard it is to classify homeless people definitively. She began her homeless life as a Kid; as an adult she sometimes survives as a Street Person, at other times as a Transitory Worker.

32. Rene I. Jahiel, "The Situation of Homelessness," in Richard D. Bingham, Roy E. Green, and Sammis B. White, eds., *The Homeless in Contemporary Society* (Newbury Park, Calif., 1987), p. 112. Again, in Santa Barbara (and presumably elsewhere) this victimization occurs overwhelmingly among the visible population.

33. See Brown et al. *Homeless of Phoenix,* p. 5, for similar findings. On the other hand, Snow et al., "Criminality," p. 539, argue that when homeless people do commit crimes, including assaults, their victims are usually other homeless people.

34. The availability of food varies considerably by location. In Fairfax, Va., finding food was rated the ninth most critical need of thirteen (Eric Goplerud, *Homelessness in Fairfax County* [Fairfax, Va. 1987], p. 31), yet a twenty-nine-city survey conducted by the U.S. Conference of Mayors found it the second most frequently cited need of homeless people after housing itself (*A Status Report on Homeless Families in America's Cities* [Washington, D.C., 1987], p. ii).

35. Physicians' Task Force on Hunger in America, *Hunger Counties 1986* (Cambridge, Mass., 1986), cited in NCH, *Homelessness in the United States* (New York, 1987), p. 8.

36. See Santa Barbara County Department of Mental Health, "Homeless Mentally Ill"; Mowbray et al., *Detroit;* Ellen Baxter and Kim Hopper, "Shelter and Housing for the Mentally Ill," in H. Richard Lamb, ed., *The Homeless Mentally Ill* (Washington, D.C., 1984), pp. 109–140.

37. Hope and Young, *Faces of Homelessness,* p. 93.

38. Rare reports claim that specific localities have kept mental patients needing aftercare from "falling through the cracks": See Phyllis Solomon, Joseph M. Davis, Barry Gordon, Paula Fishbein, and Anne Mason, *The Aftercare Mosaic* (Cleveland, 1983), p. 4, but such claims are exceptional. Homeless people, too, fall through the cracks of service delivery programs, especially the "dual-diagnosis" cases. Workers in the separate fields of substance abuse and mental health tend to accept only those whose recovery will not be complicated by other problems. See Susan Barrow, Fredric Hellman, Anne Lovell, Jane Plapinger, and Elmer Struening, *Effectiveness of Programs for the Mentally Ill Homeless* (New York, 1989); Robert H. Howland, "Barriers to Community Treatment of Patients with Dual Diagnoses," *Hospital and Community Psychiatry* 41 (1990): 1134–1135; and Wright and Weber, *Homelessness and Health,* p. 100, for data on dual-diagnosis clients at homeless medical aid stations. This reluctance has been greatly intensified in California by a 1978 decision at the state level to split alcoholism and mental health programs. Since funding guidelines now preclude treatment of one type of problem by workers in the other field, agency workers must be sure that the "primary diagnosis" of each prospective patient falls within their field. But it is virtually impossible to make a clear diagnosis of whether mental health or alcoholism is the primary problem of dual-diagnosis patients, especially those suffering at the time of diagnosis from acute

alcohol poisoning. Thus *both* programs will tend to shun such patients from fear of jeopardizing their budgets.

39. Interview with Ken Williams, September 2, 1985.

40. Seventy percent of the homeless people surveyed by the Santa Barbara County Mental Health study (which originally attempted to interview only mentally ill homeless people) reported past arrests ("Homeless Mentally Ill," p. 4), a figure significantly higher than that found in the other Santa Barbara data sets or in homeless populations elsewhere. Snow et al. find those in their sample with indicators of mental illness significantly more likely than others to have arrest records ("Criminality"). Some arrests may be for behavior that appears "crazy" rather than illegal per se. See Linda Teplin, "Criminalizing Mental Disorder," *American Psychologist* 39 (1984): 795–803; Joseph D. Bloom, Larry Faulkner, James H. Shore, and Jeffrey L. Rogers, "The Young Adult Chronic Patient and the Legal System," in David L. Cutler, ed., *Effective Aftercare for the 1980s* (San Francisco, 1983) for general discussions of the links between mental illness, criminal activity, and arrest.

41. See Leona L. Bachrach, "The Homeless Mentally Ill and Mental Health Services," in Lamb, ed., *Homeless Mentally Ill*, p. 40; H. Richard Lamb, "Deinstitutionalization and the Homeless Mentally Ill," ibid., p. 58; Ellen Baxter and Kim Hopper, "The New Mendicancy," *American Journal of Orthopsychiatry* 52 (1982): 393–408.

42. "Kids" is used throughout this work to signify a particular lifestyle subgroup. "Children" is used to refer to an age-group. For a useful summary of recent literature, see Leanne G. Rivlin, "A New Look at the Homeless," *Social Policy* 16 (Spring 1986): 4–5.

43. For similar findings regarding the local roots of homeless children, see Marjorie Robertson, Paul Koegel, and Linda Ferguson, "Alcohol Use and Abuse Among Homeless Adolescents in Hollywood," *Contemporary Drug Problems* 16 (1989): 415–452; New York State Council on Children and Families [hereafter New York State], *Meeting the Needs of Homeless Youth* (Albany, N.Y. 1984); J. Rothman and T. David, *Status Offenders in Los Angeles County—Focus on Runaway and Homeless Youth* (Los Angeles, 1985). A number of studies argue that conflict with parents occurs generally in dysfunctional families "in which parental alcohol abuse, neglect, physical and sexual abuse are common factors that impel adolescents to leave their homes" (Robertson et al., "Homeless Adolescents," p. 418). Such a background was certainly suggested by my contacts with homeless Kids in Santa Barbara, but I had insufficient data to assess how common it was.

44. The prevalence of prostitution among Kids is hard to gauge. Virginia Price reports that 17 percent of those interviewed at a Boston youth shelter were involved in prostitution, and notes that this is considerably lower than "popular misconceptions" would have it: "Runaways and Homeless Street Youth," in The Boston Foundation, *Homelessness: Critical Issues for Policy and Practice* (Boston, 1987), p. 24; Robertson et al. report similar figures: "Homeless Adolescents," p. 435.

45. Most researchers have not included hidden homeless people in their surveys, either because they are not defined as "literally homeless" (see

Peter Rossi, James D. Wright, Gene A. Fisher, and Georgianna Willis, "The Urban Homeless," *Science* 235 [1987]: 1336–1337) or because they "by definition, cannot be studied" (Peter Rossi, *Down and Out in America* [Chicago, 1989], p. 48). What could more accurately be said is that they cannot be studied using shelter and street surveys; ethnographic methods make such research possible. Whether hidden homeless people should be considered part of the homeless population, surely there is a significant difference between someone who is precariously housed but pays part or all of the rent, and someone who pays no rent and therefore has no legal rights to continued tenancy despite having a temporary roof over his or her head.

46. Hombs and Snyder note that "one can find homeless people who sleep sitting up to prevent their clothing from being wrinkled, and others who spend many hours and walk great distances to maintain a 'normal' appearance": *Homelessness in America*, p. 8. "Passing" is a strategy used by many people, housed and homeless, in a variety of situations: "Because of the great rewards in being considered normal, almost all persons who are in a position to pass will do so on some occasions by intent": Erving Goffman, *Stigma* (New York, 1986), p. 74.

47. A Santa Barbara County Department of Social Services study similarly found over half of the local homeless population hidden: "One Week Survey of Homeless DSS Service Users," internal memo (Santa Barbara, 1985). For similar findings in other areas, see Ventura County United Way, *Ventura County Homeless Report* (Ventura, Calif. 1985); Frederic G. Robinson, *Homeless People in the Nation's Capital* (Washington, D.C., 1985); Dee Roth and Jerry Bean, "New Perspectives on Homelessness," *Hospital and Community Psychiatry* 37 (1986): 712–719.

48. For similar findings, see Owen et al., *Twin City Survey*, pp. 7–8; Hope and Young, *Faces of Homelessness*, p. 89; Robinson, *Nation's Capital*, p. 9; Research Atlanta, *Impact of Homelessness*, p. 11.

49. One would expect migrant agricultural workers to show up in this subgroup (see NCH, *Malign Neglect* [New York, 1986], p. 21), but they did not. My suspicion is that such workers are instead found in the inland communities, such as Santa Maria, Lompoc, and Guadalupe, where large-scale commercial agriculture is carried on.

    The number of Transitory Workers has been augmented somewhat in recent years by normally less mobile workers who have come from other parts of the state or country expecting to find work in the area. This newer group ranges from the tail end of the nearly homeless, whose precarious financial hold has been further weakened by deindustrialization and recent recessions, to middle-class workers who will resume middle-class lives once situated in new jobs.

50. Significantly, this testimony from Hank came six weeks *after* welfare officials had agreed to loosen residency requirements.

51. Kids in Santa Barbara appear to be fairly evenly divided by gender.

52. Lower-class Anglo women scarcely showed up in the HoPP or SPA samples, although a few are found in the "Street People" subgroup. Self-reporting biases may have led some lower-class women to describe themselves as "middle-class" in origin. Alternatively, lower-class women may be less

likely to end relationships, since they are more vulnerable to the economic consequences of single parenthood.

53. See Rossi, *Down and Out*, p. 197, for evidence that those homeless people in Chicago eligible for AFDC are significantly more likely to apply than those eligible for General Assistance. Skidders, as represented in the SPA data, were twice as likely as the parents at the Church shelters (largely Street People) to be receiving AFDC; yet even among the SPA group, 88 percent of whom were low-income households, only a third were receiving AFDC.

54. "Newsletter," Spring 1985, p. 5. For evidence of this practice in other areas, see USCM, *Status Report on Homeless Families*, pp. 10, 13; NCH, *Rural Homelessness in America* (New York, 1987), p. 32. Testimony to the U.S. Congressional Committee on Government Operations indicates that children are indeed removed from homeless families in some areas: *The Federal Response to the Homeless Crisis* (99th Congress, 1st Session, House Report 99-47) (Washington, D.C. 1985), p. 21.

55. The lack of criminal activity among Skidders (and Latino Families, discussed below) may also reflect their high proportion of women, who are noted in many studies to be considerably less likely to be involved in criminal activity than homeless men: (See Mowbray et al., *Detroit*; Irving Piliavin, Michael Sosin, and Herb Westerfelt, "Conditions Contributing to Long-term Homelessness" (Madison, Wis., 1988); Merv Goldstein, Stephen Levine, and Robert Lipkins, *Characteristics of Shelter Users* (New York, 1986). This holds for the housed population as well.

56. Most local studies conducted elsewhere in the early 1980s reported women and women with children as the least likely of homeless people to use shelters, but this began changing in many areas in the mid-1980s as service providers began targeting them for help: See Alameda County, *Homelessness in Alameda County, 1988* (Oakland, Calif., 1988), p. 5; Owen et al., *Twin City Survey*, p. 19; Rossi, *Down and Out*, p. 133. Data indicating that women with children were the *most* likely of subgroups to use shelters are reported in Martha R. Burt and Barbara E. Cohen, "Differences Among Homeless Single Women, Women with Children, and Single Men," *Social Problems* 36 (1989): 518. Their study, however, was conducted at shelters and food kitchens, thus missing the hidden homeless population. In Santa Barbara, the composition of Transition House was changing toward greater numbers of women and children and fewer single men as my research ended, but available data do not allow me to say whether these women were those I call Skidders.

57. The greater likelihood of women and families to be found in such hidden arrangements has been noted in many other local studies: See Goplerud, *Fairfax County*, p. 20; Owen et al., *Twin City Survey*, p. 7.

58. The recent rapid increase in the proportion of the homeless population made up of parents with children is documented across the nation. In one typical estimate, yielded by the 1987 U.S. Conference of Mayors' twenty-nine-city survey, families made up over a third of the homeless population, and the number of families requesting emergency shelter (undoubtedly an underestimate of total need) had risen an average of 31 percent in all but one city in the previous two years: *Status Report on Homeless Families*, p. 3. For

local figures see NCH, *National Neglect;* NCH, *Pushed Out* (Washington, D.C., 1987).

59. Maintaining children's attendance at school is a major task. National figures indicate that between one-quarter and one-half of homeless children do not attend school because of residency requirements, problems with documentation, and lack of transportation: *In Just Times* 1 (June 1990): 1; 2 (July 1991): 1; *SN* 8 (April 1989): 2. These barriers persist despite the passage of the 1987 McKinney Homeless Assistance Act, which required that homeless children be guaranteed access to public schools.

60. See USCM, *Status Report on Homeless Families*, pp. 9–10; Vijaya L. Melnick and Charles S. Williams, *Homelessness in the District of Columbia* (Washington, D.C. 1987), p. 32; Ellen L. Bassuk, Alison Lauriati, and Lenore Rubin, "Homeless Families," in Boston Foundation, *Homelessness*, p. 23.

61. *SN* 9 (September 1990): 1.

62. Transition House, however, began reporting increased numbers of Latino families in the late 1980s (after my fieldwork was completed), particularly those whose breadwinners were gardeners and landscapers during the drought of 1989–90.

63. My research assistant, Guadalupe Kennedy, once saw thirty-six people using a two-bedroom apartment. Doubling-up arrangements are reflected in the data on overcrowding: Over 23.0 percent of Santa Barbara's Hispanic households were officially reported as overcrowded at the beginning of the 1980s, compared with a city average of 5.5 percent and a citywide tenant average of about 7.0 percent: Bureau of the Census, *Detailed Housing Characteristics, California* [HC80-1-B6] (Washington, D.C., 1983), pp. 53, 17, 152–157. Unquestionably, even these data are underestimates because of the hidden nature of many such arrangements, as well as the increase in homelessness during the 1980s.

Chapter 4: Hanging on and hanging out

1. David Snow and Leon Anderson, "Identity Work Among the Homeless," *American Journal of Sociology* 92 (1987): 1365.

2. Kai Erickson, "The Chronic Calamity," *The Nation* 246 (1988): 465. Exactly what "disaffiliation" means, however, is not obvious. Even within the disaffiliation school there is considerable variation in its use. It may imply an active disengagement from other people (see Howard Bahr, "Homelessness, Disaffiliation, and Retreatism," in Howard Bahr, ed., *Disaffiliated Man* (University of Toronto, 1970), pp. 39–50; Theodore Caplow, "The Sociologist and the Homeless Man," ibid., p. 9), an inability to maintain ties due to social incompetence (see Bahr, "Retreatism," p. 44), or merely a lack of ties resulting from any number of causes (see Howard Bahr, *Skid Row* [New York, 1973]). For some theorists, disaffiliation is so central a concept that they appear to define homelessness as "hearthlessness" rather than "rooflessness," so that even those with legal rights to a residence may be seen as homeless if they lack significant ties (see Howard M. Bahr, *Homelessness and Disaffiliation* [New York, 1969]; Howard M. Bahr and Gerald R. Garrett,

Women Alone [Lexington, Mass., 1976]). But these ties themselves may be defined spatially (Bahr, "Retreatism," p. 39), socially (Robert E. L. Faris, *Chicago Sociology, 1920–1932* [San Francisco, 1967], p. 66), or normatively (Sara Harris, *Skid Row, U.S.A.* [Garden City, N.Y., 1956]; Theodore Caplow, Keith A. Lovald, and Samuel E. Wallace, *A General Report on the Problem of Relocating the Population of the Lower Loop Redevelopment Area* [Minneapolis, 1958]; for a more positive view of such alternative normative frameworks, see James F. Rooney, "Societal Forces and the Unattached Male," in Bahr, ed., *Disaffiliated Man*, pp. 13–38).

3. Claude S. Fischer, "Perspectives on Community and Personal Relations," in Claude S. Fischer, ed., *Networks and Places* (New York, 1977), pp. 1–16.

4. J. Clyde Mitchell, "The Components of Strong Ties Among Homeless Women," *Social Networks* 3 (1987): 37–47.

5. Mainstream institutions: Harris, *Skid Row, U.S.A.;* Bahr, *Skid Row;* Caplow, "The Sociologist." Housed Friends and Kin: Samuel Wallace, *Skid Row as a Way of Life* (Totawa, N.J., 1965); for an opposing view, see Bahr, "Retreatism," pp. 41–42. Other homeless people: Bahr, *Skid Row*, pp. 157–168; Faris, *Chicago Sociology*, p. 66 (commenting on Nels Anderson's research); Caplow, "The Sociologist," p. 6; Leonard U. Blumberg, Thomas E. Shipley, Jr., and Joseph O. Moor, Jr., "The Skid Row Man and the Skid Row Status Community," *Quarterly Journal of Studies on Alcohol* 3 (1971): 928. A contrary view is expressed in James F. Rooney, "Group Processes Among Skid Row Winos," *Quarterly Journal of Studies on Alcohol* 22 (1961): 444–460; Jack W. Peterson and Milton A. Maxwell, "The Skid Row 'Wino,' " *Social Problems* 5 (1958): 308–316; Nels Anderson, *The Hobo* (Chicago, 1923); Wallace, *Skid Row as a Way of Life*. Douglas Harper notes that those researchers who administered surveys were far less likely to see community among homeless people than those who lived as insiders, such as Anderson and Wallace: "The Homeless Man" (Ph.D. dissertation, Brandeis University, 1975).

6. Alan Hall and Barry Wellman, "Social Networks and Social Support," in Sheldon Cohen and S. Leonard Syme, eds., *Social Support and Health* (Orlando, Fla., 1985), p. 33.

7. See Douglas K. Welch, "Homelessness in America" (B.A. honors thesis, Wesleyan University, 1989).

8. In 1983 a merchants' Committee on Alcoholism, Vagrancy, Etc. (CAVE) claimed that its survey of merchants showed that in recent years businesses in the lower State Street area had lost $1.8 million due to shoppers' avoiding the area and over $1.0 million from robberies and theft, while spending $0.5 million on security devices—all largely attributed to the increased presence of "transients": interview with Charles Parkey, chair of CAVE, April 15, 1983. Accordingly, a recurring theme in many merchants' plans to deal with "the lower State Street problem" is that homeless people should be dissuaded from staying in town: "We would like to see this become an understood fact: that Santa Barbara isn't the easiest town in the world to live in if you are going to try that lifestyle. Usually if they find that it's not easy, they'll move on to a place that's easier" (Parkey interview).

9. Santa Barbara City Council testimony, August 19, 1986.

10. Parkey interview.

11. There are, of course, exceptions, and many among the street subgroups differentiate between good and bad, or friendly and unfriendly, merchants. Some restaurants leave excess food behind their stores; some merchants do not appear to be prejudiced against homeless people who come into their stores; others are appreciated because they do not interfere with scavenging in their dumpsters.

12. The same framework of expectations exists in many other interactions, notably with employers and police. In each case, designation as homeless reduces the housed person's expectations of reciprocity (labor for wage for employers; respect for the law in return for protection and treatment as a law-abiding citizen for the police). Again, there are exceptions in which housed people try to differentiate between "types" of homeless people or even treat each as a distinct individual. For a discussion of this process in relation to police, see Chapter 5.

13. As a result, the daily rhythm of life for many homeless people is largely set by the institutions of mainstream society. When working, they are regulated by the dictates of straight time and workaday rhythms. Even when not working or seeking work, the daily cycle is heavily influenced by where and when resources (including food, shelter, clothing, and welfare) are available. The monthly cycle of homeless (and particularly street) life is also heavily influenced by mainstream society, most notably by the fact that Food Stamps and other entitlements are available on the first or third of the month. This affects the behavior of more than just those receiving benefits. At the beginning of each month, resources are pumped into the economy of the streets. Inflation results: The radio that would have been traded for five dollars in Food Stamps last week is now worth fifteen, as Food Stamps are generally more plentiful. People are more generous, more inclined to share, in the first few weeks of the month as resources are more available.

14. See Peter Rossi, *Down and Out in America* (Chicago, 1989), p. 167; James D. Wright, *Address Unknown* (New York, 1989), pp. 77, 85. Note, however, that 30 percent of males and 40 percent of females in a study of *housed* poverty-level households in Chicago reported that they had no one to provide help in a major crisis: Rossi, *Down and Out*, p. 174, based on William J. Wilson, *Urban Family Life Project* (Chicago, 1988). Similarly, the extremely low percentage of homeless people ever or currently married was often cited in the past as a "principal factor" in causing homelessness (Bahr, *Skid Row*, p. 89, citing data in Caplow et al., *General Report;* and see Rossi, *Down and Out*, p. 130, for a more recent but less strongly worded connection), even though virtually the same percentage of unmarried people is found among samples of General Assistance recipients, AFDC recipients, and SRO residents in Chicago: Rossi, *Down and Out*, p. 129.

15. See Dee Roth, Jerry Bean, Nancy Lust, and Traian Saveanu, *Homelessness in Ohio* (Columbus, Ohio, 1985); Ellen L. Bassuk, Lenore Rubin, and Alison Lauriati, "Is Homelessness a Mental Problem?" *American Journal of Psychiatry* 141 (1984): 1548–1549.

16. James Allan Davis and Tom W. Smith, *General Social Surveys 1972–1988* (Storrs, Conn., 1988). Comparison data have been recalculated from ques-

tions 426 through 437 to include deceased parents in order to permit valid comparison to studies of homeless populations.

17. Greg Owen, Paul Mattessich, and Judy Williams, *Results of the Twin City Survey of Emergency Shelter Residents* (St. Paul, 1987), table 136. Similar reports of relatively infrequent contact appear in Carol Mowbray, Andrea Solarz, V. Sue Johnson, Emile Phillips-Smith, and Claudia J. Combs, *Mental Health and Homelessness in Detroit* (Lansing, Mich., 1986), p. 17; Peter Rossi, James D. Wright, Gene A. Fisher, and Georgianna Willis, "The Urban Homeless," *Science* 235 (1987): 1339; Carl I. Cohen and Jay Sokolovsky, *Old Men of the Bowery* (New York, 1989), p. 126.

18. Irving Piliavin, Michael Sosin, and Herb Westerfelt, "Conditions Contributing to Long-term Homelessness" (discussion paper no. 853–87, Institute for Research on Poverty, University of Wisconsin–Madison, 1988), p. 25. For evidence of rates of contact approaching the national (housed) sample, see Greg Owen, Judy Williams, and June Heineman, *Emergency Shelter Survey* (St. Paul, 1986), table 128; Steven P. Segal, Jim Baumohl, and Elise Johnson, "Falling Through the Cracks." *Social Problems* 24 (1977): 393; Roth et al., *Homelessness in Ohio*, table U24 (p. 68).

19. Cohen and Sokolovsky in *Old Men*, p. 114, perceptively point out that analysis and characterization of the resulting data are affected by the different comparison points from which evaluations are made: "Bogue (1963) and Rooney (1976) found virtually equivalent levels of friendship among two skid row populations [but] the former characterized them as 'semi-isolates' whereas the latter asserted that skid row was 'clearly . . . not a population of isolates.' " For arguments that measures of disaffiliation historically have been class-biased, see Jacqueline P. Wiseman, *Stations of the Lost* (Englewood Cliffs, N.J., 1970); Charles Hoch and Robert A. Slayton, *New Homeless and Old* (Philadelphia, 1989), p. 111.

20. Researchers such as Rossi et al. ("Urban Homeless") might argue that doubled-up households are not homeless. Doing so, however, deflects attention from the social origins of an explosion in doubling-up that parallels the explosion in "literal" homelessness. While some characteristics of the two groups may differ—crucially, in this discussion, the availability of friends or kin who can temporarily provide shelter—the end result in either case is the lack of a place to live where one has legal rights to residency. See Hoch and Slayton, *New Homeless and Old*, p. 192, for a similar argument.

21. See Owen, Mattessich, and Williams, *Twin City Survey*, table 136; Roth et al. *Homelessness in Ohio*, p. 68; Knoxville Coalition, *Homelessness in Knox County* (Knoxville, Ohio, 1986), p. 17.

22. For example, from 31 percent for those homeless less than a year to 47 percent for those homeless over a year.

23. See Segal et al., "Falling Through the Cracks," for similar findings.

24. For example, when Rossi et al. report that a third of the homeless people they surveyed had no contact with any relative ("Urban Homeless," p. 1339), they are in effect also reporting that two-thirds had such contact.

25. Erving Goffman, *Stigma* (New York, 1986), pp. 144–145; Felix M. Berardo, "Survivorship and Social Isolation," in Bahr, ed., *Disaffiliated Man*, pp. 51–79. "Somewhere between 10 and 20 percent of the [general] population

can be considered as social isolates [and] an even greater percentage, probably about one-third at a minimum, are alienated from society or are self-alienated": Edgar W. Butler, *The Urban Crisis* (Santa Monica, Calif., 1977), p. 28.

26. Less pervasive contact: Ellen L. Bassuk, Alison Lauriati, and Lenore Rubin, "Homeless Families," in The Boston Foundation, *Homelessness* (Boston, 1987), p. 22; Cohen and Sokolovsky, *Old Men*, pp. 122, 131; "Tracking the Homeless" (summary of the work of Piliavin and Sosin), *Focus* 10 (1987–88): 23; cf. Davis and Smith, *Social Surveys*, p. 448, for data regarding the general population. Majority retaining contact: Roth et al., *Homelessness in Ohio*, p. 69; Eric Goplerud, *Homelessness in Fairfax County* (Fairfax, Va., 1987), p. 20; Owen, Mattessich, and Williams, *Twin City Survey*, p. 13; Knoxville Coalition, *Knox County*, p. 29.

27. Quotation from John R. Logan and Harvey L. Molotch, *Urban Fortunes* (Berkeley, 1987), pp. 104–105. For an example of this argument applied to homeless people, see Cohen and Sokolovsky, *Old Men*, p. 124.

28. See Owen, Williams, and Heineman, *Emergency Shelter Survey*, tables 71–73; Knoxville Coalition, *Knox County*, pp. 22, 32; Martha R. Burt and Barbara E. Cohen, "Differences Among Homeless Single Women, Women with Children, and Single Men," *Social Problems* 36 (1989): 515; Roth et al., *Homelessness in Ohio*, table U14 (p. 63).

29. See Hoch and Slayton, *New Homeless and Old*, p. 191; Rossi et al., "Urban Homeless," p. 1340.

30. This support, however, was unlikely to include housing. Of 112 callers to the SPA in a six-month period, only 14 reported staying with their families when they lost their residences.

31. Piliavin and Sosin report that 76 percent of those they surveyed in their mixed street and shelter population had "exited" the streets or shelters at least once in a six-month period. Apparently a majority went to the homes of friends or family, but over half of those who exited also returned to the streets in the same six-month period: Focus, "Tracking the Homeless," p. 23.

32. For example, when "Bowery men" were asked why they did not see their housed children, over a third cited the indifference or hostility of the children: Cohen and Sokolovsky, *Old Men*, p. 127; and see Roth et al., *Homelessness in Ohio*, p. 47, for similar data. Of course, there may be some amount of guilt-relieving rationalization in these responses.

33. *Stigma*, p. 65.

34. Network theorists have often speculated that "multiplex" ties (those involving several different roles, such as co-worker and neighbor) are stronger than "uniplex" ties. While the social roles of homeless people are often less defined, multiple roles—and thus multiplexity—are still present. For example, Mayor Max and Sandman were friends, "neighbors" (they often shared sleeping places), and co-workers (they gathered scrap metal together). Fischer notes that two factors that result in neighborhood cohesion are difficulty in "developing or maintaining extralocal relations" and "overlapping ties": "Network Analysis and Urban Studies," in Fischer, ed., *Networks and Places*, p. 32.

35. See Douglas Harper, *Good Company* (Chicago, 1982).
36. *Old Men,* p. 123 (original emphasis). Cohen and Sokolovksy's work is particularly important because it focuses on the population of Skid Row men that many within the disaffiliation school wrote about. Their conclusions strongly contest the representation of disaffiliation as either cause or result of homelessness, finding that most Skid Row men have contact with housed people (including kin), mainstream institutions, and other homeless people.
37. Anne M. Lovell, "Marginality Without Isolation" (paper presented at the 83rd annual meeting of the American Anthropological Association, Denver, 1984); see also Leanne G. Rivlin, "A New Look at the Homeless," *Social Policy* 16 (Spring 1986): 3–10.
38. This changed for some Skidders with the establishment of the SPA. See Chapter 5.
39. However, those who began with this overall conception of other homeless people frequently found it tempered by living with them, for instance in the Church shelters. When I told Hank, "Some people say the homeless problem is thirty winos on State Street," he replied: "That's not really true. I don't believe that. Probably at one time, I would've believed, I would've said, 'Well, they must be drunks,' or 'They must be crazies,' you know."
40. The core of the Homeless People's Association has continued for years to stage periodic eats, although the daily meals eventually died out under the combined weight of the anti-camping ordinance and unequal contributions to the meals.
41. Threats also heighten distrust of outsiders, as I learned following a crackdown on Street People in April 1983. See the Appendix for details.
42. For a view that instead attributes Kids' inability to sustain relationships for more than a few months to their inability to maintain emotional intimacy, see Virginia Price, "Runaways and Homeless Street Youth," in Boston Foundation, *Homelessness,* pp. 24–28.
43. For instance, about half of those interviewed in the Santa Barbara County Department of Mental Health study reported lacking a "supportive other" ("Preliminary Report," Santa Barbara, 1986), p. 4. Again, this figure includes some homeless people who were not mentally ill.
44. While many people spend some time at the Fig Tree (or other hangouts), a relatively small number simply "lie around the park all day," as housed people often complain. People arrive, catch up on news with their friends, leave to do business (such as checking their mail at General Delivery, applying for benefits, calling about a job, or buying rolling tobacco), and return several hours later. For a similar finding, see Louisa R. Stark, Kathleen E. MacDonald-Evoy, and Arthur J. Sage, *A Day in June* (Phoenix, 1983), p. 6.
45. See Harper, "The Homeless Man" and *Good Company* for similar findings regarding tramps of the Northwest; and Elliot Liebow, *Tally's Corner* (Boston, 1967), pp. 204–205, for a description of a similar present-time orientation to friendship among "streetcorner men."
46. For other reports of such sharing of material resources, often coupled with emotional support, see Carl Brown, Steve MacFarlane, Ron Paredes, and

Louisa Stark, *The Homeless of Phoenix* (Phoenix, 1983), p. 5; Knoxville Coalition, *Knox County*, p. 30; Rivlin, "A New Look," p. 6; Cohen and Sokolovsky, *Old Men*, pp. 119, 124; James P. Spradley, *You Owe Yourself a Drunk* (Boston, 1970).

47. For similar findings, see Jim Baumohl, "Alcohol, Homelessness, and Public Policy," *Contemporary Drug Problems* 16 (1989): 285; Mowbray et al., *Detroit*, p. 16; Snow and Anderson, "Identity Work."

48. Testimony of Community for Creative Non-Violence worker Harold Moss, in Marjorie Hope and James Young, *The Faces of Homelessness* (Lexington, Mass., 1986), p. 75.

49. Although Rossi argues that "many of the homeless are completely isolated" (*Down and Out*, p. 177), and stresses social isolation as a key variable in explaining who becomes homeless, he calculates that only 24 percent of those surveyed in Chicago (all "literally homeless," completely bypassing the hidden homeless population) are in fact isolated (p. 176).

50. Cf. J. Clyde Mitchell, *Social Networks in Urban Situations* (Manchester, Eng., 1969), p. 18.

51. Jim Baumohl, personal communication, July 14, 1992.

52. "People create networks through a series of choices, and social structure influences their choices by determining the range and relative value of available alternatives": Robert Max Jackson, Claude S. Fischer, and Lynne McCallister Jones, "The Dimensions of Social Networks," in Fischer, *Networks and Places*, p. 42.

53. "Social Networks," p. 25.

Chapter 5: T h e   h o m e l e s s   m o v e m e n t

1. Howard M. Bahr, *Skid Row* (New York, 1973), p. 30.

2. Theodore Caplow, "The Sociologist and the Homeless Man," in Howard M. Bahr, ed., *Disaffiliated Man* (Toronto, 1970), pp. 5–6.

3. Their nonvoter status appears to be due more to the conditions of homeless life and local regulations that make voting difficult for homeless people than to any atypical political apathy preceding homelessness. See Greg Owen, Judy Williams, and June Heineman, *Emergency Shelter Survey* (St. Paul, 1986), tables 34, 126; and Greg Owen, Paul Mattessich, and Judy Williams, *Results of the Twin City Survey of Emergency Shelter Residents* (St. Paul, 1987), p. 13, for data indicating that prehomeless registration and voting percentages among shelter dwellers are similar to national totals. "The right to vote has been established in only five cities: Chicago, Philadelphia, Washington, D.C., Santa Barbara, and New York": *In Just Times* 1 (July 1990):2.

4. Frances Fox Piven and Richard Cloward, *Poor People's Movements* (New York, 1977). This is not to say that this is the *only* way the homeless movement may advance. Legal challenges and appeals to the consciences of housed people have been fruitful, but these are not the same sorts of power as that implied by "leverage."

5. This became apparent to a SPA organizer when she first set up an

appointment with the news media to interview some of the people who had contacted her:

> They were especially interested in shooting footage of children living in cars and such. And most of the people who I know who are living in cars *don't* want their picture on TV. Especially the women. Two were women there with teenaged kids, and the teenaged kids don't want their friends to know that they've been living in their vehicle. Or that they're living with friends or whatever. That their mother is desperate.

6. Women in general are likely to think of the police as protectors rather than enemies:

> M A R G I E : I felt safe because . . . they were driving around and they saw me walking at nighttime. . . .
>
> Q : You weren't afraid they were going to arrest you for illegal sleeping or anything like that?
>
> M A R G I E : No, no. . . . People around here cooperate with the police, and the police have some kind of confidence [in return]. Sure they make trouble about the homeless people, but some of them are nice.

7. Interview with Sergeant John Thayer of the Santa Barbara Police, March 23, 1983.

8. Thayer interview.

9. Ironically, by 1990 the mayor of Santa Barbara was recommending that homeless people relocate to the Jungle from the downtown area: "None of them are in the jungle now, a lot better location than de la Guerra Plaza as far as I'm concerned. We're hoping to get them back there, but lots further would be even better": quoted in Ronald W. Powell, "Temptest Intensifies in De la Guerra Triangle," *Santa Barbara News-Press,* June 3, 1990.

10. Thayer interview. For evidence that clearing areas where homeless people sleep is a conscious policy of the Santa Barbara police, see Peter Finn, *Street People* (Washington, D.C. [National Institute of Justice], no date), p. 2.

11. The homeless movement in Los Angeles similarly arose in response to organized police raids against homeless people in preparation for the summer Olympics of 1984: Richard Ropers, *The Invisible Homeless* (New York, 1988), p. 198. As Richard Flacks has argued in *Making History* (New York, 1988), social movements often arise when elites deprive a population of rights they had come to expect, especially when initial individual resistance against the new order generates no tangible results.

12. At the same time, the HPA's militance alarmed others, especially older alcoholics, who feared the new police heat at their traditional gathering places like the Fig Tree.

13. Several HoPP Wingnuts had been ticketed or arrested for illegal sleeping offenses in other cities.

14. See Alaine Touraine, *The Voice and the Eye* (Cambridge, 1981). In some cases, the HPA's tactics were formulated to challenge stereotypes they felt housed people held about them. One example was the "street people for cleaner streets squad," which once a week cleaned up the parks frequented by homeless people.

15. Beginning from Bachrach and Baratz' famous formulation of a second "face

of power," which involves setting the agenda for political discussion (Peter Bachrach and Morton S. Baratz, "Two Faces of Power," *American Political Science Review* 56 [1962]: 947–953), Harvey Molotch and Deirdre Boden argue there is a third face of power, "the most basic of all; it is the ability to determine the very grounds of the interaction through which agendas are set and outcomes determined; it is the struggle over linguistic premises upon which the legitimacy of accounts will be judged": "Talking Social Structure," *American Sociological Review* 50 (1985): 273. See Charles Hoch and Robert A. Slayton, *New Homeless and Old* (Philadelphia, 1989), p. 210, for a discussion of how structural pressures have led housed advocates to stress "images of vulnerability" rather than their preferred "politics of entitlement."

16. Wingnuts, Transitory Workers, Kids, and Latino Families, by contrast, show little signs of collective organizing, probably attributable to their inability to affiliate (Wingnuts), their mobility (Kids and Transitory Workers), their lack of self-identification as homeless people (Transitory Workers, some Latino Families), or structural barriers to organization (those Latino Families who are undocumented). Some, however, joined in the political efforts of the HPA, SPA, and Homeless Coalition.

17. Rob Rosenthal, "Homeless People's Project Interim Report 2" (Santa Barbara, 1984).

18. This also tends to be how police regard the situation. As one police officer giving citations to homeless people explained to a reporter: "It's my job. . . . I'm just doing what I'm told. I'm just a beat cop" (quoted in Powell, "Tempest Intensifies").

19. Cf. Charles Tilly, *From Mobilization to Revolution* (Reading, Mass., 1978); John D. McCarthy and Mayer N. Zald, "Resource Mobilization and Social Movements," *American Journal of Sociology* 82 (1977): 1212–1241; J. Craig Jenkins, "Resource Mobilization Theory and the Study of Social Movements," *Annual Review of Sociology* 9 (1983): 527–553.

20. In a similar vein, homeless activist Theresa Funiciello complains in "Give Them Shelters," *The Nation* 246 (1988): 470, "It's worth noting that remarkably few of the public policy stars in this field are women, almost all are white—the reverse of the population 'served.' "

21. In innumerable police dramas, a suspect is first interrogated by a "bad cop" who threatens him (all players until recently were invariably men) with harm if he doesn't cooperate. Just as the bad cop appears to be ready to blow, the "good cop" sends him away and speaks nicely to the suspect, gives him a cigarette, and so forth. Within two minutes, overwhelmed by the good cop's kindness and terrified that the bad cop will return, the suspect has confessed to everything. See Rob Rosenthal, "Good Cop/Bad Cop" (paper presented at the annual meeting of the Society for the Study of Social Problems, San Francisco, August 6–8, 1989).

22. Naturally, this dynamic is not peculiar to Santa Barbara, or even to the homeless movement. See Rosenthal, "Good Cop/Bad Cop," for illustrations from the labor, civil rights/black liberation, and anti–Vietnam War movements.

23. Nor are the bad cops in most movements more conscious of the ways in

which the good cops are necessary for progress. See Rosenthal, "Good Cop/Bad Cop."

24. For examples of other victories of homeless movements across the nation, see Marjorie Hope and James Young, *The Faces of Homelessness* (Lexington, Mass., 1986), pp. 235–248; Vijaya L. Melnick and Charles S. Williams, *Homelessness in the District of Columbia* (Washington, D.C., 1987), p. 3; Ropers, *Invisible Homeless*, pp. 189–209. The best source of information about ongoing political struggles is *Safety Network*, the newsletter of the National Coalition for the Homeless: 1621 Connecticut Avenue, NW, Washington, D.C., 20009.

Chapter 6: Getting ahead and the barriers to escape

1. Over 75 percent of the HoPP group, 80 percent of the Church guests, and all of the SPA callers reported being homeless less than a year (although, of course, they were not yet housed); only 11 percent of the HoPP group and 13 percent of the Church group had been homeless for two years or longer at the time of interview or intake. Figures in other local studies show a remarkable similarity. See Richard Ropers, *The Invisible Homeless* (New York, 1988), pp. 44–46; Alameda County, *Homelessness in Alameda County, 1988* (Oakland, Calif., 1988), p. 12; William K. Woods and Edward Lee Burdell, *Homelessness in Cincinnati* (Cincinnati, 1987), p. 55; Peter Rossi, *Without Shelter* (New York, 1989), p. 45. Most data, it should be noted, were generated from people who were still homeless at the time they were interviewed.

2. Virtually all studies agree that "most homeless people are *not* chronically homeless, but are *episodically* homeless": James D. Wright, *Address Unknown* (New York, 1989), p. 140, original emphasis.

3. According to California Rural Legal Assistance figures, the average California rent in 1987 required 79 percent of AFDC payments—the highest of all entitlement programs in California: cited in Lauri Flack, *Santa Barbara Comprehensive Homeless Assistance Plan (CHAP)* (Santa Barbara, 1990), p. 9b.

4. Barry Shelby, "Assembly Cites the Plight of the Homeless," *Daily Nexus* (University of California, Santa Barbara), February 23, 1983, p. 1.

5. In Boston, for instance, while 15 to 25 percent of shelter guests receive Section 8 or similar certificates at some time during their stay, 65 to 75 percent are returned unused after ninety days: Emergency Shelter Commission [hereafter Boston Commission], *Boston's Homeless* (Boston, 1986), p. 52. Michael S. Carliner discusses the failures of the Section 8 program in "Homelessness: A Housing Problem?" in Richard D. Bingham, Roy E. Green, and Sammis B. White, eds., *The Homeless in Contemporary Society* (Newbury Park, Calif., 1987), pp. 119–128.

6. For Kids, of course, escape generally means a reconciliation with their parents or finding new guardians who will provide them with material resources, including a home.

7. AFDC recipients are eligible for subsidized child care in some states, but this provision does not guarantee available, affordable care.

8. See Boston Commission, *Boston's Homeless*, p. 40; Greg Owen, Paul Mattessich, and Judy Williams, *Results of the Twin City Survey of Emergency Shelter Residents* (St. Paul, 1987), pp. 11, 13; Merv Goldstein, Stephen Levine, and Robert Lipkins, *Characteristics of Shelter Users* (New York, 1986), p. 32; Peter Rossi, James D. Wright, Gene A. Fisher, and Georgianna Willis, "The Urban Homeless," *Science* 235 (1987): 1339. But these data were largely obtained from shelter and visible homeless populations and therefore do not reflect the considerably lower disability rates found among hidden groups.

9. Latino Family members are kept from bettering their pay in their current jobs by a number of barriers against both individual and collective action: lack of relevant job skills, competitive pressures arising from a surplus workforce, a scarcity of resources for organizing, Santa Barbara's nonunion tradition (especially in the fields in which they predominantly work—agriculture/gardening, service jobs, and light manufacturing), and the reluctance of undocumented workers to risk political involvement.

10. California Rural Legal Assistance figures cited by Flack (*Santa Barbara CHAP*, p. 9b) indicate that a household with a full-time breadwinner making minimum wage in 1987 was paying 68 percent of its income for the average statewide rent; rents in Santa Barbara are higher.

11. In fact, 53 percent of those Church guests who were working had still slept on the streets the night before (as opposed to motels, cars, campgrounds, friends' homes, etc.). Forty-three percent of Church guests with full-time jobs and 97 percent of those with part-time jobs reported seeking additional work. (These figures should be regarded as largely unbiased, since those working were already assured of high priority for admittance.)

12. See Goldstein et al., *Shelter Users*; NCH, *An Embarrassment of Riches* (New York, 1985); NCH, *Out in the Cold* (Washington, D.C., 1987); NCH, *Pushed Out: America's Homeless, Thanksgiving, 1987* (Washington, D.C., 1987).

13. For instance, a third of those in St. Paul and Minneapolis shelters reported that they could pay over $200 a month, and 35 percent of the women residents could pay over $300 a month (Owen, Mattesich, and Williams, *Twin City Survey*, p. 9). At one time some form of housing would have been available for those (real) dollars.

14. For example:
    FIELD NOTES, 3 / 28 / 83: Ran into Virginia Mike today. Said he was going home [i.e., back to Virginia] April 1: "I can be poor there just like here. At least I have my people there."

15. Sixty-nine percent stressed roots of various sorts (lifetime or long-term residency, friends or family, homeless activism, school, or job); 21 percent mentioned amenities (climate, safety, services); 9 percent said they were "tired of running" or "want to make my stand here." The advantage of staying in a town where one has preexisting networks is suggested by the HoPP figures relating length of time in Santa Barbara to where people slept: Whereas 1 of 12 HoPP members in town under a year was staying with a friend or relative, 11 of 25 of those in town longer than a year were so sheltered.

16. *Address Unknown*, p. 118.

17. Michael Perez, "Homelessness in Isla Vista" (report, Isla Vista, Calif., 1984), p. 5.
18. Erving Goffman, *Stigma* (New York, 1986), p. 2.
19. See Marjorie Hope and James Young, *The Faces of Homelessness* (Lexington, Mass., 1986), p. 27; Howard M Bahr, *Skid Row* (New York, 1973), pp. 58–86. Why housed people view unhoused people in this way is a fecund topic in itself: See Douglas K. Welch, "Homelessness in America" (B.A. honors thesis, Wesleyan University, 1989); Jonathan Kozol, *Rachel and Her Children* (New York, 1988), p. 130.
20. *Stigma*, p. 5.
21. Welch, "Homelessness in America," p. 54.
22. Michael Sloss, "The Crisis of Homelessness," *Urban and Social Change Review* 17 (Summer 1984): 18.
23. Elliot Liebow, *Tally's Corner* (Boston, 1967).
24. The only exceptions to this pattern were a small number of Street People who said they wanted to aid homeless people.
25. *Stigma*, p. 4.
26. See David A. Snow, Susan G. Barker, and Leon Anderson, "Criminality and Homeless Men," *Social Problems* 36 (1989): 542–543.
27. For instance, the percentage of HoPP interviewees arrested at least once expressed as a ratio to the percentage of those who reported having committed at least one crime is 1:2 for those who have been homeless less than a year but rises to 3:4 for those homeless over a year.
28. Snow et al., "Criminality," p. 545.
29. See Robert M. Myers, *The Homeless in Santa Monica* (Santa Monica, Calif., 1988); Snow et al., "Criminality," pp. 544–545.
30. Snow et al., "Criminality," p. 546.
31. For evidence tying substance abuse to chronic or long-term homelessness, see "Tracking the Homeless," *Focus* 10 (1987–88): 21–24; Wright, *Address Unknown*, p. 153. The regression analyses of Piliavin et al. failed to show substance abuse as a significant influence on chronic homelessness, although it "had substantial and statistically significant zero-order correlations with our measures of chronicity": Irving Piliavin, Michael Sosin, and Herb Westerfelt, "Conditions Contributing to Long-term Homelessness" (discussion paper no. 853–87, Institute for Research on Poverty, University of Wisconsin-Madison, 1988), p. 23.
32. The public identification of homelessness with alcoholism is in part a perceptual problem tied to the far greater visibility of those who drink on the streets (because they have no home to drink in) than the many who drink at home (see Bahr, *Skid Row*, p. 228; National Council on Alcoholism, Santa Barbara Chapter, "Lower State Street," *Keynotes* 5 [May 1983]: 2), and their concomitant greatly increased chance of arrest (see Snow et al., "Criminality"). CAVE's study of jail records indicated that twenty-nine people accounted for between 20 and 25 percent of all arrests for public drunkenness in Santa Barbara in 1982–83: interview with Charles Parkey, April 15, 1983; not all of these people, of course, were necessarily homeless.
33. Mary Ellen Hombs and Mitch Snyder, *Homelessness in America* (Washington, D.C., 1983), p. 115.

34. Michael Drohan, Margaret Rafferty, and Rita Zimmer, "Helping the Homeless Alcoholic," in Margaret Rafferty, Denise A. Hinzpeter, Laurie Colwin, and Margaret Knox, eds., *The Shelter Worker's Handbook* (New York, 1984), p. 136.

35. For similar data from other areas, see Stephen Crystal and Mervyn Goldstein, *The Homeless in New York City Shelters* (New York, 1984), p. 26; James D. Wright and Eleanor Weber, *Homelessness and Health* (Washington, D.C., 1987), pp. 70–77; Martha R. Burt and Barbara E. Cohen, "Differences Among Homeless Single Women, Women with Children, and Single Men," *Social Problems* 36 (1989): 517. In-depth data on substance abuse among homeless people in Santa Barbara are somewhat restricted. The Church shelters' strict and well-publicized ban of those who had been drinking limited the number who might mention alcoholism problems as well as the number of drinkers who actually gained admittance. The SPA call-in forms did not include questions about alcohol or drug use. The available evidence is therefore limited to the HoPP data, but these too have important limitations. Although my field experiences often included observation of, and encounters with, alcoholics, formal oral histories were obtained from a smaller group of people who were both willing and able to answer my questions. Only five of the forty-four HoPP respondents were people whose lives revolved around drinking, obtaining funds to drink, or the struggle to give up drinking; the comments that follow are based on both the oral histories and field observations.

36. While this is attributable in part to the presence of children and attendant feelings of responsibility, cultural factors may also play a role. Wright and Weber report that homeless Hispanics seen at medical centers were disproportionately unlikely to have drinking problems: *Homelessness and Health*, p. 71.

37. A number of studies have suggested that Kids tend to come from households in which substance abuse is common: Virginia Price, "Runaways and Homeless Street Youth," in The Boston Foundation, *Homelessness* (Boston, 1987), p. 26; Marjorie Robertson, Paul Koegel, and Linda Ferguson, "Alcohol Use and Abuse Among Homeless Adolescents in Hollywood," *Contemporary Drug Problems* 16 (1989): p. 426. I had insufficient data to assess this factor in Santa Barbara.

38. Less than 6 percent of the homeless adolescents interviewed by Robertson et al. reported daily alcohol use, while 39 percent reported getting drunk once a month: "Homeless Adolescents," p. 425. However, they characterize 49 percent of their surveyed population as having "a DSM-II diagnosis of alcohol abuse" (p. 439). See also National Network of Runaway and Youth Services, Inc., *To Whom Do They Belong?* (Washington, D.C., 1985); Robertson et al., "Homeless Adolescents," p. 419, appropriately point out that "studies on alcohol and this population . . . are plagued by serious problems" of specification and nonstandardization of assessment techniques.

39. See John Talbott, Anthony Arce, Ken Thompson, Margaret Rafferty, and Timothy O'Connor, "Psychiatric Illnesses Among the Homeless," in Rafferty et al., *Shelter Worker's Handbook*, p. 88; Ellen Baxter and Kim Hopper,

"The New Mendicancy," *American Journal of Orthopsychiatry* 52 (1982): 403; Leona L. Bachrach, "The Homeless Mentally Ill and Mental Health Services," in Richard H. Lamb, ed., *The Homeless Mentally Ill* (Washington, D.C., 1984), pp. 15–16. Such abuse has been noted among nonhomeless chronically mentally ill people as well: See James H. Shore, "The Epidemiology of Chronic Mental Illness," in David L. Cutler, ed., *Effective Aftercare for the 1980s* (San Francisco, 1983), pp. 5–12.

40. To the best of my knowledge, use of drugs during my research period was mainly restricted to marijuana and occasional psychedelics; public assistance workers (who agree with this characterization) reported in 1990 that crack and heroin had surfaced in one shelter since that time.

41. Ropers, *Invisible Homeless*, p. 62, citing an unspecified 1983 U.S. Department of Health and Human Services report. For varying estimates of the prevalence of substance abuse among street populations, see Paul Koegel and M. Audrey Burnham, "Traditional and Nontraditional Alcoholics," *Alcohol Health and Research World* 11 (1987): 29; Dee Roth and Jerry Bean, "The Ohio Study Revisited," *Alcohol Health and Research World* 10 (1985–86): 14–15; Robertson et al., "Homeless Adolescents," p. 439.

42. See James F. Rooney, "Group Processes Among Skid Row Winos," *Quarterly Journal of Studies on Alcohol* 22 (1961): 444–460, for a discussion of the "psyche-group functions or structured interpersonal contacts which fulfill emotional needs" of "bottle gang" members on Skid Row; and Baxter and Hopper, "New Mendicancy," for a similar viewpoint.

43. "Isla Vista," p. 2.

44. Many alcoholism researchers, no doubt, would question whether the reasons listed above are truly why these homeless people drink. Certainly some of the quotations are self-serving, and some come from people with long histories of drinking before they were homeless. Alcoholism clearly has deeper roots than immediate disappointment. Yet analyses and treatments that view alcoholism as a disease unconnected to people's everyday realities merit criticism. People seem to have greater or lesser tendencies to alcoholism from some combination of genetics and background. But within those tendencies, the desire to drink and the ability to *stop* drinking are clearly affected by a sense of fulfillment or lack of fulfillment within daily life. See Wright and Weber, *Homelessness and Health*, pp. 77–78, for a similar assessment.

45. These include social interactive problems as well as effects on health: D E M O   D A N : Drinking, it's just a craziness. . . . You know, when [homeless] people are arguing, most of the time it's behind drinking. . . . And a lot of times it's like if you get drunk, you're an easy pigeon. . . . Like one night I . . . went behind the Star Bar and was drinking with a bunch of people. . . . The cops came and they checked me for ID. . . . I couldn't find my ID, and I couldn't find my money either. I was looking for my wallet at the time going, "What happened to all that money I had in my pocket?"

46. See Wright and Weber, *Homelessness and Health*, p. 77.

47. For an instructive discussion of the "planned" versus the "unplanned" drunk," see Douglas A. Harper, *Good Company* (Chicago, 1982), p. 158.

48. In 1986 a psychiatric worker at the jail told me, "You could get fifty people out of this jail immediately if the County had a detox facility." A joint private/County "sobering unit" was created in 1989; in its first year, staff reported serving 88 homeless individuals out of 2,000 clients: Flack, *Santa Barbara CHAP*, p. 7. Shipley et al. argue that the detoxification process is of particular importance for homeless alcoholics "to promote the first steps in rehabilitation" and avoid an endless "revolving door" of arrest, detoxification, release to the streets, and rearrest: Thomas E. Shipley, Irving W. Shandler, and Michael L. Penn, "Treatment and Research with Homeless Alcoholics," *Contemporary Drug Problems* 16 (1989): 511.

49. Kay Whitney, "Summary of Alcoholism Services to Street Alcoholics," appendix to Michelle Jackman et al., "Task Force on Lower State Street Problems: Summary Report" (Santa Barbara, 1983). In the late 1980s, a privately funded "Project Recovery" began using acupuncture for the treatment of substance abuse. It reported seeing 420 clients in 1987 (Flack, *Santa Barbara CHAP*, p. 7), but the housing status of clients is unknown. Robertson et al. report that only 13 percent of homeless adolescent alcohol abusers in their Hollywood study had ever received inpatient alcohol treatment; only 18 percent had received alcohol treatment of any kind in the past year: "Homeless Adolescents," p. 436.

50. Gerald Garrett's review of recent studies leads him to estimate that 10 to 15 percent of homeless people are drug abusers, and 3 to 4 percent daily drug users, compared with his estimate of 30 to 40 percent (presumably with some overlap) being alcohol abusers: "Alcohol Problems and Homelessness," *Contemporary Drug Problems* 16 (1989): 320–321. Again, these studies largely neglected the hidden homeless population. Regarding etiology, Jim Baumohl, for instance, points out that the demise of SROs and the adoption of stricter admission policies at state mental hospitals removed two traditional housing havens for low-income alcoholics: "Alcohol, Homelessness, and Public Policy," *Contemporary Drug Problems* 16 (1989): 292.

51. Proposition 13, passed in California in 1978, severely limited property taxes and hence local government revenue and spending.

52. See Wright and Weber, *Homelessness and Health*, pp. 77–78; Kim Hopper, "Deviance and Dwelling Space," *Contemporary Drug Problems* 16 (1989): 391–414; Friedner D. Wittman, "Housing Models for Alcohol Programs Serving Homeless People," *Contemporary Drug Problems* 16 (1989): 483–504.

53. See Charles Hoch and Robert A. Slayton, *New Homeless and Old* (Philadelphia, 1989), pp. 94–98.

54. See Robertson et al., "Homeless Adolescents," p. 443, for this argument concerning homeless adolescents.

55. Baumohl wisely cautions in "Public Policy," p. 288, that "advocates for the homeless cannot simply deny that there is widespread pathology (or harmful behavior) among the homeless when there is good evidence of it." The question is how good—and how representative—the available evidence is. The extent of substance abuse, the variations among subgroups, and particularly the importance of such abuse as either cause of homelessness or barrier to escape have yet to be definitively established.

56. See James P. Spradley, *You Owe Yourself a Drunk* (Boston, 1970).

57. The presence of meaningful affiliations between homeless people that I stressed in Chapter 4 "might actually prolong a state like homelessness because of the commitment one develops to others" (Jim Baumohl, personal communication, July 14, 1992); this suggestion is certainly consistent with social network theories concerning the ways in which people retain group membership through close ties: See J. Miller McPherson, Pamela A. Popielarz, and Sonja Drobnic, "Social Networks and Organizational Dynamics," *American Sociological Review* 57 (1992): 153–170; Claude S. Fischer, "Network Analysis and Urban Studies," in Claude S. Fischer, ed., *Networks and Places* (New York, 1977), pp. 19–37. I did not, however, find such ties to be an impediment to escape except for some women who attached themselves to a man for protection on the streets but were then drawn into his counterproductive activities such as drinking or crime.

58. It could well be argued that the slackers and sliders were unlikely to be interviewed because of the way in which HoPP interviewees were selected, yet the Church data also suggest that most homeless people are trying to escape their state. There is little long-term use of the shelters; the employment rate of Church guests, while dismal, rises continuously with time in Santa Barbara; and the percentage of *employed* Church guests seeking further work is quite high (43 percent of those Church guests working full-time and 97 percent of those working part-time). See Wright's calculation that "the 'undeserving homeless,' or, if you will, the 'just plain shiftless,' . . . account for about 5% of the total [homeless] population": *Address Unknown*, p. 66. Even the declarations of the few who say they "choose" homelessness freely can only be understood in context: "Homelessness may indeed be a matter of choice for some people, but perhaps only when there is a scant number of alternatives that are no more palatable than life on the street. To the extent that this is true, the choice is of the lesser of evils and takes on a rather different meaning than if it were made in the face of more attractive options": David Snow and Leon Anderson, "Identity Work Among the Homeless," *American Journal of Sociology* 92 (1987): 1364.

59. Much more dramatic impacts on health are noted in most studies. See Wright and Weber, *Homelessness and Health;* Rafferty et al., *Shelter Worker's Handbook;* Rossi et al., "Urban Homeless," p. 1337; Burt and Cohen, "Differences," p. 516.

60. For arguments that homelessness at the very least can lead to disorientation and depression, see Kozol, *Rachel and Her Children*, p. 152; Carl I. Cohen and Jay Sokolovsky, *Old Men of the Bowery* (New York, 1988), p. 201; Peter Rossi, *Down and Out in America* (Chicago, 1989), p. 148; Leanne G. Rivlin, "A New Look at the Homeless," *Social Policy* 16 (Spring 1986): 8–9. Schwartz et al. point out that mentally ill people often have periods in which they seem to be "basically healthy people," but "difficulties in fulfilling practical needs . . . [may] become stressful enough to trigger decompensation": Stuart R. Schwartz, Stephen M. Goldfinger, Michael Ratener, and David L. Cutler, "The Young Adult Chronic Patient and the Care System," in Cutler, ed., *Effective Aftercare*, p. 32.

61. For example, less than half of those with serious mental problems who made

it into the Church shelters were receiving SSI or SSDI, and fewer than one in seven was in touch with a social worker.

62. See Robert H. Howland, "Barriers to Community Treatment of Patients with Dual Diagnoses," *Hospital and Community Psychiatry* 41 (1990): 1134–1135; Bachrach, "Homeless Mentally Ill"; Barbara I. Larew, "Strange Strangers," *Social Casework* 61 (1980): 107–113.

63. Hombs and Snyder report in *Homelessness in America*, p. 51, that 600,000 mentally ill Americans are arrested every year; see also Joseph D. Bloom, Larry Faulkner, James H. Shore, and Jeffrey L. Rogers, "The Young Adult Chronic Patient and the Legal System," in Cutler, ed., *Effective Aftercare*, pp. 37–50; Linda Teplin, "Criminalizing Mental Disorder," *American Psychologist* 39 (1984): 795–803. Homeless mentally ill people are particularly likely to be arrested: 70 percent of those interviewed in the Santa Barbara County Mental Health study reported arrest records ("Preliminary Report" [Santa Barbara, 1986], p. 4), compared with about a third of the HoPP group.

    Although the jail social workers are empowered to invoke "a 5150," authorizing a seventy-two-hour confinement for observation and psychological evaluation, or "a 5250," authorizing a fourteen-day stay in a mental health facility, current legal restrictions and the lack of facilities make that improbable. One jail worker commented, "If you can get to the [Rescue] Mission on your own, you're not a 5250."

64. The Santa Barbara Rescue Mission, for instance, has a 15 percent success rate: Ronald W. Powell, "Homeless Need More Than a Roof Over Their Heads," *Santa Barbara News-Press*, June 4, 1990.

65. If it is true, as interactionists have long posited, that our sense of self is developed from the reflection we see in the mirrors of others' reactions, what kind of damage do we do to people when we not only present an undesirable reflection but in many cases simply pretend that there is nothing in front of us to cast an image?

66. *Stigma*, p. 37.

67. See Kozol, *Rachel and Her Children*, pp. 33, 67, for vivid examples of this paralysis. He notes: "Physicians often hear these words, 'I can't breathe,' in interviews with homeless patients" (p. 39).

68. For similar findings, see Vijaya L. Melnick and Charles S. Williams, *Homelessness in the District of Columbia* (Washington, D.C., 1987), p. 5; Ropers, *Invisible Homeless*, pp. 198–209; Hope and Young, *Faces of Homelessness*, pp. 243–248.

69. "Mere desire to abide by the norm—mere good will—is not enough, for in many cases the individual has no immediate control over his level of sustaining the norm. It is a question of the individual's condition, not his will": *Stigma*, p. 128.

70. See Snow and Anderson, "Identity Work," for an extensive discussion of how homeless people use verbal constructions to create and sustain personal identities.

71. Peter Rossi, Gene Fisher, and Georgiana Willis, *The Condition of the Homeless in Chicago* (Amherst, Mass., 1986); Marjorie Robertson, Richard Ropers, and Richard Boyer, *The Homeless of Los Angeles County* (Los Angeles, 1985); Dee Roth, Jerry Bean, Nancy Lust, and Traian Saveanu, *Homelessness in Ohio*

(Columbus, Ohio, 1985); Focus, "Tracking the Homeless"; Piliavin et al., "Long-term Homelessness."

72. Focus, "Tracking the Homeless," looks at the presence of children but makes no theoretical argument.

73. For example, 80 percent of married Church guests could give an emergency contact, compared with 62 percent of single guests.

74. Wright and Weber, *Homelessness and Health*, p. 71; Burt and Cohen, "Differences," pp. 517–518.

75. For an argument that networks of employed friends are essential for escaping unemployment, see Martha Van Haitsma, "A Contextual Definition of the Underclass," *Focus* 12 (Spring/Summer 1989): 27–31.

76. However, those Church guests and HoPP respondents who are working do not show shorter periods of homelessness on average than those not working (especially when one removes those homeless less than six months, who may still be holding on to their old jobs). This reflects the low wages paid for the jobs homeless people can get and the high cost of renting an apartment. On ties to housed friends and family, see Wright and Weber, *Homelessness and Health*, p. 54.

77. Some studies, however, present evidence that parents are likely to be homeless for shorter periods: See Burt and Cohen, "Differences," p. 514; Wright, *Address Unknown*, p. 74; Focus, "Tracking the Homeless," p. 24. Similarly, no SPA caller had been homeless over a year.

78. See Focus, "Tracking the Homeless," pp. 23–24; Owen, Mattessich, and Williams, *Twin City Survey*, pp. 20–21; Snow and Anderson, "Identity Work," pp. 1350–1351, 1358.

79. The HoPP data are very similar, although the differences in likelihood of receiving welfare are more pronounced and contrary results are found regarding full-time workers; the HoPP group contained more short-term-homeless women not working but receiving entitlements and some long-term homeless Latino Families whose breadwinners continue working full-time. Of course these variables work both ways. Those who do not work or receive public assistance will tend to remain homeless longer; those who are homeless longer become discouraged and less inclined to work or apply for assistance. Additionally, variables like work are subject to many contingencies, most of which may be out of the control of the individual homeless person, and therefore may not necessarily demonstrate disaffiliation. Emergency contact, however, remains a strong indicator of affiliation.

80. But see Wright and Weber, *Homelessness and Health*, p. 54, for a finding that length of homelessness does not correlate with migration.

81. See Boris M. Levinson, "The Homeless Man," *Mental Hygiene* 47 (1963): 596; Bahr, *Skid Row*, p. 288. On the other hand, some of their contemporaries found no such normative isolation in post–World War II Skid Row populations: See James F. Rooney, "Societal Forces and the Unattached Male," in Howard M. Bahr, ed., *Disaffiliated Man* (Toronto, 1970), pp. 13–38; Theodore Caplow, "The Sociologist and the Homeless Man," ibid., pp. 3–12.

82. For similar findings, see Ann Marie Rousseau, *Shopping Bag Ladies* (New York, 1981), p. 17; Hope and Young, *Faces of Homelessness*, pp. 31–32; Baxter and Hopper, "New Mendicancy," p. 403.

83. This emphasis on freedom and autonomy mixed with patriotism was a common thread of Street People interviews (especially among veterans), as the American flag was a common prop at HPA demonstrations and gatherings. (Skidders not only shunned this concept of freedom but were far more likely to be critical of the country and the Reagan administration.) As Segal and his co-workers found in Berkeley, "the high value street people . . . place on self-sufficiency and autonomy cannot be over-emphasized": Steven P. Segal, Jim Baumohl, and Elise Johnson, "Falling Through the Cracks," *Social Problems* 24 (1977): 394; this value is seen in Henry's refusal to get on GR, since it would make him "dependent," or Kevin's giving up Food Stamps as a "bribe."

84. Rescue Mission: Interview with Charles Pope, director of Santa Barbara Rescue Mission, March 22, 1983. See also Sara Harris, *Skid Row, U.S.A.* (Garden City, N.Y., 1956), p. 15.

85. *Tally's Corner.*

86. Hyman Rodman, "The Lower-class Value Stretch," *Social Forces* 62 (1963): 205–215. Of course, it is likely that *all* people engage in value-stretching from time to time.

87. Robert Merton, *Social Theory and Social Structure* (New York, 1968 [1949]).

88. Rousseau, *Shopping Bag Ladies*, p. 17.

89. "Learning the ways of the streets" is commonly seen as one of the few positive things about being homeless:

    M A R G I E : Homelessness teaches me how to survive, it's a big lesson. I have always wanted to know what it was to be smart, street-wise. This is good because, you know, I've never had it easy, but still, now I know better. Now I know more than I knew before. And I don't feel as naive as I was before.

90. *Tally's Corner*, pp. 64–66. For similar reports regarding homeless people, see Kozol, *Rachel and Her Children*, pp. 37, 129; Kim Hopper and Ellen Baxter, "The Experiment Continues," in U.S. Congress, Subcommittee on Housing and Community Development, *Homelessness in America—II* (Washington, D.C., 1984), p. 517. For arguments regarding working-class people generally, see Lillian Breslow Rubin, *Worlds of Pain* (New York, 1976); Hylan Lewis, "Culture, Class and the Behavior of Low Income Families" (paper presented at the National Conference on Social Welfare, New York City, May 29, 1962).

91. Harry Murray, "Time in the Streets," *Human Organization* 43 (1984): 154–161.

92. For arguments that shelters and other "caretaker" arrangements breed dependency, see Hoch and Slayton, *New Homeless*, pp. 82–83, 196–198; Cohen and Sokolovsky, *Old Men*, pp. 132–133.

Chapter 7: H o m e l e s s n e s s   a n d   t h e   A m e r i c a n   P a r a d i s e

1. I have retained the construction "the homeless" here because the arguments against aiding homeless people indeed treat them as a homogeneous group.

2. The National Coalition for the Homeless noted sardonically in 1985 that the mayor of Elizabeth, New Jersey, had recently "joined a list of nearly 50 different mayors, governors, or county executives who claim their area is the mecca for the nation's homeless": *SN 2* (February 1985): 1.

3. King County, *Homelessness Revisited* (Seattle, 1986), p. 16, based on uncited NCH figures.

4. Cited in James D. Wright and Eleanor Weber, *Homelessness and Health* (Washington, D.C., 1987), p. 52.

5. Just under half of HoPP interviewees had lived in Santa Barbara for five years or more, while 74 percent of Santa Barbara city residents in 1980 had lived in Santa Barbara County in 1975. These figures are calculated from data in Santa Barbara City, *Housing Element Addendum, 1985 Update* (Santa Barbara, 1986), p. 93. In general, families, and particularly women with children, appear to migrate much less often than single men: See Manhattan Task Force, *A Shelter Is Not a Home* (New York, 1987), pp. 16–17; Eric Goplerud, *Homelessness in Fairfax County* (Fairfax, Va., 1987), p. 19; Merv Goldstein, Stephen Levine, and Robert Lipkins, *Characteristics of Shelter Users* (New York, 1986), p. 12.

6. In all parts of the country, cities located near areas undergoing local depressions show comparatively higher percentages of migrants, though these are typically people from surrounding states: See Knoxville Coalition, *Homelessness in Knox County* (Knoxville, Ohio, 1986), p. 16; USCM, *Homelessness In America's Cities* (Washington, D.C., 1984), p. 6; Dan Salerno, Kim Hopper, and Ellen Baxter, *Hardship in the Heartland* (New York, 1984), p. 133. For a general critique of "mobility theory" see Barret A. Lee, "Residential Mobility on Skid Row," *Demography* 15 (1978): 285–300.

7. Certainly some homeless people move to the Sunbelt because survival seems easier there:

   J U L I A : South. Warm. Cover your basic needs. Stay alive. Do not freeze to death. Do not cause yourself to go into any mental abuse because of not having your basic human needs covered.

   For other reasons see Knoxville Coalition, *Knox County*, p. 16; Greg Owen, Paul Mattessich, and Judy Williams, *Results of the Twin City Survey of Emergency Shelter Residents* (St. Paul, 1987), p. 9; Mary E. Stefl, "The New Homeless," in Richard D. Bingham, Roy E. Green, and Sammis B. White, eds., *The Homelessness in Contemporary Society* (Newbury Park, Calif., 1987), pp. 48–49.

8. When asked why they came to Santa Barbara, nonnative HoPP interviewees were less likely to cite the availability of services than a past stay in the city, being dropped off in town by chance, or work opportunities; they were about twice as likely to cite the climate or the presence of friends or family. Throughout the period of study, Santa Barbara County's GR payments were the highest in California, 76 percent above the state median, yet not a single person in the Homeless People's Project (nor any other homeless person I met in my travels) mentioned GR as a reason for coming to or staying in Santa Barbara. See Carl Brown, Steve MacFarlane, Ron Paredes, and Louisa Stark, "Executive Summary of *The Homeless of Phoenix*" (Phoenix, 1983), pp. 8–10, for similar findings.

9. Attract: Howard M. Bahr, *Skid Row* (New York, 1973), p. 107; Leona L. Bachrach, "The Homeless Mentally Ill and Mental Health Services," in H. Richard Lamb, ed., *The Homeless Mentally Ill* (Washington, D.C., 1984), p. 15. Repel: William H. Friedland and Robert A. Marotto, "Streetpeople and Straightpeople in Santa Cruz" (manuscript, University of California at Santa Cruz, 1985), pp. 29–30.

10. Dallas: NCH, *National Neglect/National Shame* (Washington, D.C., 1986), p. 18. New York: *New York Times*, January 10, 1987, cited in Jonathan Kozol, *Rachel and Her Children* (New York, 1988), p. 14.

11. Research Atlanta, *The Impact of Homelessness on Atlanta* (Atlanta, 1984), p. 55.

12. Rob Rosenthal, "Homeless People's Project Interim Report 2" (Santa Barbara, 1984). While much of this amount went for fixed costs such as police salaries, other parts were highly variable, such as jail services and patrol car costs.

13. Health workers also point out that hospital costs tend to be higher for homeless people than for others, since doctors often keep them in hospital beds for longer periods rather than releasing them to the streets, where their condition would quickly regress. The huge pool of untreated disease among homeless people affects the general public as well (for instance, through exposure to homeless children at school; see Wright and Weber, *Homelessness and Health*, p. 107). Recent studies documenting the spread of AIDS and HIV infection through the homeless population indicate that such costs may be greatly enlarged in the near future: See National Commission on Acquired Immune Deficiency Syndrome, "Open Letter to President George Bush" (Washington, D.C., April 24, 1990); NCH, *Fighting to Live* (Washington, D.C., 1990).

14. People who are judged to be potentially dangerous to themselves or others are usually taken by the Santa Barbara police to the local Psychiatric Health Facility (PHF), at a cost of $288 per day in 1985. Mental health officials estimate that 25 percent of these people are homeless. The average length of stay is five to six days, but, here again, those who are homeless are generally detained another three to five days while housing is sought. Many of those most disoriented and without a home are seen again and again at the PHF unit. Research Atlanta estimates that three-quarters of the more than $20 million in annual costs of homelessness in Atlanta are in mental and physical health costs: *Impact*, p. 55.

15. The Santa Barbara merchants of CAVE argued that a bed in an alcohol rehabilitation program would cost $5,000 per year (in 1983), compared with jail costs of $27,000 per year: interview with Charles Parkey, chair of CAVE, April 15, 1983. Other cities: See Kozol, *Rachel and Her Children*, pp. 48–49; Richard Neuner and David Schultz, *Borrow Me a Quarter* (Anoka, Minn., 1986).

16. Philip L. Clay, *At Risk of Loss* (Washington, D.C., 1987).

17. Kozol, however, argues that small, nonprofit shelters in New York are typically both cheaper *and* offer more services than large city-run "barracks" shelters: *Rachel and Her Children*, pp. 17–18. See Robert Trobe, "Understanding the City Approach to the Problem," *CBC Quarterly* 2 (1982): 4–6, for a city administrator's rejoinder to such criticisms.

18. A Legal Aid attorney, for instance, points out "the futility of a [New York] state policy which denies [potentially homeless AFDC] recipients the [additional] $60 or $80 they need to meet monthly rental costs while spending literally thousands of dollars to provide them with emergency shelter once they become homeless": *SN* 9 (May 1990): 2.

19. For instance, until 1987 federal tax laws allowed landlords to use accelerated depreciation allowances to offset other income, thereby encouraging turnover of properties (with consequent raising of rents to cover new mortgage costs) every five years, the period of most accelerated depreciation. Ironically, the 1986 Tax Reform Act, which phased out depreciation allowances for part-time landlords and capital gains treatments, has made landlording considerably less attractive as a tax shelter, necessitating a rapid rise in rents to make up the lost income.

20. Peter Dreier and John Atlas, "Mansion Subsidy Revisited," *Shelterforce* 13 (May/June 1991): 16.

21. Appropriations for public housing in the last Reagan budget of 1989 were $381 million, about 8 percent of their level in the average Carter administration budget: *SN* 10 (January 1991), p. 2. Although Section 8 total outlays tripled in the 1980s because of rising costs, annual net new commitments dropped 44 percent in that period: Sar A. Levitan, *Programs in Aid of the Poor* (Baltimore, 1990), pp. 93–94. With the elimination of the Section 8 construction program for all units except those to be occupied by elderly and handicapped people, the great bulk of Section 8 funds were channeled to existing housing rather than production of additional housing (ibid., p. 94).

22. U.S. Congressional Budget Office, *Current Housing Problems and Possible Federal Responses* (Washington, D.C., 1988). Regulations have further restricted eligibility for housing assistance. For instance, single people (unless elderly or disabled) may not occupy more than 15 percent of public housing or Section 8 units in most projects, despite the fact that single people make up the majority of homeless people in the country: *SN* 9 (May 1990): 4.

23. *SN* 9 (January 1990): 3.

24. See IPS, *The Right to Housing* (Oakland, Calif., 1989), p. 7; Teresa Riordan, "Housekeeping at HUD," *Common Cause Magazine*, March/April 1987, p. 26; *Shutting the Back Door* is an invaluable source for ongoing and extensive discussions regarding the loss of privately owned subsidized housing: "An Occasional Newsbrief from the National Anti-Displacement Project on the Loss of Privately Owned Assisted Housing," Low Income Housing Information Service, 1012 14th St., NW, Suite 1500, Washington, D.C. 20005. While the 1990 National Affordable Housing Act provided guidelines (and very attractive incentives to owners) to save many of these units as low-income housing, it by no means guarantees that this will occur. Protections for rural low-income housing built under similar conditions under the Section 515 program were considerably weakened within a year after enactment, following an onslaught of protests from the construction and real estate lobbies: see Robert Wiener, "Prepayment Hits Countryside Hard," *Shelterforce* 12 (March/April 1990): 18–21.

25. Thus welfare benefits declined 35 percent in real dollars from 1970 to 1987: *New York Times*, July 30, 1987, cited in Kozol, *Rachel and Her Children*, p. 81.

This pattern was repeated at the local level: For example, public assistance shelter allowances in New York rose only 25 percent from 1975 to 1986, while the median gross rent rose 100 percent: Manhattan Task Force, *A Shelter Is Not a Home,* p. 43.

26. This prohibition was abolished nationally beginning in October 1990 by the 1988 Family Support Act.

27. One result is that many homeless mentally ill people are now in danger of being "reinstitutionalized" in homeless shelters that have become semi-permanent warehouses without any therapeutic services. See Marta Elliott and Laura J. Krivo, "Structural Determinants of Homelessness in the United States," *Social Problems* 38 (1991): 126, for an argument that "greater per capita expenditures on residential beds and higher total per capita expenditures on mental health care are strongly associated with lower [local] rates of homelessness."

28. For instance, testimony before the Human Resources Committee of the House of Representatives indicates the misuse of perhaps $100 million in federal funds by existing local mental health centers: reported in *SN* 9 (May 1990), p. 2.

29. The federal government's potential role as a leader in the struggle against homelessness was circumscribed from the very creation of the Federal Interagency Task Force on Homelessness, founded in October 1983 with the following assumptions: "1. Homelessness is essentially a local problem. 2. New federal programs for the homeless are not the answer. 3. Knowledge of strategies in many communities to help the homeless needs to be transferred to other communities": (GAO, *Homelessness: A Complex Problem and the Federal Response* [GAO-HRD-85-40] (Washington, D.C., 1985), p. 41, citing the "Briefing Book" for the U.S. Department of Health and Human Services (HHS) Task Force on the Homeless.

30. Boston Commission, *Boston's Homeless* (Boston, 1987–88), p. iv. The federal response to Hurricane Andrew in 1992 bears out this observation.

31. Marjorie Hope and James Young, *The Faces of Homelessness* (Lexington, Mass., 1986), p. 47.

32. *Homelessness: Access to McKinney Act Programs Improved but Better Oversight Needed* [GAO/RCED-91-29] (Washington, D.C., 1990), pp. 2, 8.

33. See GAO, *McKinney Act Programs Improved;* GAO, *Homelessness: HUD's and FEMA's Progress in Implementing the McKinney Act* (Washington, D.C., 1989).

34. NCH, *Precious Resources* (Washington, D.C., 1988). Faced with these figures, a District Court judge ruled in July 1989 that HUD's implementation of the "HUD homes" program was invalid; a similar legal scenario was played out for the HHS: See *In Just Times* 1 (August 1990): 1; 2 (April 1991): 1. But despite these rulings, few properties have been transferred to homeless people or advocacy groups.

35. *In Just Times* 2 (June 1991): 1. This continues a pattern evident for some time within the federal government. For instance, although $8 million was appropriated in FY1984 to the Department of Defense for renovation of vacant military facilities for use as emergency shelters, "only $900,000 was obligated by DoD for two facilities. The balance of the funds was used for

the maintenance of Army Reserve facilities": congressional testimony of
Paul Wright, GAO, cited in U.S. Congress, Committee on Government
Operations, *The Federal Response to the Homeless Crisis* (99th Congress, 1st
Session, House Report 99-47) (Washington, D.C., 1985), p. 15.
36. NCH, *Pushed Out: America's Homeless, Thanksgiving, 1987* (Washington, D.C.,
    1987), pp. 80–81.
37. See Manhattan Task Force, *A Shelter Is Not a Home*, pp. 8–10. This
    irrationality was often mirrored at the local level. In the most famous
    example, throughout the 1980s New York City housed homeless families in
    welfare hotels at enormous cost rather than creating new housing by
    renovating the more than 100,000 vacant units in buildings seized by the
    city for nonpayment of taxes. Kozol points out that if the average rehabilita-
    tion cost of each unit was $50,000, "even this—a one-time cost—is less than
    what the city spends to house a family of five for two years in" a welfare
    hotel: *Rachel and Her Children*, p. 93.
38. *SN* 9 (February 1990): 2.
39. *SN* 10 (January 1991): 4.
40. See *In Just Times* 2 (November 1991).
41. Proof of residence: *In Just Times* 1 (February 1990): 2. Outreach: Grants
    under the Homeless Veterans' Reintegration Project of the McKinney Act
    now include a review of applicants' outreach strategies. Funding in FY1989
    and 1990, however, was only $1.9 million: Wendy Chris Adler, *Addressing
    Homelessness* (Washington, D.C., 1991), p. 36. State agencies that adminis-
    ter Food Stamps may now receive funding to support outreach efforts.
42. GAO, *Progress*.
43. Ibid.
44. See NCH, "Stewart B. McKinney Homeless Assistance Act Funding
    Levels" (Washington, D.C., 1991), p. 1; NCH, *Necessary Relief* (Washington,
    D.C., 1988), p. 24. Until early 1992, alcoholism was not defined as a
    disabling condition in applications for most McKinney Act housing grants; it
    is still not defined as such for some programs.
45. Homeless people who are HIV positive or stricken with AIDS are routinely
    denied admission to most shelters in the country: *SN* 9 (April 1990): 1, 4.
    The Bush proposals for FY1991 specifically excluded them from HUD
    housing programs for disabled people. The "Shelter Plus Care" and "AIDS
    Housing Opportunities" programs authorized in 1991 under the McKinney
    Act appeared finally to address this problem, but while $75 million was
    authorized for the latter program in 1991, no funds were appropriated
    (Adler, *Addressing Homelessness*, p. 17), nor were any requested in the
    president's FY1992 budget.
46. Military spending: Kozol, *Rachel and Her Children*, p. 134. Despite talk of a
    "peace dividend" resulting from the end of the Cold War, the Bush
    administration was successful in instituting prohibitions against the transfer
    of funds from military spending to domestic programs until at least 1994.
    S&Ls: Nancy Folbre notes that "the amount of money set aside every year
    to save the banking industry from self-destruction far exceeds expenditures
    on Aid to Families of Dependent Children (AFDC). Yet Republicans never
    worry that bankers are 'trapped in a spider's web of dependency' ": "Where

Has All the Money Gone?" *Village Voice Literary Supplement,* April 1990, p. 12.

47. Dreier and Atlas, "Mansion Subsidy Revisited," p. 16; Peter Dreier and John Atlas, "Eliminate the Mansion Subsidy," *Shelterforce* 12 (May/June 1990): 10–11, 21.

48. See John Atlas, "What to Expect from the Bush-Kemp Team?" *Shelterforce* 11 (December/January 1989): 6–7.

49. See Chester Hartman, "Not Good Enough," *Shelterforce* 13 (July/August 1991): 9; Barry Zigas, "Whole New Ballgame," *Shelterforce* 13 (July/August 1991): 6–8; *Shutting the Back Door,* November 1990, January 1991, May 1991. Projects with expiring Section 8 contracts are left largely unprotected against owner decisions to leave the program and convert to market-level rents: National Housing Law Project, "Summary of the 'Low-Income Housing Preservation and Resident Homeownership Act of 1990' " (Berkeley, 1990), p. 19.

50. "Not Good Enough," p. 9.

51. Robert Fitch, "Put 'Em Where We Ain't," *The Nation* 246 (1988): 468.

52. *Rachel and Her Children,* p. 39.

53. *Faces of Homelessness,* p. 269. Those countries calling themselves "socialist" in the 1980s generally reported little or no homelessness (see Antonin Kerner, "Affordable Housing in a Socialist Country," in Jurgen Friedrichs, ed., *Affordable Housing and the Homeless* [Berlin, 1988], pp. 75–88), although it is uncertain to what extent hidden homelessness and doubling up masked the phenomenon. Celestine Bohlen notes the recent growth of Hungary's "hard-core homeless, whose numbers have surged as Hungary evolves into a capitalist society": "Hungary's New Burden," *New York Times,* October 23, 1990.

54. Keeping in mind the extreme amount of guesswork in all estimates of homeless populations, see Arne Karyd, "Affordable Housing and the Market," in Friedrichs, ed., *Affordable Housing,* pp. 59–74; Naomi Carmon and Daniel Czamanski, "Israel," in Willem van Vliet, ed., *International Handbook of Housing Policies and Practices* (New York, 1990), pp. 517–536; Hope and Young, *Faces of Homelessness,* p. 270; Debbie C. Tennison, "Homeless People Grow Numerous in Europe Despite Welfare State," *Wall Street Journal,* April 25, 1983; Dan Ferrand-Bechmann, "Homeless in France," in Friedrichs, ed., *Affordable Housing,* pp. 147–155; William Tuohy, "Homeless: A Problem in Europe Too," *Los Angeles Times,* February 9, 1985.

55. For detailed discussions from a similar perspective, see Rachel G. Bratt, Chester Hartman, and Ann Meyerson, eds., *Critical Perspectives on Housing* (Philadelphia, 1986); John I. Gilderbloom and Richard Appelbaum, *Rethinking Rental Housing* (Philadelphia, 1988); Chester Hartman, *America's Housing Crisis* (Washington, D.C., 1985); David C. Schwartz, Richard C. Ferlauto, and Daniel N. Hoffman, *A New Housing Policy for America* (Philadelphia, 1988); IPS, *Right to Housing.*

56. George Sternlieb and James W. Hughes, "The Post-Shelter Society," in George Sternlieb and James W. Hughes, eds., *America's Housing* (New Brunswick, N.J., 1980), p. 41.

57. *Faces of Homelessness,* p. 138.

58. The 1975 and 1983 New Jersey Supreme Court decisions in the "Mount Laurel I" and "Mount Laurel II" cases provide legal precedent for overcoming local opposition to inclusionary zoning. Statutorily mandated affirmative planning would be more effective in promoting an equitable distribution of affordable housing than the "developers' remedies" prescribed in the Mount Laurel cases (as the court itself acknowledged); see Alan Mallach, "Opening the Suburbs," *Shelterforce* 11 (August/September 1988): 12–15.

59. For the short term, some "demand side" programs (like Section 8) will also need to be reauthorized until production equals demand.

60. Kozol, *Rachel and Her Children*, p. 200.

61. See Gilderbloom and Appelbaum, *Rethinking Rental Housing;* Emily P. Achtenberg and Peter Marcuse, "Toward the Decommodification of Housing," in Bratt et al., eds., *Critical Perspectives*, pp. 474–483; IPS, *Right to Housing*, p. 13. The actual funding mechanism might be a housing trust fund, as Schwartz et al. have suggested in *New Housing Policy*. California already operates a trust fund totaling $20 million per year, generated from offshore oil taxes.

62. Wright and Weber, *Homelessness and Health*, p. 153. At the same time, they characterize a national right to housing as "the ultimate solution" to homelessness. On local programs see IPS, *Right to Housing*, pp. 35–37.

63. *Rethinking Rental Housing*, p. 192. One immediate target for third-stream housing is the enormous number of subsidized units vulnerable to prepayment of mortgage and conversion to market-level rents. Saving them will require providing downpayment grants and technical support in most cases. The 1990 National Affordable Housing Act made a first (though vastly underfunded) step in this direction.

64. See Gilderbloom and Appelbaum, *Rethinking Rental Housing*, chap. 8. I am indebted to their work in this section. While housing availability appears to have been a problem in many of the formerly "socialist" countries of Eastern Europe, the proportion of household income spent on housing costs was typically much lower than in capitalist countries: See Kerner, "Socialist Country."

65. *Right to Housing*, pp. 62–63.

66. *Rethinking Rental Housing*, p. 199; for details of their plan, see pp. 190–196.

67. Theresa Funiciello, "Give Them Shelters," *The Nation* 246 (1988): 471; Victor Bach and Renee Steinhagen, *Alternatives to the Welfare Hotel* (New York, 1987), p. 26.

68. *A Shelter Is Not a Home*, pp. 98–102.

69. See David C. Schwartz, Richard C. Ferlauto, and Daniel N. Hoffman, "A New Housing Policy for America," *Shelterforce* 10 (April/May 1988): 13–14.

70. Dreier and Atlas point out that the rate of homeownership in Canada and Australia, neither of which has a homeowner deduction, is about the same as in the United States: "Eliminate the Mansion Subsidy," p. 11. However, the expectation of such tax relief is now part of family budgeting in the United States, and the deduction could not be eliminated without significant impact.

71. See Dreier and Atlas, "Mansion Subsidy Revisited," p. 11.

72. "How to Expand Homeownership," *Shelterforce* 15 (September/October 1992): 6–8. Eliminating the deduction entirely for households earning over $100,000 a year would produce an estimated $11.6 billion in annual government revenue: Dreier and Atlas, "Mansion Subsidy Revisited," p. 11.

73. For fuller discussions of public entitlements and social services, see Tom Joe and Cheryl Rogers, *By the Few for the Few* (Lexington, Mass., 1985); Levitan, *Programs;* Michael Katz, *The Undeserving Poor* (New York, 1989); Fred Block, Richard A. Cloward, Barbara Ehrenreich, and Frances Fox Piven, eds., *The Mean Season* (New York, 1987); John Schwarz, *America's Hidden Success* (New York, 1983).

74. For discussions on this point, see *Focus* 12 (Spring 1990).

75. This argument, of course, can instead be read as saying that workers who are not threatened with hunger and deprivation are an unruly bunch. This, Piven and Cloward have argued, was the reasoning behind the Reagan administration's assault on the welfare state: Frances Fox Piven and Richard Cloward, *The New Class War* (New York, 1982).

76. See Michael Harrington, *The New American Poverty* (New York, 1984), p. 93; Robert Kuttner, *The Economic Illusion* (Boston, 1984).

77. See Levitan, *Programs*, pp. 102–103; Hope and Young, *Faces of Homelessness*, p. 203; Funiciello, "Give Them Shelters," p. 471.

78. For examples currently in place on the local level, see Schwartz et al., "New Housing Policy," p. 15; NCH, *Out in the Cold* (Washington, D.C., 1987), p. 26; Manhattan Task Force, *A Shelter Is Not a Home*, pp. 2, 78–82.

79. *Faces of Homelessness*, p. 97.

80. See David T. Ellwood, *Poor Support* (New York, 1988); James Tobin, "The Case for an Income Guarantee," *Public Interest* 4 (Summer 1966): 31–41; Alicia H. Munnell, ed., *Lessons from the Income Maintenance Experiments* (Boston, 1986). At the same time, the minimum wage should be indexed to inflation to keep businesses from shifting their labor costs to the taxpayers.

81. Setting the minimum level at the current poverty line (adjustable upward for areas or households with extra costs) seems a politically defensible standard. But, further, future levels of aid in all programs must be indexed to inflation, as they are in universal programs like Social Security. Available evidence, however, suggests that poor families, given their other pressing needs, do not devote marginal additional income to housing (Urban Institute, "Uncoordinated Policies Leave Poor Inadequately Sheltered," *Urban Institute Policy and Research Report*, Summer 1988, pp. 11–13), underlining the need for the simultaneous creation of affordable housing and imposition of rent controls.

   In the Food Stamp program, the federal government has successfully set uniform (albeit unrealistically low) standards that take into account household characteristics and ensure equitable levels in disparate geographic areas. In contrast, the continuing failure of the federal government to mandate minimum AFDC levels has resulted in average AFDC payments per person in 1989 that range from $39 in Alabama and Mississippi to $198 in California: Levitan, *Programs*, pp. 49–51.

   The general perception of Social Security (and other non-means-tested programs) as an earned right, but AFDC (and other means-tested programs) as a gift, speaks eloquently to the need eventually to replace all public assistance programs with one unified, non-means-tested program, though, of course, the *level* of benefits will vary by income.

82. Despite conservatives' long-time emphasis on work incentives, the Omnibus Budget Reconciliation Act of 1981 virtually embraced disincentives for AFDC recipients to work. At the same time, "workfare" and other job or job-training requirements have never been realistic: Typically, those recipients required to enroll far outnumber training spots or eventual jobs; training is often for dead-end jobs; and many recipients are unable to work because of disabilities or responsibility for young children. Job training should be readily available and directed at careers rather than menial work; earnings should not be deducted from assistance payments until a household is well above the poverty line; transportation and affordable child care should be available.

83. For detailed discussions regarding family stability and related issues, see Diana Pearce and Harriette McAdoo, *Women and Children* (Washington, D.C., 1981); Ellwood, *Poor Support;* Children's Defense Fund, *Children in Poverty* (Washington, D.C. 1985); Ruth Sidel, *Women and Children Last* (New York, 1986); Lenore J. Weitzman, *The Divorce Revolution* (New York, 1985).

84. Children up to the age of nineteen in poverty-level families will be covered by Medicaid by the year 2003 if recently enacted policies are not reversed.

85. For fuller discussions regarding mental health care, see Leona L. Bachrach, ed., *Deinstitutionalization* (San Francisco, 1983); David L. Cutler, ed., *Effective Aftercare for the 1980s* (San Francisco, 1983); IAPRS, *Homeless Mentally Ill and Backlash Against Deinstitutionalization* (McClean, Va., 1985); Lamb, ed., *Homeless Mentally Ill;* Howard H. Goldman and Joseph P. Morrissey, "The Alchemy of Mental Health Policy," *American Journal of Public Health* 75 (1985): 727–731.

86. See John Talbott and H. Richard Lamb, "Summary and Recommendations," in Lamb, ed., *Homeless Mentally Ill*, p. 8; Stuart R. Schwartz, Stephen M. Goldfinger, Michael Ratener, and David L. Cutler, "The Young Adult Chronic Patient and the Care System," in Cutler, ed., *Effective Aftercare*, p. 32.

87. See Schwartz et al., "Young Adult," p. 32; Knoxville Coalition, *Knox County*, p. 26; and David Whitman, "Hope for the Homeless," *U.S. News and World Report*, February 29, 1988, pp. 25–35, for a popular treatment of this question.

88. See Phyllis Solomon, Joseph M. Davis, Barry Gordon, Paula Fishbein, and Anne Mason, *The Aftercare Mosaic* (Cleveland, 1983), p. 14; Susan Barrow, Fredric Hellman, Anne Lovell, Jane Plapinger, and Elmer Struening, *Effectiveness of Programs for the Mentally Ill Homeless* (New York, 1989).

89. In some cases states will have to override local zoning restrictions that exclude institutions as a way of keeping mentally ill people out of their communities—a policy change consistent with the recent Americans with Disabilities Act.

90. *Faces of Homelessness*, p. 98.

91. At present, care is generally paid for by patient fees and private insurance and delivered by private, for-profit agencies, which creates built-in incentives to discourage independence while stressing "client management": Hope and Young, *Faces of Homelessness*, pp. 170–172. An independent audit of federally funded community mental health centers (reported in *SN* 9 [May 1990]: 2) found almost half to be noncompliant with federal standards, and a quarter seriously so. Clearly, adequate funding and zealous oversight will be required to prevent such abuse in the public sector as well.

92. For detailed discussions of substance abuse, generally and among homeless people, see Arnold S. Trebach and Kevin B. Zeese, eds., *Reformer's Catalogue* (Washington, D.C., 1989); Ethan A. Nadelmann, "Drug Prohibition in the United States," *Science* 245 (1989): 939–947; Wright and Weber, *Homelessness and Health;* and the Fall 1989 issue of *Contemporary Drug Problems.*

    The term "endway" was suggested by shelter volunteer Jane Jansak, quoted in Hope and Young, *Faces of Homelessness*, p. 98. On chronic abusers see Gerald R. Garrett, "Alcohol Problems and Homelessness," *Contemporary Drug Problems* 16 (1989): 301–332; Thomas E. Shipley, Irving W. Shandler, and Michael L. Penn, "Treatment and Research with Homeless Alcoholics," *Contemporary Drug Problems* 16 (1989): 505–526.

93. For discussions of various aspects of the relationship of physical health to homelessness, see Wright and Weber, *Homelessness and Health;* Richard Lander, "Medical Needs of the Homeless," in Margaret Rafferty, Denise A. Hinzpeter, Laurie Colwin, and Margaret Knox, eds., *The Shelter Worker's Handbook* (New York, 1984), pp. 1–37.

94. Levitan, *Programs,* p. 80, citing U.S. Congress, House Committee on Education and Labor, *Health Insurance and the Uninsured* (Washington, D.C., 1988), p. 95.

95. For instance, providing Medicaid payments for all those below 140 percent of the poverty line who are not covered by private insurance (as currently envisioned by federal plans by the year 2003); providing federally generated regulations for payment and eligibility; replacing state block grants in Medicaid with direct payments, as in Medicare; and guaranteeing treatment and support services, with a parallel attack on discrimination in housing, for those who are HIV positive.

96. See Hope and Young, *Faces of Homelessness*, p. 224, for a review of some of these data.

97. For more detailed discussions of employment, unemployment, and deindustrialization, see Barry Bluestone and Bennett Harrison, *The Deindustrialization of America* (New York, 1982); Bennett Harrison and Barry Bluestone, *The Great U-Turn* (New York, 1988); Harrington, *New American Poverty;* S. M. Miller and Donald Tomaskovic-Devey, *Recapitalizing America* (Boston, 1983).

98. See Christopher Jencks, *Inequality* (New York, 1972), for a masterful statement of this argument, and *Who Gets Ahead?* (New York, 1979) for a subsequent reassessment.

99. As Harrington has pointed out, the conservative dogma that raising the minimum wage lowers employment among the poverty population has been

repeatedly shown to be false over the past thirty years: *New American Poverty*, p. 111.

100. Recent expansion of the Earned Income Tax Credit is a step in the right direction; raising the tax threshold would further help. See Joe and Rogers, *By the Few*, pp. 138, 142. Our entire tax structure needs to be overhauled so that it truly becomes a progressive system, rather than one in which the poorest tenth of the nation in 1985 paid an average tax rate of 29 percent while the wealthiest tenth paid an average 25 percent rate: *New Republic*, February 18, 1985, p. 7, cited in Hope and Young, *Faces of Homelessness*, p. 284.

101. *New American Poverty*. See also Helen Ginsburg, *Full Employment and Public Policy* (Lexington, Mass., 1983); Andrew Levison, *The Full Employment Alternative* (New York, 1980).

102. John Tierney, "Using Housing Projects for Welfare Angers Tenants," *New York Times*, June 28, 1990.

103. See Manhattan Task Force, *A Shelter Is Not a Home*; USCM, *Homelessness in America's Cities*, p. 8.

104. For current examples see Connecticut Department of Human Resources, *People Without Homes* (Hartford, 1988), pp. 23–24; Kozol, *Rachel and Her Children*, p. 27; Manhattan Task Force, *A Shelter Is Not a Home*, pp. 108–110. Recent McKinney Act reauthorizations have included some limited funding for "shelter-plus-care" housing.

105. See NCH, *Necessary Relief*, pp. 13, 16. However, the U.S. Conference of Mayors reported in 1989 that transitional housing had increased twice as fast as shelters in surveyed cities the previous year—an encouraging sign: *Status Report on Hunger and Homelessness in America's Cities: 1989* (Washington, D.C., 1989), p. 3.

106. *Alternatives to the Welfare Hotel*, p. 36 and appendix B.

107. See *In Just Times* 1 (June 1990): 1; NCH, *Necessary Relief*, p. 29.

108. See Friedner D. Wittman, "Housing Models for Alcohol Programs Serving Homeless People," *Contemporary Drug Problems* 16 (1989): 483–504; Shipley et al., "Treatment and Research."

109. *Health and Homelessness*.

110. Some of the "Family Support Centers" funded by the 1990 McKinney Act reauthorization provide public housing residents with such job-related services as training and child care.

111. Suggested readings on providing emergency services to homeless people include California State Senate Office of Research, *Shelter and Services* (Sacramento, 1985); Robert Mayer, *Developing Shelter Models for the Homeless* (New York, 1985); Rafferty et al., *Shelter Worker's Handbook*; Manhattan Task Force, *A Shelter Is Not a Home*.

112. *Status Report, 1989*, p. 3.

113. New York City paid a quarter of its enormous shelter bill for homeless families—$159 million in FY1987—while the state paid a quarter and the federal government half: Manhattan Task Force, *A Shelter Is Not a Home*, pp. 23–24.

114. See *New Approaches* (the newsletter of the Emergency Food and Shelter National Board Program) (October 1988); USCM, *Status Report, 1989*, pp. 2–3.

115. *Rachel and Her Children*, p. 196.

116. Ibid., p. 17.
117. *Homelessness and Health,* particularly chap. 10.
118. As Cohen and Sokolovsky warn, however, "it is imperative to eschew pronouncements that tout the use of indigenous support systems as a panacea for service delivery problems": Carl I. Cohen and Jay Sokolovsky, *Old Men of the Bowery* (New York, 1989), p. 215.
119. NCH, *Homelessness In America: A Summary* (Washington, D.C., n.d.), p. 4; see also Madeleine R. Stoner, "An Analysis of Public and Private Sector Provisions for Homeless People," *Urban and Social Change Review* 17 (Winter 1984): 3–8.
120. Massachusetts: Nancy K. Kaufman, "Homelessness: A Comprehensive Policy Approach," *Urban and Social Change Review* 17 (Winter 1984): 21–26. Similar models: Cohen and Sokolovsky, *Old Men,* p. 205.
121. Kozol, *Rachel and Her Children,* p. 200. See also Funiciello, "Give Them Shelters."
122. See Christine Reed, "Why Housing the Homeless Is an Issue for the Cities," *Western City* 62 (March 1986): 7–8. This is true of housing and welfare policies generally. As long as taxing powers and spending requirements are even in part locally based, there will be an incentive for local governments to seek to avoid inclusionary policies (which may lower tax bases while raising costs) and practice exclusionary policies. Home rule, while in part progressive because of its empowering of local communities to determine their fates, is in large part regressive and a barrier to the type of policies that must be enacted to overcome poverty, discrimination, homelessness, and the general crisis in housing.
123. For example, a Washington Post/ABC poll taken in September 1989 found that 71 percent of those questioned favored an increase in taxes for homeless shelters, and 75 percent believed that homelessness was largely caused by "circumstances beyond [homeless people's] control," but by May 1990 the percentage supporting these views had fallen to 58 percent and 63 percent respectively: reported in E. A. Torriero, "Public Getting Fed Up with the Homeless," *San Jose Mercury News,* June 6, 1990.
124. Similar resolutions have been passed by the European Commission (an advisory board to the Common Market), the Parliament of the United Kingdom, and, in the United States, the Massachusetts state legislature. A simple declaration of the right to housing is insufficient, as the 1949 Housing Act demonstrates, without the kinds of programs I have been proposing.
125. Income inequality in the United States in the late 1980s was more pronounced than at any time since the Great Depression (Harrison and Bluestone, *Great U-Turn,* pp. 129–131), the culmination of a trend that began in the late 1970s (see Salerno et al., *Hardship in the Heartland,* p. 25).

Appendix: Researching homelessness

1. For additional discussion of the methodological questions raised here, see Rob Rosenthal, "Straighter from the Source," *Urban Anthropology* 20 (1991): 110–126.

2. William H. Friedland and Robert A. Marotto, "The New Homeless and Community Public Policy" (paper presented at the annual meeting of the American Sociological Association, Washington, D. C., August 26–30, 1985), p. 3.

3. Elliott Liebow, *Tally's Corner* (Boston, 1967); James P. Spradley, *You Owe Yourself a Drunk* (Boston, 1970).

4. *The Hobo* (Chicago, 1923), p. 106.

5. See Rosenthal, "Straighter from the Source." Mostly importantly, most research has been conducted at shelters, but virtually all researchers have come to see that "homelessness is not a one-to-one predicator of use of temporary shelter": Kenneth Winograd, *Street People and Other Homeless* (Pittsburgh, 1983), reprinted in U.S. Congress, Subcommittee on Housing and Community Development, *Homelessness in America—II* (Washington, D.C., 1984), p. 1350. James Cleghorn suggests, using data from various studies, that less than half of the homeless population ever take up shelter residency: James Stephen Cleghorn, "Residents Without Residences" (master's thesis, University of Alabama, Birmingham, 1983), reprinted in U.S. Congress, *Homelessness in America—II*, pp. 1104–1233. For other discussions of the validity and representativeness of shelter surveys, see Richard Ropers and Marjorie Robertson, *The Inner-City Homeless of Los Angeles* (Los Angeles, 1984), p. 5; Liebow, *Tally's Corner*, p. 8; Dan Salerno, Kim Hopper, and Ellen Baxter, *Hardship in the Heartland* (New York, 1984), p. 177.

6. See Task Force on Emergency Shelter, *Homeless in Chicago* (Chicago, 1983); Sara Rimer, "The Other City," *New York Times*, January 30, 1984; Nancy K. Kaufman and Janet L. Harris, "Profile of the Homeless in Massachusetts" [publication no. 13239-24-400-5-83-C.R] (Springfield, Mass., 1983), reprinted in U.S. Congress, *Homelessness in America—II*, pp. 481–504. Jamshid A. Momeni, ed., *Homelessness in the United States*, vol. 1 (New York, 1989), presents a collection of local estimates. Peter Rossi, James D. Wright, Gene A. Fisher, and Georgianna Willis, "The Urban Homeless," *Science* 235 (1987): 1336–1341, is notable for its attempt to attain a level of methodological sophistication and accuracy previously lacking, although the study remains flawed; see Rosenthal, "Straighter from the Source."

7. U.S. Department of Housing and Urban Development, *A Report to the Secretary on the Homeless and Emergency Shelters* (Washington, D.C., 1984). For instance, while HUD reported a " 'reliable' low estimate of 12,000" homeless people in New York in January 1984, over 16,000 people were then receiving shelter: Jonathan Kozol, *Rachel and Her Children* (New York, 1988), p. 9; the original source of this comparison appears to be Kim Hopper, "Ironies of a Lost Reform," *SN* 1 (June 1984): 3. For other critiques see Richard Appelbaum, "Testimony on *A Report to the Secretary on the Homeless and Emergency Shelters*," in Jon Erickson and Charles Wilhelm, eds., *Housing the Homeless* (New Brunswick, N.J., 1986), pp. 156–165; Chester Hartman, "Testimony on *A Report to the Secretary on the Homeless and Emergency Shelters*," in Erickson and Wilhelm, eds., *Housing the Homeless*, pp. 150–155. For defenses of, or figures close to, HUD's count, see Barret A. Lee, "Homelessness in Tennessee," in Momeni, ed., *Homelessness in the United States*, pp. 181–204; Marta Elliott and Laura J. Krivo, "Structural Determi-

nants of Homelessness in the United States," *Social Problems* 38 (1991): 113–131; Peter Rossi, *Down and Out in America* (Chicago, 1989). Some researchers have suggested that the differences between HUD's count and that of advocates may be seen as the difference between counts on a given night versus counts for an entire year: see Leanne G. Rivlin, "A New Look at the Homeless," *Social Policy* 16 (Spring 1986): 3; Richard Ropers, *The Invisible Homeless* (New York, 1988), p. 35.

8. *Homelessness in America's Cities* (Washington, D.C., 1984), p. 4.
9. The service providers' estimates were invariably accompanied by three warnings: that there were many more homeless people than those they saw; that some proportion of the homeless population was seen by more than one provider; and that there were certainly far more homeless people in Santa Barbara over the course of a year than there were at any one point in time.
10. Michael Perez, "Homelessness in Isla Vista" (report, Isla Vista, Calif., 1984), p. 1.
11. Such comparisons, of course, are dangerous. Since each locality experiences the same difficulties in making a count, no estimate is likely to be very accurate. In addition, there is a danger of circularity: New York makes an estimate, San Francisco makes an estimate based on New York's estimate in proportion to San Francisco's total population, Los Angeles uses that figure to estimate its homeless population, and a year later the researchers in New York hear the Los Angeles estimate and believe it verifies their original figures. I made these comparisons not to claim proof of the estimations I was coming up with in Santa Barbara, but to see whether such figures were even plausible.
12. Lineworkers and supervisors in the Food Stamp program estimated that 60 percent of those applying for Food Stamps were homeless, based on their inability to give a local residential address. If we use this estimate, therefore, of 1,512 recipients in the metropolitan area, approximately 907 would be homeless, as would perhaps another 90 individuals receiving Food Stamps through the AFDC program, for a total of about 1,000 homeless Food Stamp recipients.

As we have seen, not all homeless people apply for Food Stamps or indeed any entitlement program. The data obtained later from Church guests and HoPP interviewees indicated that between 10 and 25 percent of the homeless population were receiving Food Stamps. Combining these use-percentages with the Food Stamp and AFDC lineworker estimates of 1,000 homeless Food Stamp recipients would yield an estimate, within the city itself, of 4,000 to 10,000 homeless people—a number to be corrected downward by some unknown factor to reflect the fact that some homeless people not receiving Food Stamps had in fact applied for them and were thus counted in the original estimate of 1,000.

Similarly, lineworkers in the GR program estimated in 1985 that 50 to 60 homeless people a week were applying for GR, with a "small percentage" of duplicated applications. Such estimates would indicate a metropolitan-area estimate (since other parts of the county have their own intake offices) of 2,600 to 3,120 homeless applicants per year, although not all of these people would be remaining in Santa Barbara at the same time. Again, when the low rate of application among the homeless population is factored in, the resulting estimates become quite large.

13. See Pamela J. Fischer, "Estimating the Prevalence of Alcohol, Drug and Mental Health Problems in the Contemporary Homeless Population," *Contemporary Drug Problems* 16 (1989): 333–390.

14. See Liebow, *Tally's Corner;* Kathy Davis, *Power Under the Microscope* (Rotterdam, 1988); Harvey Molotch and Deirdre Boden, "Talking Social Structure," *American Sociological Review* 50: 273–288.

15. See Rossi et al., "Urban Homeless"; Carl Brown, Steve MacFarlane, Ron Paredes, and Louisa Stark, *The Homeless of Phoenix* (Phoenix, 1983); Winograd, *Street People.*

16. Rob Rosenthal, "The Interview and Beyond," *Public Historian* 1 (1979): 58–67.

17. See David Snow and Leon Anderson, "Identity Work Among the Homeless," *American Journal of Sociology* (1987): 1336–1371; Richard Ropers and Marjorie Robertson, *Notes on the Epidemiology of Homeless Persons* (Los Angeles, 1984).

18. Howard M. Bahr and Kathleen C. Houts, "Can You Trust a Homeless Man?" *Public Opinion Quarterly* 35 (1971): 376. In perhaps the most detailed recent investigation of this problem, Robertson et al. compared responses they were given by homeless women in interviews with those given by the same women as part of the intake process at the Los Angeles Transition House shelter and found 92 percent agreement between the two, a powerful demonstration of reliability if not necessarily validity: Marjorie Robertson, Richard Ropers, and Richard Boyer, *The Homeless of Los Angeles County* (Los Angeles, 1985).

19. See Ropers and Robertson, *Epidemiology;* Bahr and Houts, "Trust a Homeless Man?" Douglas A. Harper, *The Homeless Man* (Ph.D. dissertation, Brandeis University, 1975).

20. See John Lofland, *Analyzing Social Settings* (Belmont, Calif., 1971).

21. See footnote to Chapter 2 for the symbols used in oral history and field note transcriptions.

22. Rosenthal, "Interview and Beyond." For similar findings by researchers of homeless populations, see Marjorie Hope and James Young, *The Faces of Homelessness* (Lexington, Mass., 1986); Robertson et al., *Los Angeles County.*

23. See Lofland, *Social Settings.*

24. "The stigmatized individual may . . . wait to 'fault' the self-appointed wise, that is, continue to examine the others' actions and words until some fugitive sign is obtained that their show of accepting him is only a show": Erving Goffman, *Stigma* (New York, 1986), p. 114.

25. Although we originally planned to have me sit in on interviews and have Kennedy serve as translator rather than interviewer, both the amount of time this would have added to interviews and the nervousness of some respondents (in some cases because of their noncitizen status) indicated that having Kennedy do the interviews alone was a better strategy.

26. *Social Settings,* pp. 117–118.

27. *Tally's Corner,* pp. 243–246.

28. *Stigma,* p. 28.

29. It is also important to mention who was *not* interviewed. Interviewing depended on a willingness and ability to be interviewed. In particular, those impaired by alcoholism or mental illness were less likely to be interviewed (just as I was less likely to have spent much time hanging out with them). Further, my desire to have a personal relationship with those I interviewed (in order to ensure greater candor) limited the number of "transients" in the study. Of 44 interviews, 4 were with those I would describe as mentally ill, 5 with those I would describe as alcoholic, and 4 with those I would describe as transient.

30. *Social Settings*, p. 76.

31. Ibid., p. 90.

32. For similar findings elsewhere, see Robertson et al., *Los Angeles County;* Ellen Baxter and Kim Hopper, "The New Mendicancy," *American Journal of Orthopsychiatry* 52 (1982): 393–408.

33. For example, more unaccompanied children, alcoholics, and mentally ill people appear in the HoPP data, but these groups are probably underrepresented in all three data sets.

34. *Homeless Man*, p. 52.

35. See Howard S. Becker, "Afterword" to Douglas Harper, *Good Company* (Chicago, 1982), pp. 169–172.

36. Obviously, as a housed researcher of homelessness, I am not arguing that investigations can only be conducted by "insiders." See Robert Merton, "Insiders and Outsiders," *American Journal of Sociology* 78 (1972): 9–47.

Index

Affiliations, 77–94; constrains on, 93–94; defined, 77; desire for, 93–94, 169; factors affecting, 133–135, 137; of homeless people to housed friends and family, 34, 72–74, 75, 80–84, 94, 116, 144, 192; of homeless people to mainstream society, 78–80, 172; of homeless people to other homeless people, 77, 85–94, 95, 109, 126, 134–135, 235nn.42, 45, 237n57, 252n118. *See also* Disaffiliation; Homeless people: emotional resource networks of; Homeless people: material resource networks of

Agency and constraint, 3, 118–120, 127–128, 135, 141

AIDS, 150, 160, 242n13, 250n95

Aid to Families with Dependent Children (AFDC): child care provisions of, 231n7; levels of, 21–22, 158, 231n3, 248n81; regulation problems in, 112, 117, 120, 147, 149, 157, 163; use of, by homeless people, 66, 71–72, 73, 74–75, 120, 254n12. *See also* Public assistance

Alcohol abuse and use. *See* Substance abuse and use

Alcohol abusers, 91, 205n14, 215n6, 229n12, 256n29

Anderson, Elijah, 178

Anderson, Nels, 166, 175

Appelbaum, Richard, 40, 154, 155

Bach, Victor, 163

Bahr, Howard, 132, 178

Biker John, 184

(Boston) Emergency Shelter Commission, 147

Bret, 27, 36, 48, 49–50, 138, 180, 181

Bruce, 31, 72, 86, 98, 132

Bush administration, 146, 150, 165, 171

Camilia, 131

Capitalism, 151

Caplow, Theodore, 95, 132

Catholic Social Service, 74, 75, 76, 115, 184

Charlie, 52, 56, 57, 87, 91, 92, 99, 102, 119

Child abuse, 208n33, 219n43

Child care, 71, 113, 135, 158, 161, 249n82; shared with friends, 83, 84

Children: as barrier to escape for parents, 113, 117, 135; as contributing cause of

Children *(cont.)*
parent's homelessness, 25–26, 33–34, 41; discrimination against, in housing, 33–34, 41, 114, 135; effects of homelessness on, 73–74, 76, 145; employment difficulties of homeless, 66, 113; in homeless families, 73–76, 192; as incentive for escape for parents, 134, 234n36; likelihood of becoming homeless, 210n46; removal of, from homeless families, 71, 74, 75; runaway and throwaway, 17, 209n41; schooling of homeless, 164, 222n59; in single-parent families, 17; vulnerability of, to homelessness, 26. *See also* Kids
Child support, 25, 158
Christine, 34, 112, 131
Cloward, Richard, 96
Cohen, Carl, 85
Community Development Block Grants (CDBG), 163
Community Mental Health Centers, 161
Community Mental Health Centers Act, 14, 158
Comprehensive Homeless Assistance Strategies (CHAS), 149
Constraint, *See* Agency and constraint
Consuela, 32
Cost argument, The, 145–146
Cottage industries, 52, 66
Criminal activity: and acting out by mentally ill people, 64–65; as adaptation to homelessness, 121, 126–127, 128, 137–138; against homeless people by housed people, 58–60; by homeless people, according to police and merchants, 97–98, 223n8; by homeless people for economic reasons, 53–55, 64, 66–67, 115; and intrahomeless people, 87, 136; lack of, by some subgroups, 70, 72; status offenses as, 45, 121, 233n32

Danita, 30
Deindustrialization, 13
Deinstitutionalization (individual): 24, 32–33, 210n47

Deinstitutionalization (programmatic): aftercare programs (and lack of), 24, 32–33, 129, 159, 207n22, 218n38, 251n104; as contributing cause of homelessness, 14–16, 147, 236n50; history of, 14–16, 158
Demo Dan, 87, 90, 97, 181, 191
Deserving poor, 93, 174–175
Disabled persons. *See* Handicapped persons
Disaffiliation: as cause of homelessness, 3, 4, 27, 36–37, 77–78, 224n14; countering, 132–135; as result of homelessness, 3, 4–5, 27, 77, 84–85, 130–137, 141
Disaffiliation theory, 2, 77–78, 85, 95, 109
Disenfranchisement. *See* Homeless people: voting by
Disengagement. *See* Disaffiliation
Displacement, 3–4, 12–13, 28–36, 37
Displacement theory, 3, 77–78, 143
Divorce. *See* Families: break-up of, as contributing cause of homelessness
Doonesbury (cartoon strip), 12, 106, 115
Dora, 34, 128
Doubling up. *See* Housing, doubling up in
Drug abuse and use. *See* Substance abuse and use
Drug abusers, 205n14
Drug dealing, 54, 66–67, 160
Dual diagnosis patients, 218n38
Dula, 88, 131

Efficacy, 134–135, 140–141, 169
Eli, 32, 51, 60, 124, 126, 136, 138
Emilio, 75
Employment of homeless people: and affiliation, 80, 134, 135; as escape strategy, 112–114, 237n58; factors affecting and barriers to, 49–52, 62, 66, 71, 74, 118, 120, 127, 138–139, 207n26; problems of, as contributing cause of homelessness, 20–21, 27, 28–29; structural aspects of, 13, 29, 200n2; by subgroup, 49–52, 62, 66, 69–70, 71, 74,

192; and training, 157, 161, 166; and
unemployment, 13–14, 20–21, 29
Empowerment, 134–135
Evictions. *See* Housing: evictions from

Families: break-up of, as contributing
cause of homelessness, 25–26, 32;
change in structure of, as contributing
cause of homelessness, 16–17; characteristics of homeless, 207n29, 221n57,
241n5; conflicts in, as contributing
cause of homelessness, 27, 29; escape
problems of homeless, 113, 149;
growth in number of homeless,
221n58; stabilizing vulnerable, 157–
158; use of emergency shelters by
homeless, 221n56
Farmer's Home Administration
(FmHA), 148, 152
Federal Emergency Management
Administration (FEMA), 147–148,
167
Federal Housing Administration (FHA),
152
Fig Tree, The, 1, 54, 86, 90, 91, 92,
178–181; battle for control of, 99–100;
and "Fig Tree types," 56, 93, 107;
regulars at, 87, 100, 183, 186
Fitch, Robert, 151
Food stamps: as currency of the streets,
91, 215n13; uniform standards for,
248n81; use and limitations on use of,
by homeless people, 60, 69, 73, 149,
205n10, 254n12. *See also* Public assistance
Friedland, William, 174
Future orientation, 120, 132, 138–141,
203n1, 227n45

Gavina, 139
General Accounting Office (GAO), 148,
150
General Relief (GR): levels of, 21, 112,
241n8; use of, by homeless people, 52,
53, 63, 64, 69, 241n8, 254n12. *See also*
Public assistance

Gilderbloom, John, 40, 154, 155
Glen, 49, 54, 61, 79, 80, 92, 111, 118, 119,
120, 121, 123, 127, 130, 138, 139
Goffman, Erving, 82, 84, 117–118, 120,
130, 132, 189
Greg, 32, 87–88, 136
Greyhound therapy, 24

Handicapped persons, 21, 22, 42, 112–
113
Hank, 31, 48, 69, 70–71, 86, 89, 119, 122,
139
Harper, Douglas, 178, 193
Harrington, Michael, 161
Harris, Sara, 136
Hartman, Chester, 151
Health care, 105, 145, 160, 165–166; and
health problems of homeless people,
129–133
Henry, 36–37, 53, 54, 99, 100, 119, 133,
136–137, 138, 140–141
Homeless Coalition. *See* Santa Barbara
Homeless Coalition
Homeless movement, The, 95–109; activist groups in, 9–10, 96–109, 133;
author's participation in, 186–189;
backlash against, 10–11, 106; barriers
to organizing, 96, 103, 232n9; and battle against illegal sleeping laws, 11,
87–88, 102, 106–109, 187; and battle
for right to vote, 101; divisions within,
103–104, 108; effect of participation
in, 98–99, 134; good cop/bad cop dynamic in, 105–108; and Homeless People's Association (HPA), 96–108, 133,
134, 178, 186–188, 194, 227n40; mobilization of resources by, 103; precipitating events of, 9–10, 96–98, 101, 133;
reaction by local government to, 11,
102, 105–109; and Santa Barbara
Homeless Coalition, 101–108, 134,
188; and Single Parent Alliance (SPA),
4, 71, 101–108, 115, 133, 134, 175, 183,
187, 189, 192; sources of power of, 11,
96, 105–109, 133; victories of, 11, 109.
See also Housed people: role of, in the
homeless movement

Homelessness: adaptations to, 120–128; amelioration of, 166–168; causes of, 2–4, 12–17, 42–43, 143, 146–147, 151, 171, 198n9; criminalization of, 45, 121, 168; definitions of, 5, 149, 225n20; downward cycles of, 116–132; economic costs of, 102, 145–146, 171, 187; effects of, 116–132, 137–141; effects of length of time of, 121, 135, 141, 232n15; episodic and chronic, 89, 111, 133; escape from, 80, 92, 111–141, 162–166; factors influencing length of time of, 133–135, 233n31; framing of the issue of, 97, 100, 107, 171; government response to, 11, 105–109, 147–151; growth of, 3, 9; historic review of, 2–3; paths to, 4, 19–43; precipitating events leading to, 28–37; prevention of, 152–162; rates of, in different countries, 151; researching, 173–195; resulting from inability to find substitute housing, 37–43; social costs of, 145; voluntary, 2, 26–27, 35–37, 50, 128, 141, 144, 147; vulnerability to, 19–28. *See also* Homeless people; Methodological and analytical issues, problems, and caveats

Homeless people: animosity of, toward other homeless people, 85–87, 90, 93, 102, 104, 108, 130; arguments against aiding, 144–146; attempts to live "normally" by, 77; class backgrounds of, 19, 38, 71, 74, 83, 128, 134, 139–140; classifications of, 48, 194, 214n6, 217n31; clothing sources of, 61, 65, 67, 70, 73, 75–76; daily lives of, 4, 45–76, 78–94; distancing by, from other homeless people, 92, 93, 96, 130, 133; diversity of, 3, 4, 48, 240n1; educational levels of, 20, 66; emotional resource networks of, 78, 85, 88, 90, 94, 111, 135, 232n15; feelings of solidarity and community among, 85–88, 91, 92, 95, 109, 126; food sources of, 60–61, 65, 67, 70, 73, 75; health problems of, 129–133, 165–166; hidden, 68–76, 79–80, 96, 126, 176; lack of home base of, 5, 117; marriage among, 134, 135, 224n14; material resource networks of, 47–76, 80–83, 86–87, 91–94, 111–116, 128, 134, 135; mobility of, for escape purposes, 115–116, 135, 144; norms and values of, 87, 109, 120, 121, 128, 136–141; personal hygiene of, 61, 70, 73, 75, 79, 117; political views of, 95, 102; romantic relationships of, 88; self-images of, 92, 93, 98–101, 121,126–127, 130–135, 137; sleeping places of, 55–60, 65, 66–67, 68–69, 70, 72–73, 75, 81, 82, 84; social competence and incompetence of, 2–3, 19, 27, 33, 42–43, 78–79, 93–94, 222n2, 227n42; specialized knowledge of, 45–46, 138; violence against, 10–11, 58–60, 66–67, 87; visible, 48–67, 80, 96, 126–127; voting by, 96, 101. *See also* Employment of homeless people; Homeless movement: activist groups in; Homelessness; Housed people: attitudes of, toward homeless people

Homeless People's Association (HPA), 96–108, 133, 134, 178, 186–188, 194, 227n40

Homeless People's Project, 3

Homeless political groups. *See* Homeless movement, The

Homeowner deduction, 150, 152, 155–156

Home Ownership for People Everywhere (HOPE), 150

Home rule, 252n122

Hope, Marjorie, 16, 148, 151, 152–153, 157

Housed people: attitudes of, toward homeless people, 10, 49–50, 78–80, 84, 118–119, 121, 127, 130, 133, 141, 171, 172, 215n94; relations of, with homeless people, 78–84; role of, in the homeless movement, 103–105, 106, 107, 108

Housing: affordable, defined, 12–13; cost of, 13, 19, 50, 210n42; cost of, as barrier to escape, 114, 117, 231n3, 232n10; cost of, as contributing cause of homelessness, 19, 21, 25, 27, 28–30, 40–41, 212n71; decommodification of, 150,

154–155, 162–163; discrimination in, 33–34, 41–42, 114, 160; doubling up in, 34–35, 38, 42, 75, 81, 82, 149; evictions from 28–30, 33–35, 37; gentrification of, 35, 146, 152, 153; ideological beliefs about, 153–154; in other countries, 154; precarious, 35; public, 39–40, 112, 146, 149, 154, 162; Section 8, in Santa Barbara, 21, 29–30, 39, 40, 112, 115; Section 8, nationally, 40, 162, 164, 231n5, 243nn.21, 22, 246n49, 247n59; Section 202, 164; Section 515, 243n24; shortage of affordable, as contributing cause of homelessness, 12–13, 38–43, 114, 143; subsidized, and funding for, 12, 146, 150, 151, 154–156, 163; subsidized, and government regulations regarding, 148, 210n52, 243n22; subsidized, and prepayment of mortgage in, 147, 150–151, 213n77, 247n63; transitional, 163, 164; vacancy rates in, 38–40; vouchers for, 213n75. *See also* Single Room Occupancy hotels

Housing Act of 1949, 152

Housing and Urban Development, Department of (HUD), 148, 149, 150, 163, 175

Houts, Kathleen, 178

HPA. *See* Homeless People's Association

Illegal sleeping and camping, 58, 87–88, 100, 121, 168, 215n9; costs of enforcing laws against, 145, 187; responses to prohibition of, 99, 102. *See also* Homeless movement: and battle against illegal sleeping laws; Santa Barbara City Council

Immigration. *See* Migration and immigration

Incarceration, 23–24

Institute for Policy Studies, 154

Institutionalization, 23–24

Interfaith Task Force on Homelessness (ITFH), 56, 105–108

Isolation. *See* Disaffiliation

Jack, 23, 27, 28–29, 38, 42, 46–47, 48, 80, 84, 125, 140

Javiar, 122

Job training, 157, 161, 166

Jonathan, 23, 89–90, 118, 123, 140, 181–182

Jose, 41

Juanita, 34–35, 76, 131

Julia, 32, 62, 83, 89, 130, 131–132, 139–140, 188, 241n7

Jungle, The, 9, 98, 178

Kaiser Commission, 152

Kathie, 29–30, 33, 35, 40, 64, 112, 129, 131

Kennedy, Guadalupe, 175–176, 183

Kevin, 50, 55, 83–84, 87, 99–100, 102, 116, 124, 126, 136

Kids (introduced and defined), 66–67

Kozol, Jonathan, 28, 151, 167

Labeling: as barrier to escape, 117–119, 194; as drinker, 126–127; as ex-convict, 24; of homeless people, 9, 80, 93, 96, 97, 121, 127, 130; rejection of, 132–133. *See also* Homeless people: self-images of

Latino Families (introduced and defined), 74–76

Liebow, Elliot, 120, 137, 138, 174, 178, 186

Lisa, 26, 29, 48, 66–67, 121, 123, 139

Liz, 20, 74, 85, 88, 101, 116, 130, 131

Lofland, John, 180, 186, 191

Lovell, Anne, 85

Lynn, 25, 27, 41, 73, 84, 112, 113

McKinney Act (Stewart B. McKinney Homeless Assistance Act), 146–150, 163, 164, 166–167, 222n59

Magnet (or Mecca) theory, The, 144, 170–171

Malinowski, Bronislaw, 178

Manhattan Task Force, 155

Manuel, 130

Margie, 30, 36–37, 59, 66, 69, 84, 130, 132, 229n6, 240n89
Mark, 51–52, 57, 58, 84, 91, 92, 93, 117, 124, 125, 128, 136, 140
Marotto, Robert, 174
Marx, Karl, 137
Mayor Max, 20, 28, 45–46, 48, 49, 52, 79, 86–87, 91–92, 99, 124, 128, 136, 182, 214n6, 226n34
Medicaid, 147, 158, 159, 161
Medicare, 161
Mental illness and stress: as contributing cause of homelessness, 14–16, 22–23, 41–43; as result of homelessness, 129–132
Mentally ill people: confinement of, 15, 159–160, 238n63, 242n12; criminal activity of, 64–65, 217n22; criminalization of, 238n63; growth in numbers of, 214n83; isolation of, 65–66, 86, 89–90; mobility of, 33, 62–63, 129; problems finding housing by, 41–42, 112–133, 164; problems receiving public assistance by, 22, 33, 62–64, 129; as proportion of homeless population, 205n13; substance abuse by, 23, 33, 123; treatment for, 129, 150, 159–160, 164–165, 171. *See also* Deinstitutionalization (individual); Deinstitutionalization (programmatic); Wingnuts
Merchants, 78–79, 130
Merton, Robert, 137
Methodological and analytical issues, problems, and caveats: characteristics of homeless population, 53, 81, 208n31, 210n48, 215nn.7, 8, 216n19, 231n1, 232n8, 239n79; definitions, 214n6, 217n31, 222n2, 225nn.19, 20; hidden homeless population, 68, 126, 176, 177; methods of investigation, 177–178, 223n5, 237n58, 253n5, 256n29; objectivity, 174, 189; resource use, 176, 192, 221n56, 253n5; size of homeless populations, 174–177, 253n7, 254n11; substance abuse, 126, 205n14, 233n32, 234nn.35, 38, 236nn.50, 55
Michael, 66, 209n41

Migrant (agricultural) workers, 220n49
Migration and immigration, 24, 31–32, 75, 239n80. *See also* Transiency
Minimum wage, 232n10, 248n80, 250n99
Minorities. *See* People of color
Mobility of homeless people. *See* Homeless people: mobility of, for escape purposes; Mentally ill people: mobility of; Migration and immigration; Transiency
Moral argument, The, 144
Mount Laurel court decisions, 247n58

National Affordable Housing Act of 1990, 150, 213n77, 247n63
National Coalition for the Homeless, 101, 149, 170, 187
National health care, 159, 160, 161, 166
National Housing Institute, 155–156
National Housing Trust Fund, 155, 247n61
Negative income tax, 157
Nonprofit housing. *See* Housing: decommodification of

Omnibus Budget Reconciliation Act of 1981, 249n82
Oral history gathering, 4, 177–178, 189–191, 194–195
Outreach: 149, 156–160, 163–166, 168, 169
Overcrowded housing. *See* Housing: doubling up in

Passing (as housed), 68, 79–80, 121, 135, 228n5
Pat, 114–115, 120
People of color, 204n5. *See also* Latino Families; Racial discrimination
Perez, Michael, 117, 124
Piliavin, Irving, 81
Piore, Michael, 20
Piven, Frances Fox, 96

Police: interactions of, with homeless people, 96–102, 107, 109, 121, 130, 224n12; Jungle raids by, 9, 98; proactive tactics of, 97–98, 182

Population, homeless, 3, 145, 174–177, 198n10

Poverty, 14, 28, 37, 116, 156

Problem populations, 194–195

Prostitution, 64, 66, 67, 121

Public assistance: effect of, on rhythm of daily life, 140; failure of, to serve homeless people, 52–53, 62–64, 69–70, 71–72, 74–75, 156; low levels of, as contributing cause of homelessness, 21–22, 29–30, 147; low levels of, in preventing escape, 112, 216n17; as magnet for homeless people, 144; in other countries, 156; problems receiving, as contributing cause of homelessness, 14, 21, 33, 147, 156; program boundaries in, 64; regulations in, 112, 117, 120, 147, 149, 163, 243n22; use of, by homeless people, 52, 62, 66, 69, 71, 74–75, 192, 237n61, 254n12. *See also* Aid to Families of Dependent Children; Food stamps; Housing: Section 8; Public policies (past and present); Public policies (recommended); Reagan administration; Social Security; Social Security Disability Insurance; Supplemental Security Income

Public housing. *See* Housing: public

Public policies (past and present), 146–151; on employment, 161, 166, 249n82; on health care, 160–161; on housing, 146–147, 150–151, 152–153; on mental health, 150, 158–160; on public assistance, 147, 156–157; on tax laws, 146, 153, 155–156, 251n100. *See also* Substance abuse and use: treatment for

Public policies (recommended), 151–170; on centralization and coordination of services, 163, 165, 166, 168–170, 171; on decriminalizing homelessness, 168; on employment, 157, 161–162, 166; general principles of, 168–170; on health care, 160–161, 165–166; on housing, 152–156, 162–163; on mental health care, 158–160, 164–165, 171; on public assistance, 156–157, 163–164, 171; on role of federal government, 153–156, 157, 170–171; on shelters, 166–168, 170; on stabilizing vulnerable families, 157–158, 164; on substance abuse treatment, 160, 165; on tax laws, 155–156, 157, 161

Rachel, 22–23, 24, 27, 35, 38, 41–42, 64, 65–66, 89, 95, 97, 112, 184–186

Racial discrimination, 41, 114, 204n5, 211n58

Ray, 57, 128, 131, 208n35

Reagan administration: approach of, toward homelessness, 147; cutbacks in housing problems by, 146–147, 171, 213n75; cutbacks in social services and public assistance by, 33, 147, 171, 216n16; mental health policies of, 171

Reciprocity, 77–80, 84, 91, 94, 109

Rent control, 153, 210n43

Rents. *See* Housing

Resolution Trust Corporation (RTC), 148

Riordan, Suzanne, 101, 175

Rodman, Hyman, 137

Roger, 71–72, 73, 85, 114

Rossi, Peter, 28

Runaways, 17, 209n41

Safety net. *See* Public assistance

Sandman, 52, 182, 226n34

Santa Barbara (as a research setting), 6–17

Santa Barbara City Council, 1–2, 11, 88, 102, 106–109

Santa Barbara Homeless Coalition, 101–108, 134, 188

Santa Barbara Rental Housing Task Force, 41

Savings and Loan Bailout Bill (Financial Institutions Reform, Recovery, and Enforcement Act of 1989), 148

Secondary labor market, 20, 29
Shelter, right to, 166–167
Shelter dependency, 56–57, 167–168,
  240n92
Shelter poverty, 19, 200n7
Shelters, homeless (in Santa Barbara):
  beds in, compared to need, 55;
  Church of the Month, 56–57, 70–71,
  105, 169, 184, 192; and Klein Bottle/
  Social Advocates for Youth (KBSAY),
  8, 17, 66, 183; material needs met by,
  56, 70; National Guard Armory, 109;
  opposition to, 56–57; problems or lack
  of problems at, 57, 70, 140–141,
  217nn.26, 27; psychological needs met
  by, 56; reasons not used, 57, 72–73, 75;
  regulations of, 55–56, 65, 89, 120; Rescue Mission, 45–47, 55, 117, 120, 125,
  136, 238nn.63, 64; Salvation Army, 8,
  45–47, 56, 59, 124, 125, 184, 198n10;
  Transition House, 70, 105, 109,
  221n56, 222n62; triaging within, 93;
  Wings of Love, 47, 55
Shelters, homeless (nationally): conversion of, to low-income housing, 155;
  cost of, 145–146, 170; exclusions from,
  151, 167–168; three-tiered model of,
  170; use of, by homeless people,
  253n5; use of, for reinstitutionalizing
  mental patients, 244n27
Shriver, Linda, 178–180, 181
Single Parent Alliance (SPA), 4, 71, 101–
  108, 115, 133, 134, 175, 183, 187, 189,
  192
Single Room Occupancy hotels (SROs):
  and definition of homelessness, 5; loss
  of, 13, 42, 114, 146–147; loss of, and
  effect on substance abusers, 236n50;
  protection of, 164; rent inflation at, 53,
  212n71
Skidders (introduced and defined), 71–74
Skid Row, 2, 95, 227n36
Sloss, Michael, 119
Snyder, Mitch, 11, 106–107
Social margin, 4, 38, 93, 120–121, 128,
  134; and escape, 111, 117
Social networks. *See* Affiliations; Homeless people: emotional resource net-

works of; Homeless people: material
  resource networks of
Social ownership of housing. *See* Hous-
  ing: decommodification of
Social Security, 21, 248n81
Social Security Disability Insurance
  (SSDI), 62, 165, 237n61
Social services, 74–75, 144, 156–160,
  215n10
Sokolovsky, Jay, 85
Sonja, 21, 33, 95, 115, 120, 130
SPA. *See* Single Parent Alliance
Spradley, James, 174, 178
Steinhagen, Renee, 163
Stewart B. McKinney Homeless Assis-
  tance Act. *See* McKinney Act
Stigmitization. *See* Labeling
Stone, Michael, 19
Street People (introduced and defined),
  48–62
Substance abuse and use: as contributing
  cause of homelessness, 23, 28–29,
  121–122, 141; as disaffiliation indicator, 134; effect of, on affiliations, 23,
  235n45; as escape barrier, 121–127,
  233n31; in families of children who
  become homeless, 234n37; interaction
  of, with structural problems, 23, 42–
  43, 126; prevalence of, in homeless
  population, 124–125, 127, 205n14,
  236n50; reasons for, 124–126, 137–
  138, 139–140, 160; as result of homelessness, 121–127; by subgroups, 122–
  125; treatment for, 125–126, 129, 150,
  160, 165, 235n44
Supplemental Security Income (SSI),
  21, 62, 63, 64, 112, 150, 165, 237n61

Tax Reform Act of 1986, 153, 243n19
Ted, 92
Teen pregnancies, 158
Tenants' rights legislation, 153
Third stream housing. *See* Housing: de-
  commodification of
Transiency: appearance of, 49; among
  subgroups, 62–63, 69, 82, 86, 89, 129,
  192. *See also* Homeless people: mobil-

ity of, for escape purposes; Mentally ill people, mobility of

Transient, as label synonymous with homeless, 9, 53, 100, 107, 118, 174, 177

Transitory Workers (introduced and defined), 69–71

Tremaine, Kit, 173–174, 187

Unemployment, 13–14, 20–21, 29. *See also* Employment of homeless people

U.S. Conference of Mayors, 175

Value stretch, 137

Veterans, 27, 100, 210n47

Veterans Administration (VA), 148, 152, 161

Violence against homeless people, 10–11, 58–60, 66–67, 87

Weber, Eleanor, 154, 168

Welfare. *See* Public assistance; Social services

Welfare hotels, 5, 245n37

Wendi, 27, 37, 48, 49, 58, 60, 128, 180, 181

Wingnuts (introduced and defined), 62–66. *See also* Mentally ill people

Women: abuse of, as contributing cause of homelessness, 25; economic discrimination against, as contributing cause of homelessness, 17. *See also* Women, homeless

Women, homeless: contacts of, with mainstream society, 81, 229n6; and likelihood of being hidden, 221n57; mobility of, 241n5; use of emergency shelters by, 221n56. *See also* Families; Skidders

Wright, James, 154, 168

Young, James, 16, 148, 151, 152–153, 157

Youth, homeless. *See* Children; Families; Kids

Zeke, 53, 56, 133

Zoning, 153, 155, 167, 171, 249n89